Employment  Cultures

NEW HORIZONS IN MANAGEMENT

Series Editor: Cary L. Cooper, CBE, *Professor of Organizational Psychology and Health, Lancaster University Management School, Lancaster University, UK*

This important series makes a significant contribution to the development of management thought. This field has expanded dramatically in recent years and the series provides an invaluable forum for the publication of high quality work in management science, human resource management, organisational behaviour, marketing, management information systems, operations management, business ethics, strategic management and international management.

The main emphasis of the series is on the development and application of new original ideas. International in its approach, it will include some of the best theoretical and empirical work from both well-established researchers and the new generation of scholars.

Titles in the series include:

The Handbook of Human Resource Management Policies and Practices in Asia-Pacific Economies
Volume One
Michael Zanko

The Handbook of Human Resource Management Policies and Practices in Asia-Pacific Economies
Volume Two
Michael Zanko and Matt Ngui

Human Nature and Organization Theory
On the Economic Approach to Institutional Organization
Sigmund Wagner-Tsukamoto

Organizational Relationships in the Networking Age
The Dynamics of Identity Formation and Bonding
Edited by Willem Koot, Peter Leisink and Paul Verweel

Islamic Perspectives on Management and Organization
Abbas J. Ali

Supporting Women's Career Advancement
Challenges and Opportunities
Edited by Ronald J. Burke and Mary C. Mattis

Research Companion to Organizational Health Psychology
Edited by Alexander-Stamatios G. Antoniou and Cary L. Cooper

Innovation and Knowledge Management
The Cancer Information Service Research Consortium
J. David Johnson

Managing Emotions in Mergers and Aquisitions
Verena Kusstatscher and Cary L. Cooper

Employment of Women in Chinese Cultures
Half the Sky
Cherlyn Skromme Granrose

Employment of Women in Chinese Cultures

Half the Sky

Edited by

Cherlyn Skromme Granrose

Berry College, Georgia, USA

NEW HORIZONS IN MANAGEMENT

Edward Elgar

Cheltenham, UK • Northampton, MA, USA

Published by
Edward Elgar Publishing Limited
Glensanda House
Montpellier Parade
Cheltenham
Glos GL50 1UA
UK

Edward Elgar Publishing, Inc.
136 West Street
Suite 202
Northampton
Massachusetts 01060
USA

A catalogue record for this book
is available from the British Library

Library of Congress Cataloging in Publication Data
Employment of women in Chinese cultures : half the sky / edited by
Cherlyn Skromme Granrose.
    p. cm. – (New horizons in management)
  Includes index.
    1. Women–Employment–China. I. Granrose, Cherlyn S. II. Series.

HD6200.E47 2006
331.4′0951–dc22   2005049822

ISBN 1 84542 293 7

Printed and bound in Great Britain by MPG Books Ltd, Bodmin, Cornwall

Contents

PART III: CONCLUSIONS

Figures and tables

FIGURES

TABLES

Contributors

Irene K.H. Chew received her PhD in organizational behavior from the Australian Graduate School of Management of University of New South Wales and is currently an associate professor at the Nanyang Technological University. She has published in many journals. Furthermore, she contributed chapters in books such as *New Approaches in Employee Management*, and *International Review of Selection and Assessment*. She was a council member of the Singapore Institute of Human Resource and a member of the board of management of the Singapore Training and Development Association. She has also acted as consultant and trainer for organizations in both public and private sectors. Currently, she is a consultant to the Asian Productivity Organization in a cross-cultural management research project and a committee member of the Institute of Policy Studies on structural unemployment.`

Irene Hau-Siu Chow is a professor in the Department of Management, the Chinese University of Hong Kong. Dr Chow earned her BBA at the Chinese University of Hong Kong and her MBA and PhD from Georgia State University. Her academic experience includes appointments in Hong Kong, Singapore and the USA. She has published widely in international journals. Her current research interests include gender and cultural issues in Chinese societies, Chinese networks and comparative human resources management practices.

Yong-Qing Fang is a faculty member of Nanyang Business School, Nanyang Technological University, Singapore. Prior to joining NTU, Dr Fang taught in Chinese and Canadian universities. He has published in several international journals and his co-authored papers have won awards in Academy of Management (USA) and Administrative Science Association of Canada conferences. He has acted as a consultant for organizations in Canada, China, and Southeast and East Asia, and served in management capacities in China and Canada. He has been an invited speaker to prestigious industrial organizations and institutions, and has appeared in television and radio programs. His areas of research include human resource management strategies and practices, international human resource management, and cultural and cross-cultural issues in management.

Cherlyn Skromme Granrose is professor of management at Berry College in Rome, GA. She received her PhD from Rutgers University in 1981. From 1981 to 1993 she was an assistant professor and associate professor of organizational behavior and human resources at the Temple University School of Business and Management. From 1993 to 2000 she was professor in the School of Behavioral and Organizational Science at Claremont Graduate School. She has had Fulbright Awards to South Korea, Taiwan, Singapore and the People's Republic of China. Her research publications include articles and books on Asian managers' careers, women's work–family choices, and participative decision making. She is an active member of the Association of International Business and of the Academy of Management International Management Division, and has served on the boards of the Gender and Diversity Division and the Careers Division of the Academy of Management.

Naresh Khatri earned his PhD in organizational behavior and human resource management from the State University of New York, Buffalo and MBA from the Indian Institute of Management, Ahmedabad. He is currently a faculty member in strategic human resource management and transformational leadership in the Department of Health Management and Informatics, School of Medicine, University of Missouri, Columbia. Dr Khatri's research and teaching interests focus on unleashing the human potential in organizations. He recently authored the book *The Human Dimension of Organizations*. In addition, he has published over 25 research articles and book chapters on human resource management, leadership, strategic decision making, and cross-cultural behavioral issues in refereed journals. He has presented his research in over 40 conferences and seminars and conducted executive workshops on leadership and strategic human resource management for Matsushita, Samsung, the Ministry of Defense, Singapore, and the Ministry of Environment, Singapore.

Rita V. Kong (Mei Hui Jiang) earned her MA in psychology, specializing in evaluation and organization behavior, and her MBA at Claremont Graduate University. She is currently a market intelligence specialist at Hewlett Packard, carrying out research in strategic planning and product development.

T.K. Peng is professor and head of the Graduate School of Management, I-Shou University, Taiwan. He obtained his PhD from Texas Tech University. His areas of interest center on comparative organizational behavior and human resource management, with a focus on Pacific Rim countries. He has worked in both public and private sectors and carried out research in leadership, work values and attitudes, career beliefs, harmony and conflict, and gender issues. Some of his papers have appeared in the *Journal of Organizational Behavior*, *Journal of International Business Studies*, *Organizational Dynamics*, *Asian Pacific Journal of Management*, *International Business Review*, *International Journal of Cross-Cultural Management*, *Thunderbird International Business Review*, *Journal of Developing Societies*, *Journal of Asian Business*, among others, and he has contributed chapters to several books.

Tsai-Wei Wang is an assistant professor of the Graduate Institute of Multicultural Education, National Hualien Teachers College, Taiwan. She obtained a PhD from the University of Pittsburgh. Tsai-Wei's research interests include gender studies, sociology and education as well as history. Some of her publications focus on women's movements, women's organizations, and female workers in contemporary Taiwan.

Introduction: Chinese women with different government systems

Cherlyn Skromme Granrose

Government policies related to taxation, health, reproduction, welfare, childcare, educational access and non-discrimination in employment affect women's employment directly and indirectly. Policies and laws vary widely in Chinese societies from the egalitarian, socialist provisions of Singapore and Taiwan, to the laissez-faire policy the British advocated for the Hong Kong government. In each of the following chapters we can see the influence on women's employment of some common cultural traditions. We can also begin to discover how these traditions are enacted as they have been influenced by Chinese cultural history and economic differences from 500 BCE to the political events of the twenty-first century.

This volume contains chapters which describe the status of government policies and the status of employed women in different Chinese nation-states at the beginning of the twenty-first century. In addition to a chapter on Singapore, we include the People's Republic of China, Hong Kong and Taiwan (the Republic of China) as separate chapters, even though they are currently considered by some to be a single nation, because each of these entities has a distinctive history as well as different legal and economic systems that provide different options and constraints for women who work for pay outside the domestic sphere.

The volume concentrates on paid work for women and includes discussion of workers in high government and management positions as well as those working in difficult factory or service conditions. The book does not attempt to address uncompensated work even though many women labor for no compensation. It also does not include analyses of the employment concerns of women working in the underground or illegal economy. We hope there are other scholars who will address the concerns of these women in another volume.

For each of the chapters that summarize a specific location, the author listed first is a scholar whose personal background is from the culture being described, to ensure that the interpretation of statistics and laws and government actions is consistent with internal perceptions. In addition to these 'insider' perspectives, the authors of all chapters have reviewed the work of each chapter in the volume and contributed suggestions from their different perspectives. We chose this process in the hope that through this dialogue of opinions, each work could be strengthened. The final authority, however, has always rested with the credited authors.

The idea for this volume arose out of a symposium proposal for the Academy of Management meetings about Chinese women's lives in different parts of the world. It was shaped by the interests of the women scholars we were able to locate in various Chinese societies and grew to the present volume after almost five years of research, writing, reviewing and editing. Because national statistics are collected in different ways and published in different years using different formats, the authors could not always produce parallel data and information for each country; however each author tried to provide a picture at the beginning of the new century with additional background data from the twentieth century where it was available. The authors also come from different academic cultures that have different views about relevance and appropriateness. We have tried to honor each tradition while creating enough similarity to provide relevant information to the reader. These differences have prevented us from conducting statistical comparisons between entities; however the global picture described of each nation-state can give the reader some sense of possible similarities and differences even with the lack of statistical tests for significant differences.

The book is divided into three sections: Part I, 'Western theory and Chinese culture', provides a theoretical introduction from both Chinese and Western perspectives; Part II, 'Government policies and the employment status of Chinese women', provides summaries from each nation-state; Part III, 'Conclusions', provides a comparative summary. The contributors hope that this work will provide a story of Chinese women at the turn of the twentieth to twenty-first century that will be a useful benchmark for government officials, organizational policy makers, scholars and women themselves to build upon for the rest of the twenty-first century.

The book begins in Part I with 'Theoretical perspectives on women's employment careers in a national government context' by Cherlyn Skromme Granrose, Irene Hau-Siu Chow and Irene K.H. Chew. This chapter outlines major theories of careers of employed women taken primarily from a Western academic tradition. Some might question the need or even propriety of including Western theories in a collection of descriptions about Chinese women; however almost all of the previous empirical and theoretical work on employment of women in the twentieth century has focused on this tradition, and the training of most of the authors of this volume has occurred in the Western academic tradition. To ignore this background or to pretend that it has not shaped the perspective of the authors and many readers would be misleading.

It would be equally misleading to ignore the Chinese cultural and scholarly tradition that shapes the everyday lives and assumptions of authors and women and readers of this volume. The Chinese traditional perspective is described in Chapter 2, 'Images of women and government in the Chinese cultural heritage', by Cherlyn Skromme Granrose. By reading from the Western tradition presented in Chapter 1 in juxtaposition to the Taoist, Confucian, Buddhist and Legalist cultural influences presented in Chapter 2, the first two chapters provide the Chinese and Western perspectives that form a foundation for the rest of this volume. Both of these traditions are also used in the concluding chapter, Chapter 8, to provide different frameworks with which to interpret the authors' findings.

In Part II, the third chapter, 'National policy influence on women's careers in the People's Republic of China', by Yong-Qing Fang, Cherlyn Skromme Granrose and Rita V. Kong (Mei Hui Jiang), begins the descriptive section of different Chinese national systems. This chapter examines legislation, policy and constitutional provisions about women and the status of women in mainland People's Republic of China (PRC) under the current government system of Chinese socialism with market characteristics.

In addition to being the motherland from which most of the women's ancestors in all other chapters come, the nation of the PRC has a unique government history. During the first half of the twentieth century this nation moved from an empire, through a brief period of democracy, to warlord and Kou Min Tang (KMT) governments. In the second half of the twentieth century the current government controlled by the Chinese Communist Party (CCP) has also explored aspects of a market economy. Thus the PRC is the only situation described here where communist and socialist and market political and economic philosophies have all had an influence on the cultural traditions of the Chinese. While the chapter cannot review each of these political periods separately, it describes the situation at the turn of the twenty-first century that resulted from the influences of each of these systems. This chapter also reports the situation of the largest numerical population of Chinese women in the world.

The fourth chapter, 'Women in Taiwan: social status, education and employment', by T.K. Peng and Tsai-Wei Wang describes how the government has experienced influences from the ancient indigenous island culture, Chinese mainland immigration over many years, recent government by the Kuomingtang fleeing the Communist army on mainland China at the end of the 1940s, and finally a non-KMT elected government to start the new century. Because this society has not felt the influence of the CCP,

or Western colonial rule, it may be closer than the others described here to
the evolution of a traditional Chinese culture in a market economic system.

Chapter 5, 'The impact of government policy on working women in
Hong Kong', by Irene Hau-Siu Chow, also relates the tale of a Chinese
island flooded with immigrants from the Chinese mainland over most of its
history. In this case the political system has had a different British Empire
colonial history during most of the twentieth century. Hong Kong returned
to PRC rule in 1997 but has permitted the territory to maintain the market
economy left as the British legacy, with some continuing tension about the
extent of independence from PRC influence. Thus we have a Chinese
culture influenced by a British view of a free market economy within a colonial political system recently transformed by renewed political influence of
the PRC.

'The impact of government and family responsibilities on the career
development of working women in Singapore' by Irene K.H. Chew and
Naresh Khatri is the sixth chapter. This presents the status of working
women on another Chinese-dominated island, this time off the tip of
Malaysia, which experienced British colonial rule for the first half of the
twentieth century until it became independent from Britain and Malaysia
in 1959. The first decade after independence was a time of turmoil,
separating from Malaysia and fighting insurgent Chinese Communists. For
most of the latter half of the twentieth century the Singaporean government reflected the strong paternalistic and centralized government of a
Chinese majority with some influence of the Malay, Indian and British
minorities operating under a market economic system.

This section concludes with an in-depth study of the specific implemen-
tations of national policies at the local level in one Chinese province near
Beijing. 'Women's development in Hebei Province, PRC' by Yong-Qing
Fang presents an evaluation of public policy and provides one indication
of the problems and triumphs of local efforts to implement policies to
support women at the time the international women's conference was
meeting in the PRC. This chapter also serves to illustrate both the triumphs
and the gaps in policy administration as local governments seek to apply
national policy directives.

In Part III of this volume, Chapter 8, 'Chinese women, half the sky, little
ground: comparative comments on Chinese women's lives under various
government systems', Cherlyn Skromme Granrose uses the theoretical
frameworks from the first part of the book to provide an analysis of the
effects of the various political systems on the lives of Chinese women and
to cast a critical eye toward the descriptive and empirical findings from the
different settings. Because it was not possible to obtain trustworthy equivalent statistics that are comparable across countries, the final comparison

cannot rest on a quantitative analysis of the country data but must examine the collective experience portrayed by the whole chapter from each location. In every case, a clear gap remains between the employment lives of women and of men in each of these Chinese societies, and this gap is clearly tied to gender roles prescribed by family obligations arising from Chinese cultural traditions and gender discrimination that exists in both Chinese and Western societies. The chapter concludes with some recommendations for change captured from each of the authors' work.

The contributors hope that through the juxtaposition of work on women of a similar culture heritage living under different government systems, some scholars, women and government leaders might gain new insights that will benefit Chinese working women wherever they live.

PART I

Western theory and Chinese culture

1. Theoretical perspectives on women's employment careers in a national government context

Cherlyn Skromme Granrose, Irene Hau-Siu Chow and Irene K.H. Chew

At the turn of the twenty-first century, women held all kinds of occupations from corporate presidents, engineers, lawyers and doctors, to construction workers, homemakers and maids. But in many locations women were not distributed among these occupations in the way that men were distributed, and they were not paid the same as men who held these same occupations (Blackwell, 2003; Cohen, 2004; Burress and Zucca, 2004). This chapter is devoted to theoretical explanations of the careers of women, why the careers of women might differ from the career patterns of men, and in what way the national settings in which women and men live influence their careers. First, the chapter introduces some basic career vocabulary and career perspectives. The second part of the chapter reviews the competing theoretical models that are used to explain why women's careers most often result in fewer women attaining top positions in organizational hierarchies, and in women more often being paid less than men. These theoretical perspectives are derived from European and American literature and are supplemented with examples from both Western and Asian empirical work. The chapter also includes a simple theoretical model for how national-level career constructs have an impact on careers, and discusses how these national differences might affect gender differences in careers.

THEORETICAL CAREER PERSPECTIVES

In American and European theory a career is 'the evolving sequence of a person's lifelong series of work related experiences and attitudes' (Hall & Associates, 1986). A career is both a system of positions that an individual holds throughout his or her life, and the internal feelings, attitudes and beliefs that a person might hold about those positions. An occupation is a career to a person if the individual associates his or her self-identity, self-definition and self-concept to it (Jackson et al., 1994).

Career Development Theories

The two broad schools of theories explaining career development and career choice are matching theories and process theories (Hall, 1976). Major representative examples of the main theories are presented in Table 1.1. Matching theories analyse different personalities and traits of individuals, and recommend suitable occupations. Some examples of matching theories are the Work Adjustment Theory, the Trait and Factor Theory, and Holland's Theory of Types (Holland, 1973; Adeymo, 2002). As one president of Harvard University discovered to his dismay when making comments to the contrary, the extent that men and women are born with or are socialized to hold different characteristics (Browne, 2002; Eccles et al., 2000) is not a primary explanation for occupational segregation by gender, even though these theories recommend that individuals select occupations that match their personal characteristics. In addition, these theories do not primarily address processes of occupational choice or the processes that occur as people change jobs throughout a career. Since most people hold multiple positions and even multiple occupations throughout their careers, for the purpose of this research we shall focus on the descriptive process theories that seek to explain patterns of behavior and processes of choice within careers, rather than theories that focus on the prescriptive choice of a single best occupation.

Process theories often are based on Erikson's (1968) view of development. His theory of life-cycle development explains how changes in individual needs and competencies over time and age affect career development. Erikson's work focused on the lives of men, but does not explain how women's career development may differ from the career development of men when women consider family roles to be as important, or more important, than employment roles, and when women seek to balance their employment and family roles. Because of the particular pattern of family and employment roles associated with many women's lives, some career theories have been developed or adapted specifically to address the careers of women.

Early female career development research looked mainly at career patterns based on the central proposal that the central life role of a woman is that of 'homemaker'. Zytowski (1969) used three dimensions – the age of entry, span of participation and degree of participation in the labor force – as the backbone of a description of women's career development patterns. In reality, interruptions and time lags are common in many of the career

Table 1.1 Career development theories

Name of theory	Authors/contributors	Year	Perspective
Matching theories			
– Trait and Factor Theory	Frank Parson	1909	• Focuses on the match between an individual's aptitudes, achievements, interests, values and personality, and the requirements and conditions of occupations
	Edmund G. Williamson	1939/ 1965/1972	• Relies heavily on use of test and inventories
– Work Adjustment Theory	Rene Dawis and Lloyd Lofquist	1984	• States an individual's abilities and values can predict work adjustment and length of time on the job
– Holland's Theory of Types	John Holland	1966/ 1973/ 1985	• Defines 6 personality types (Realistic, Investigative, Artistic, Social, Enterprising, Conventional) that can be matched with a corresponding environment
			• Congruence is achieved when the type of client is assessed and matched with appropriate occupations

Table 1.1 (continued)

Name of theory	Authors/contributors	Year	Perspective
Matching theories			
– Myers-Briggs Type Theory	Carl Gustav Jung	1921/1971	• States 2 different ways of perceiving (sensing, intuition) and judging (thinking, feeling) • Relates these styles to career decision making and work adjustment
Process theories			
– Super's Lifespan Theory	Super	1957/1970	• Shows relationship between life roles and developmental stages • Phases career development into 4 stages (Exploration, Establishment, Maintenance, Disengagement)
– Triple Helix Theory	Rapoport & Rapoport	1980	• Network model which depicts the career behavior as triple helix • Takes into account the interaction of career with the family
Boundaryless Career; Protean Careers	Arthur & Rousseau; Hall	1996 2002	• Individual not tied to one organization; tied to network or occupation • Individual guided by growth in core value or identity

patterns of women due to differences in life-stage events like marriage, pregnancy, childbirth and childcare (see Table 1.2). Thus the three patterns used by Zytowski seem too simplistic for current times and fail to take into account the nature of jobs and other external environmental factors in the society. Later adaptations have added multiple ages or stages at which women may enter or leave the labor force due to family or leisure obligations (for one example see Rapoport and Rapoport, 1980).

Larwood and Gutek (1987) identified five concerns to take into consideration in the pattern of career development of women. They are career preparedness; opportunities available in the society; the influence of marriage, pregnancy and childbirth; age; and timing. 'Career preparedness' refers to the kind and quality of education that a woman receives, the kind of information that she manages to gather for a particular career, and the mental and physical preparation for a job. 'Opportunities available in the society' refer to the possible chance of employment in the society, which can be subject to the rate, degree and type of economic development in the society. It also depends on the suitability of the kind of jobs available in the society and the mindset of the society at large. The 'influence of marriage, pregnancy and childbirth' are major and critical events in a woman's life and women may be willing to give up their career temporarily or permanently to accommodate to such concerns. 'Age' and 'timing' are the age that a woman is at a particular stage in her life that may affect her career development. For example, if a woman has her first child at the peak of her career at age 35 or before her career has even begun at age 18, the timing may influence whether or not she may decide to give up or modify her employment role.

Super (1957) introduced seven career patterns for women, shown in Table 1.2, that include those who adopt the role of homemaker for most or part of their lives, as well as those who are continuously employed. In today's context, the seven patterns introduced by Super are still valid except that certain patterns such as stable homemaking and the conventional career pattern may describe a smaller percentage of women compared to the findings in 1957, since more mothers work outside the home now than in the previous generation, and today's research focuses on women in all roles – homemakers, managers and non-managerial women (Benham, 2000; Hite and McDonald, 2003; Mayrhofer et al., 2004).

Because the careers patterns of many women are drawing closer to the career patterns of men, separate career theories that describe careers of men and women are less common today. Contemporary career theories address careers of both men and women, and a different set of theories try to express the reasons for the existence of gender differences between the careers of men and women.

Table 1.2 Female career patterns

Type	Author, year	Premise	Description
Mild vocational pattern	Zytowski, 1969	Age of entry, span of participation and degree of participation	Early or late entry and brief participation
Moderate pattern	Zytowski, 1969	Age of entry, span of participation and degree of participation	Early and lengthy participation, but low degree of participation
Unusual career pattern	Zytowski, 1969	Age of entry, span of participation and degree of participation	Early entry, lengthy and uninterrupted span and high degree of participation
Stable homemaking	Super, 1957	Interruptions and time lags, life stage events	Marry while in or shortly after leaving school and have no significant working experience
Conventional career pattern	Super, 1957	Interruptions and time lags, life stage events	Work outside the home until marriage
Stable work pattern	Super, 1957	Interruptions and time lags, life stage events	Work continuously- i.e. have a career
Double track	Super, 1957	Interruptions and time lags, life stage events	Combine work and home
Interrupted	Super, 1957	Interruptions and time lags, life stage events	Women returners
Unstable	Super, 1957	Interruptions and time lags, life stage events	Irregular and repeated pattern of home or work involvement
Multiple trial	Super, 1957	Interruptions and time lags, life stage events	Unstable job history

Between the First World War and the 1980s, career development usually meant a system of jobs a person held in one or two organizations, often characterized by a career path of upward mobility, and career development theories, whether addressing the careers of men or the careers of women, assumed employment aimed toward upward mobility within a small number of organizations. Separate career theories of women's careers arose to explain what happened when women left this path of upward mobility to raise a family. During the 1990s, a newer concept of boundaryless careers became applied to both men and women as the psychological contract between individuals and organizations changed and organizations could no longer promise a lifetime employment of upward mobility (Arthur and Rousseau, 1996; Rousseau, 1995; Arnold, 2002). Boundaryless careers span multiple organizations and are defined by individuals who are tied more to their profession or occupations or to a network of peers than to particular organizations (Arthur and Rousseau, 1996). Boundaryless careers include not only upward mobility, but also lateral mobility and mobility through a network of jobs and related occupations in multiple organizations. This concept of careers is especially useful in many service industries and in management or professions where the product of work is knowledge or information rather than tangible goods.

Some individuals follow a career not committed to a single organization but committed to individual career goals. Hall describes these careers as 'protean careers' (Hall, 2002). In protean careers individuals have a guiding commitment related to particular personal career values, which might be upward mobility, or a particular occupation, or personal values in which the individual defines the value as part of his or her own identity and growth.

An individual's identity can be seen as a combination of many different sub-identities (Hall, 1976). The way in which individuals integrate multiple occupational and personal identities and move between roles that depend on different sub-identities is a growing concern in contemporary career theory and has always been a key question in women's careers (Ashforth, 2001; Law et al., 2002; Rothman, 2005). For example employed women with families often take on the sub-identities of a wife, mother and career woman. In the protean career it is possible that a guiding value might be to integrate the multiple sub-identities into a balanced life, and this balanced life would be the value an individual was more committed to than the traditional organizational commitment of previous careers (Reitzes and Mutron, 2002).

Empirical work examining both boundaryless careers and protean careers have had mixed results and it is not yet certain to what extent these concepts are distinctly different, and to what extent they are held by the individuals they propose to describe; however boundaryless careers do seem to have some gender differences. In some empirical studies women more often experience inter-organizational mobility whereas men more often experienced intra-organizational mobility. A differential impact was found on the accompanying spouse of both men and women who experienced inter-organizational mobility in boundaryless career moves. The accompanying spouse experienced a negative impact on pay and upward mobility and little effect on intrinsic outcomes such as job satisfaction (Eby, 2001; Valcour and Tolbert, 2003).

The most recent way of conceptualizing careers breaks from the organization completely. In knowledge work and in information technology industries in particular, careers have become 'extra-organizational', that is outside organizations altogether. In this type of career, the individual has a contract or temporary position in one organization after another and is essentially self-employed. In these instances, the ultimate boundaryless career is enacted with the professional network and staffing agencies becoming the extra-organizational career development vehicle for both men and women in these new types of careers (Muryn-Kaminski and Reilly, 1984; Bidwell, 2005; Fernandez-Mateo, 2005).

The old implied contract was that a worker gave loyalty and labor in exchange for pay and lifetime employment. In the newer context of corporate downsizings, mergers and lay-offs, when many employees know they cannot count on continuous employment with any employer, careers have become more self-managed, and more the responsibility of the individual employee (Shore and Coyle-Shapiro, 2003). Some forward-looking employers are being persuaded that they must invest in human career capital and project-based learning to enter into a more collaborative career management partnership with their employees (Inkson and Arthur, 2002). Whether individuals see themselves as guided by personal values and growth as in the protean career, or committed to an occupation or personal network of a boundaryless career because the organization cannot be trusted to look out for their own long-term career welfare, or in an extra-organizational career, moving from one employment contract to another, most employees believe that the balance of career development has shifted from counting on the organization for career management to taking care of one's career oneself (Aselage and Eisenberger, 2003). In order to meet the needs of their clients, career counselors inside and outside of organizations have been forced to go to the internet and web pages to meet the needs of these individuals, which also may have significant gender implications for many women with limited access to appropriate technology at home (Harris-Bowlsbey, 2002).

Neither the theories that addressed the careers of women as distinctly separate entities because they include the occupation of homemaker, nor the newer ways of looking at careers as boundaryless or protean or extra-organizational, can account for the persistent fact that in most circumstances, women do not have the same employment experiences as men. An entirely different set of social science theories has arisen that address this question.

THEORIES OF GENDER DIFFERENCES IN EMPLOYMENT

Four primary theories are commonly used to explain careers differences between men and women: gender role socialization theory, human capital theory, dual labor force theory and discrimination theory. In some cases these theories are compared to each other to determine which provides a better explanation for gender differences; more commonly they are used within different social science traditions to explain different parts of the phenomenon of women's careers. In this case we will explain each basic theory and provide a few Western and Asian examples of recent empirical findings which describe common women's career situations, to enable the reader to see how each of these theories is currently being used and to indicate how the theory might serve as a potential explanation for the data found in the more complete description of Chinese women's experience to follow in later chapters.

Gender Role Socialization Theory

Gender role socialization theory explicitly defines gender roles within the family and affects the roles people adopt outside the family as well (Eagly, 1987; Eccles et al., 2000). Boys are taught that a man's role is that of the breadwinner outside of the family and decision maker inside the family, while girls are taught that a woman's role is largely domestic, as a mother, wife and homemaker. The paid 'work' role refers to the direct contribution to the production of goods and services consumed by society, while the 'family' role refers to the bearing, nursing, caring and raising of children, and the feeding and caring of adult men, as well as care for elderly parents and their siblings (Lim, 1982).

Gender role socialization also affects women's career choices as young girls, causing them to prepare for careers that fit their stereotype of those appropriate for women, or to prepare only for the roles of wife and mother, even though statistically most will be employed at some time during their lives (Sen, 2003). Gender role socialization further reinforces the sexual division of labor, with the family as women's primary role obligation, even when both spouses are working outside home.

Because of the physiological characteristics of childbirth and nursing, many cultures, including Chinese cultures, consider the family role of women to be a primary life role regardless of whether a woman works in the home without wages or for pay outside the family. The work of a house-wife and mother is not just something you do, it is somebody you are, that is, a sub-identity (Rowbotham, 1973).

According to gender role socialization theory, being female can have a negative effect on women's employment in several ways. First, paid work roles and unpaid family work roles affect each other. Role conflict may arise when a woman desires or has no choice but to take on the work and family roles at the same time (O'Leary, 1977; Adams, 1984; Pleck, 1985). Working women today often face inter-role conflict (Noor, 2004). The emotional stress and psychological pressure from competing demands of having to handle the two roles, combined with guilt arising from being unable to play the two roles well, make it even more difficult to undertake each role effectively and efficiently and require frequent trade-offs that may have a negative effect on either role (Mennino and Brayfield, 2002).

Enacting more than one role may also have positive effects up to certain limits. Even though there are most certainly time conflicts, enacting mul-tiple roles such as employee and mother or wife may create benefits such as added income, positive mental health and increased opportunities for success, as well as buffering effects against failure in one role, more social support, expanded frames of reference, increased self-complexity and increased marital satisfaction due to an increase in similarity of male and female roles (Barnett and Shibley-Hyde, 2001; Edwards and Rothbard, 2000; Rothbard, 2001).

A second effect on women's employment is that devotion to family roles may increase her time spent out of the labor force. Childbirth and childrearing often cause the intermittent pattern of a woman's employment career. A bi-modal work profile (leaving work to care for children and returning when the children go to school) provides the basis for employer prejudice. If employers expect to lose women to childrearing, they are less willing to hire them and less willing to train them (Sullerot, 1971).

Third, gender role socialization also affects job opportunities available for women in several different ways. When girls prepare for careers that they believe are appropriate for gender roles that fit their stereotype of what is female, they also limit the types of occupations open to them later in life. Later, in trying to adapt and make personal adjustments to balance their working and family life, their career paths and patterns may vary greatly from that of a man. When women are socialized into jobs consist-ent with traditional gender roles corresponding to their primary responsi-bility of home management and childcare, these jobs are feminized, and as a result women are segregated in low-paid, boring, monotonous, routine jobs (Geib and Lueptow, 1996).

The empirical research finds many examples of gender role socialization in contemporary society. Although both men and women in contemporary careers say they expect to be employed, gender differences in expectations about the importance of family roles persist in both European and Asian cultures. For example in PR China, husbands were found to be more highly devoted to the paid work role than their wives, and there is open discussion of the conflict between male and female roles in family and employment (Aifeng, 2000; Zuo, 2003). Among Singaporean women, when both career-priority and family-priority women were interviewed, they openly discussed their responsibilities to family roles as well as to their employment roles as a factor that had an impact on their career decisions (Burke and Kong, 1996). Hong Kong professional women experienced significant role conflict between employment and family role expectations, and greatly desired more flexible working hours, a solution amenable to both employer and government policy reforms (Lo, 2003).

Recent studies of gender occupational segregation in the US concluded that by including the occupation of housewife in the analysis, measures of occupational segregation declined over time, revealing that in fact occupational desegregation was not due as much to changes in the gender composition of various occupations as it was to the movement of women out of the occupation of housewife (Cohen, 2004). This means that even as more women enter the paid workforce, they join co-workers who are also women, and this stereotyping of occupations is as much a result of gender role socialization as is women choosing to inhabit the occupation of housewife. American men still find the worker role more salient to their identity, while women find other roles such as mother, wife and homemaker more salient and central (Reitzes and Mutran, 2002). US women also continue to do more housework than their spouses, and some do not perceive this to be unfair (Grote et al., 2002).

Socialization of traditional gender roles exists among young people as well as adults. Among Canadian and Chinese college students, career success was an important value for both men and women, but the young women were more likely to rate work–family balance more highly in their work goals than were young men, and similar samples of college students could predict occupations based on gender stereotypical information (Bu and McKeen, 2001; Zhou et al., 2004). US high school youth are apparently similar in their job-related values. Both girls and boys valued extrinsic rewards (such as pay and promotions) equally, but girls were much more interested in intrinsic rewards and in work–leisure or work–social contribution balance, although boys seemed more interested in having time for family, a definite change from earlier findings (Marini et al., 1996).

In each of these instances, women and girls were conscious of their non-work roles or of balancing family and employment roles in a way that gender socialization theory predicts to have an impact on their careers, while the men in every study (but one study of US boys' values) were less likely to take family roles into account.

Human Capital Theory

Another explanation of gender differences in careers is human capital theory. Human capital theory views women as accumulating less human capital than men through obtaining less education or by gaining fewer years of work experience when they leave the labor force for family responsibilities or when firms refuse to give women training (Mincer, 1962; Becker, 1975). Much of the access to human capital investment is structured by employers' policies within firms. Low investment by women may not be through personal choice, but through discrimination in access to training for women workers. Consequently lack of training affects the quality of the female labor supply and also affects the opportunities available to women who have lower human capital.

The recent empirical evidence related to human capital theory is voluminous and varies by nation, occupation and the aspect of human capital to which one refers – training or experience. For example, Shu and Bian (2003) analysed the gender gap in wages in PR China and found that the portion of the wage gap due to differences in education and occupational segregation increased between 1988 and 1995, while the portion due to affiliation with party membership or state economic sector had decreased during the same time period of great market economic reform. In Taiwan, gender differences in training in high-tech firms still exist (Huang, 1999). A recent analysis in Korea concluded that both differences in human capital (including less education and less time in the labor force) as well as institutional discrimination of less frequent promotions and job segregation, accounted for gender differences in pay between 1988 and 1999 (Yoo, 2003). However one study of hiring of female college graduates in Japan found that forms of social capital such as youth and a Home Economics major which would make a woman good marriage material for managers had more positive impact on hiring decisions than traditional human capital variables such as graduating from a four-year versus two-year college (Fujimoto, 2004). The women in Hong Kong however are postponing marriage in order to obtain more education, in hopes of increasing their human capital advantages for employment (Wong, 2003).

In the United States, there is some indication that previous gender differences in training may be less common in some occupations (Simpson and Stroh, 2002), perhaps due to particular training needs in computer-related, gender-segregated, women-dominated clerical jobs, although some traditional average labor market experience gaps, while narrowing, still remain (Blau et al., 1997). Explanations of the paucity of women at the top of US corporations continue to rely on human capital theory even though the differences in job tenure and experience do not account in total for the great differences in the numbers of men versus women heading US firms (Tharenou, 2001; Burress and Zucca, 2004).

More recent discussions of human capital theory are more complex than simply looking at total amount of education or labor force participation. For example a path-analytic study that included multiple predictors of career success did find that education and career impatience influenced willingness to relocate, which led to exposure to more powerful networks, and for men but not for women this exposure led to more promotions and thus higher levels and more pay, a finding that combines human capital theory and discrimination theory described later (Eddleston et al., 2004).

A more recent discussion about the mechanisms of gender differences in pay arising from gender segregation in occupations is related in part to human capital claims by Tam (1997, 2000) that men are more likely than women to invest in specialized human capital (training in firm-specific skills). These investments in firm-specific learning make job shifts more costly for workers and are compensated by firms just as are other capital investments. This has generated a healthy debate and mixed empirical work (for example see Tomaskovic-Devey and Skaggs, 2002) but support seems to be present for women still obtaining less on-the-job training than men, and therefore having lower human capital for future jobs and future compensation.

In summary, while more women are seeking and obtaining extra training, they may still receive less on-the-job training and still may have less total job tenure or total number of years in the labor force in later years of their careers than men, and this may account for some, but not all of the gender differences in pay and higher positions.

Dual Labor Market Theory

A third explanation for gender differences in careers is the dual labor market theory that states that women may be more likely to take part-time jobs to fit in with their family responsibilities (Bosanquet and Doeringer, 1973). Women seeking part-time jobs are often confined to the disadvantaged secondary sector of low-paid, less secure, less skilled and less rewarding jobs. A dual labor market does not need to occur only in low-status jobs; it may also occur in professional occupations where women are segregated into less desirable positions because they have taken time off for childbearing or because they want to have part-time work to be with their families.

Effects of different labor markets are more commonly cited in studies on ethnicity and race than they are in studies on gender, as this theory has received less attention and support than the other theories since it was proposed in the 1970s (McNabb and Psacharopoulos, 1981). However dual labor markets according to gender still seem to exist in empirically detectible forms when examining occupational prestige in the United States (Lemelle, 2002) across many occupations, as well as when looking at something as detailed as the labor market among academics in the legal profession (McBrier, 2003). In each of these instances, the pay and prestige of the labor market containing jobs in which women were more often employed were lower than the pay and prestige of the labor market composed of jobs held more often by men.

Gender Discrimination Theory

Discrimination can be viewed as arising from institutional and structural aspects deeply embedded in the organization's systems, practices and assumptions (Meyerson and Fletcher, 2000) as well as from individual cognitive processes. The gender gap in career progression has often been linked to institutional barriers as well as individual choices made by people in positions of power. For example the lack of attribution of competency that may occur when a women is hired or evaluated is one mechanism of discrimination in individual choice (Cole et al., 2004; Fuegen et al., 2004). This attribution error is one of the reasons for slow progression in women's careers (Lyness and Thompson, 1997). Discrimination bias in attribution favors men, that is, the success of men is attributed to ability while the success of women is attributed to luck (Burke and McKeen, 1992; Swim and Sanna, 1996). Another individual perception bias occurs through role incongruity. In this instance, the gender role expectations for the female gender role are incongruous with the role expectations for the role of leader or manager. This incongruity leads to bias, prejudice and less positive evaluations than the evaluations of male individuals whose gender roles more closely follow the roles congruous with expectations of leader roles (Harris, 2004; Eagly and Karau, 2004).

The institutional biases are biases built into employment policies. Biased employment policies have resulted in women not having equal access to career-enhancing resources and opportunities. For example in many organizations women receive fewer training and development opportunities, and are denied valuable line positions or opportunities for working overseas that are considered essential to further promotions.

Unfortunately many empirical examples of discrimination still exist, although many younger women believe gender discrimination is diminishing. Recent US studies of managerial and professional employees, doctors and lower-level government employees have found evidence of discrimination in hiring, promotions, opportunity structures and pay that could not be accounted for by differences in human capital, occupational preferences or other alternative non-discrimination-related explanations (Heilman, 2001; Baker et al., 2002; Carr et al., 2003; Chernesky, 2003; Ngo et al., 2003; Petersen and Saporta, 2004). Women can experience negative emotional reactions to discrimination that may have negative work outcomes (Schmitt et al., 2003). Women recognized they were being discriminated against in Asia as well. When encountering discrimination, women in Hong Kong were more likely to recognize the gender discrimination, more likely to complain and less likely to resign or neglect their work if they had more education (Ngo et al., 2002).

Each of the four theories of gender differences has its proponents and has provided some evidence of different experiences of men and women in the labor force in Western and Asian settings in the beginning of the twenty-first century. Changes are occurring as organizations become more flexible and as individuals adjust to taking more responsibility for their own careers. Just as we have examined the organizational and individual forces that cause gender differences to occur in careers, we must also examine the role of national governments in shaping women's careers.

Some believe that with the onset of global organizations, global migrations of labor, and cross-governmental or regional alliances, the impact of national boundaries is becoming less important in today's business environment; while others claim that national laws and trade restrictions as well as cultural characteristics maintained by a common national heritage still have a strong influence on the ways business is conducted and how societies organize themselves to have the ability to create innovative capabilities if firms in a knowledge-based economy (Sassen, 1990; Nachum, 2003). While acknowledging the role of flow of individuals and knowledge across borders, this volume retains the perspective that national units of analysis are important. The following section outlines the key factors of nationality that influence individual and organizational careers of women.

NATIONAL GOVERNMENT EFFECTS ON CAREERS

While many cultural groups have identifiable shared belief and behavior patterns of employment, nations have two characteristics which make them especially useful units for career research: (1) particular geographic locations with generally recognized physical boundaries; and (2) specific political-legal systems which formally regulate economic activity within this geophysical space. The geographic unit is important because it provides the physical resources and limitations available for individuals and organizations to use in economic or work activities. The political-legal system is important because it defines the resources not available internally that may be imported, the products which may be exported, and the mechanisms which may or may not be used within the national boundaries to transform raw materials into marketable products or to provide needed services (Porter, 1990). Since these laws and regulations shape economic activity, they have a powerful impact on employing organizations and the careers possible within them. In addition, national units have a history of political leaders, economic development and recessions, wars, colonialism and forms of economy that create powerful shared history even when political parties or national boundaries change as a result of these leaders and wars. Internal reforms, such as the change to a market economy of the PR China, can have profound effects on wages, promotions and other career dynamics within a nation (Steensma et al., 2000; Cao, 2001).

In an era of international alliances and instant communications, these national legal entities are influenced even more strongly by specific international trade agreements and alliances. The European Union and ASEAN have very different levels of inter-nation agreement, but both of these entities now influence trade and commerce in their respective spheres and have an influence on intra-national economic activity (Verdier and Breen, 2001). In addition, organizations such as the World Trade Organization (WTO) that establishes rules for international trade, also influence the rise and fall of trade barriers between nations. In particular for this study, the addition of PR China into WTO membership is having a major impact on many industries around the globe.

The effect of this international activity on an individual career occurs through the effect of government policy on organizational strategy (Jackson et al., 2003). This volume is not seeking to explain the flow of women across national borders, nor are we focusing on explaining the current phenomenon of jobs migrating from high-wage locations to low-wage locations across national borders (Collins, 2002). Rather, by using the nation as the unit of analysis, we focus on the national policy effects on women who occupy the jobs available to them, including both jobs and individuals that have entered the country from other nations (Kupferberg, 2003).

If we look at careers using a national level of analysis, there are several types of information that can be useful to describe how nations differ in career patterns and how government patterns influence those careers.

Allaire and Firsirotu (1984) have described the interrelationships between the society, the organization and the individual in a way that is particularly useful when thinking about cognitive processes important to knowledge workers. In their conceptual framework the ambient society's national culture influences organizational and individual beliefs and processes. Individual beliefs influence the organizational beliefs and processes which create individual and collective behavior as organizational and individual output. These relationships have been applied to a model of cross-cultural careers by Granrose (1997) as seen in Figure 1.1. This model is useful primarily in outlining the key characteristics of a nation that have a specific impact on careers.

To focus on the national level of analysis, scholars must examine the national identity, national career-related beliefs, national career-related behaviors and national career-related processes that describe how these characteristics influence organizations and individual lives.

1. National career identity: the unique characteristics of a nation which define itself and its economic relationship to other nations. The career-relevant characteristics include political history, religions, number and relative size and power of ethnic groups, languages, political and

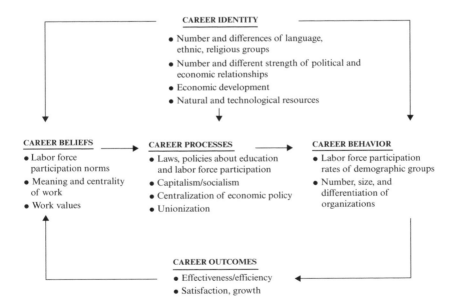

Figure 1.1   National career model

trade relationships, and natural and technological resources which are available for economic activity. The international trade relationships and intergovernmental relationships entered into by a nation would fall in this domain.

2. National career-related beliefs: evaluative and descriptive thoughts about work which are commonly held by members of a national unit, such as norms for appropriateness of gender, age and ethnic group participation in the labor force, nationally shared beliefs about the meaning of work, and nationally shared work values. Beliefs and norms about the appropriateness of mothers entering the labor force or normative obligations of daughters to undertake the work of caring for ageing parents would be examples of this domain.

3. National career-related behavior patterns: national patterns of labor force distribution extending across time, across organizations and across occupations. Examples of behavioral patterns include the structure and distribution of the labor force as well as the structure and distribution of organizations in the nation.

4. National career-related processes: formal and informal governmental policies addressing or structuring work behavior patterns. These include capitalist or socialist economy, policies oriented toward preservation of stability versus tolerance of social turbulence, provisions for educational preparation for work, as well as centralization or dispersion of economic planning and control. Policies relevant for this study would be whether or not a nation had childcare policies or policies promoting equal employment opportunities for women and men.

In order to understand how careers of women of a common Chinese ethnic culture might differ depending upon the nation in which they live or work, these characteristics of each nation can be identified. The international influences of global business and world trade affect the national policies about imports and exports as well as policies about immigration and expatriation (Linehan and Walsh, 2001; Selmer and Leung, 2003). These national policies in turn influence organizational strategies such as whether or not to locate a particular service operation or production facility in a particular nation, as well as whether to staff it with local employees or home office managers. These organizational strategic choices influence whether or not a given woman is presented with a given job opportunity or has that opportunity foreclosed to her. If we identify these processes and characteristic beliefs and behaviors, the patterns may provide information about what has shaped the careers of women in this nation.

We can also use this model to identify aspects of the theories of gender differences that might differ by nation. For example gender socialization theory has as its key characteristic the norms about family and work roles for men and women. To the extent that these roles are defined by a common Chinese heritage, one would expect that all Chinese women would be socialized in similar ways. But the national careers model also indicates that there are significant national differences in the gender norms for men and women, and sociological and economic analysis bear out national differences in family gender roles (Esping-Andersen, 1999). To the extent that these norms differ in the different nations that we include in this volume, we would expect that gender differences in family and work roles would have a different effect on gender differences in the careers of men and women in different Chinese nations.

Human capital theory relies on differences in education, training and labor force experience as explanations for gender differences in careers. The national careers model indicates that nations differ in the extent to which national policies encourage access to education and training, and they also differ in the norms and laws for age of labor force participation for both men and women. Thus we might expect these areas of government policy and social norms to be potential sources of impact on the careers of Chinese women.

Dual labor market theory suggests that women are segregated into a separate labor market when they seek work or are shunted into part-time jobs that combine well with childcare responsibilities. To the extent that a national government has policies that provide alternative daycare support, provide mechanisms or rewards for organizations to give fringe benefits for part-time workers, or contain social norms that segregate domestic and childcare work from other occupations by status or pay, we would expect to see national differences related to this theory. Studies of US work–family policies and programs show how these government policies affect the employed lives of women (Grosswald et al., 2001).

National policies related to prevention of gender discrimination such as equal pay or equal employment laws or constitutional clauses or amendments are obvious ways in which national differences might appear in accordance with discrimination theory. In addition to these obvious mechanisms, there may also be more subtle ways in which national policy might support or discourage discrimination. These include the extent to which government employee policies are non-discriminatory, or the extent to which the government takes a leadership role in encouraging non-discriminatory actions by industry and business leaders that operate within its boundaries, as well as the kinds of cross-border relationships and actions related to stopping gender discrimination that the government undertakes. A recent study of six European, African and Asian nations, including the US, India and Malaysia, did find national differences in affirmative action policies that made a difference in working lives of women and men in the nations involved (Jain et al., 2003), so it seems possible that similar differences might be found in the Chinese nations included in this volume.

In conclusion, women's careers can be described by the occupations they choose, by the extent to which their employment career and their family career interact, the extent to which they are tied to a single, or many, or no organization, or the extent to which they are guided by their own concept of identity and commitment to individual goals. The differences between men's and women's careers may be attributed to women's socialization to different gender roles, their limits in education and training, the smaller amounts of time they spend in the labor force, their segregation into separate occupations or the part-time labor force, or to discrimination. Some empirical work with UN and other data-sets suggest that national gender equity measures predict levels of work–family support in organizations, union support of women and equitable pay, all of which directly affect women's work lives (Jain et al., 2003; Lyness and Kropf, 2005).

A limited number of empirical studies have examined national differences in family-oriented policies and practices to determine the impact of government policy differences on women's employment in North America and in European nations. One study found that women's employment continuity was highest in nations with welfare-related economic systems, and with governments with specific policies that support working mothers (Stier and Lewin-Epstein, 2001). Another study of OECD countries found that no one economic system provided the best support for women's employment, but those countries with specific policies that supported women had the largest effects (Gornick et al., 1996).

Each of the gender-difference theoretical forces may vary by national career-related history, policy, norms and national career-related behavior patterns that may vary from the common Chinese cultural heritage that the women in this volume share. These theoretical backgrounds available to us from a Euro-American tradition do not point to one theory as better, or more appropriate, than another for the Chinese situation. Rather, we have chosen to present the major perspectives in broad terms that are more likely to cross cultural borders. What evidence is available from a Western perspective tends to indicate that it is specific policies and laws rather than broad economic systems that make a difference between nations in women's employment experience. In the following chapters we will look first at the common Chinese cultural heritage that the women in all of these nations share, and then examine the experience of Chinese women in each Asian nation individually.

REFERENCES

Adams, J.M. (1984), 'When working women become pregnant', *New England Business Journal*, February, 18–21.

Adeymo, S.A. (2002), 'The determinants of occupational choice: a literature survey (1980–1989)', *Psychology and Education: An Interdisciplinary Journal*, **39** (3–4), 25–35.

Aifeng, J. (2000), 'The conflict between males and the role of contemporary female professionals', *Chinese Education and Society*, **33** (6), 37–44.

Allaire, Y. and M.E. Firsirotu (1984), 'Theories of organizational culture', *Organizational Studies*, **5** (3), 193–226.

Arnold, J. (2002), 'Careers and career management', in N. Anderson, D.S. Ones, H.K. Sinangil and C. Viswesvaran (eds), *Handbook of Industrial, Work and Organizational Psychology*, vol 2, Thousand Oaks, CA: Sage Publications, pp. 115–32.

Arthur, M.B. and D.M. Rousseau (1996), *The Boundaryless Career: A New Employment Principle for a New Organizational Era*, New York: Oxford University Press.

Aselage, J. and R. Eisenberger (2003), 'Perceived organizational support and psychological contracts: a theoretical integration', *Journal of Organizational Behavior*, **24**, 491–509.

Ashforth, B.E. (2001), *Role Transitions in Organizational Life: An Identity-based Perspective*, Mahwah, NJ: Lawrence Erlbaum Associates.

Baker, B., A. Wendt and W. Slonaker (2002), 'An analysis of gender equity in the federal labor relations career field', *Public Personnel Management*, **31** (4), 559–67.

Barnett, R.C. and J. Shibley-Hyde (2001), 'Women, men, work and family', *American Psychologist*, **56** (10), 781–96.

Becker, G. (1975), *Human Capital*, New York: National Bureau of Economic Research.

Benham, B. (2000), 'Oh, Mother!' *Working Woman*, **25** (10), 16.

Bidwell, M.J. (2005), 'Reworking contingent employment', paper presented to the Academy of Management annual meeting, Honolulu, HI.

Blackwell, L. (2003), 'Gender and ethnicity at work: occupational segregation and disadvantage in the 1991 British census', *Sociology*, **37** (4), 713–31.

Blau, F.D., M. Ferber and A.E. Winkler (1997), *The Economics of Women, Men and Work*, New York: Prentice Hall.

Bosanquet, N. and P.B. Doeringer (1973),'Is there a dual labor market in Great Britain?', *Economic Journal*, **83** (330), 421–35.

Browne, K.R. (2002), *Biology at Work: Rethinking Sexual Equality*, New Brunswick, NJ: Rutgers University Press.

Bu, N. and C.A. McKeen (2001), 'Work goals among male and female business students in Canada and China: the effects of culture and gender', *International Journal of Human Resource Management*, **12** (2), 166–84.

Burke, R.J. and Y.P. Kong (1996),'Career-priority patterns among managerial and professional women in Singapore', *Psychological Reports*, **78** (3), 1304–7.

Burke, R.J. and C.A. McKeen (1992), 'Women in management', in C.I. Cooper and I.T. Robertson (eds), *International Review of Industrial and Organizational Psychology*, **78**, pp. 245–84.

Burress, J.H. and L. Zucca (2004), 'The gender equity gap in top corporate executive positions', *Mid-American Journal of Business*, **19** (1), 55–62.

Cao, Y. (2001), 'Careers inside organizations: a comparative study of promotion determination in reforming China', *Social Forces*, **80** (2), 683–712.

Carr, P.L., L. Szalacha, R. Barnett, C. Caswell and T. Inui (2003), 'A "ton of feathers": gender discrimination in academic medical careers and how to manage it', *Journal of Women's Health*, **12** (10), 1009–18.

Chernesky, R.H. (2003), 'Examining the glass ceiling: gender influences on promotion decisions', *Administration in Social Work*, **27** (2), 13–18.

Cohen, P.N. (2004), 'The gender division of labor: "keeping house" and occupational segregation in the United States', *Gender and Society*, **18** (2), 239–52.

Cole, M.S., H.S. Field and W.F. Giles (2004), 'Interaction of recruiter and applicant gender in resume evaluation: a field study', *Sex Roles*, **51** (9/10), 597–609.

Collins, J.L. (2002), 'Mapping a global labor market: gender and skill in the globalizing garment industry', *Gender and Society*, **16** (6), 921–40.

Dawis, R.V. and L.H. Lofquist (1984), *A Psychological Theory of Work Adjustment*, Minneapolis, MN: University of Minnesota Press.

Eagly, A.H. (1987), *Sex Differences in Social Behavior: A Social-role Interpretation*, Hillsdale, NJ: Lawrence Erlbaum Associates.

Eagly, A.H. and S.J. Karau (2004), 'Role congruity theory of prejudice toward female leaders', *Psychological Review*, **109** (3), 573–98.

Eby, L.T. (2001), 'The boundaryless career experiences of mobile spouses in dual-earner marriages', *Group and Organization Management*, **26** (3), 343–68.

Eccles, J.S., C. Freedman-Doan and P. Frome (2000), 'Gender-role socialization in the family: a longitudinal approach,' in T. Eckes and H.M. Trautner (eds), *Developmental Social Psychology of Gender*, Mahwah, NJ: Lawrence Erlbaum Associates, pp. 333–60.

Eddleston, K.A., D.C. Baldridge and J.F. Veiga (2004), 'Toward modeling the predictors of managerial career success: does gender matter?', *Journal of Managerial Psychology*, **19** (4), 360–85.

Edwards, J.R. and N.P. Rothbard (2000), 'Mechanisms linking work and family: clarifying the relationship between work and family constructs', *Academy of Management Review*, **25** (1), 178–99.

Erikson, E.H. (1968), *Identity: Youth and Crisis*, London: Faber & Faber.

Esping-Andersen, G. (1990), *The Three Worlds of Welfare Capitalism*, Cambridge: Polity Press.

Fernandez-Mateo, I. (2005), 'Beyond organizational careers: information, learning and trust in mediated employment arrangements', presentation to the Academy of Management annual meeting, Honolulu, HI.

Fuegen, K., M. Biernat, E. Haines and K. Deaux (2004), 'Mothers and fathers in the workplace: how gender and parental status influence judgments of job-related competence', *Journal of Social Issues*, **60** (4), 737–55.

Fujimoto, K. (2004), 'Feminine capital: the forms of capital in the female labor market in Japan', *Sociological Quarterly*, **45** (1), 91–111.

Geib, A.E. and L.B. Lueptow (1996), 'Sex, gender stereotypes and work', in P.J. Dubeck and K. Borman (eds), *Women and Work: A Handbook*, New Brunswick, NJ: Rutgers University Press, pp. 243–6.

Gornick, J.C., M.K. Meyers and K.E. Ross (1996), 'Supporting the employment of mothers: policy variation across fourteen welfare states', *Journal of European Social Policy*, **7**, 45–70.

Granrose, C.S. (ed.) (1997), *The Careers of Business Managers in East Asia*, Westport, CT: Quorum.

Grosswald, B., D. Ragland and J.M. Fisher (2001), 'Critique of US work/family programs and policies', *Journal of Progressive Human Services*, **12** (1), 53–81.

Grote, N.K., K.E. Naylor and M.S. Clark (2002), 'Perceiving the division of family work to be unfair: do social comparisons, enjoyment and competence matter?', *Journal of Family Psychology*, **16** (4), 510–22.

Hall, D.T. (1976), *Careers in Organizations*, Santa Monica, CA: Goodyear.

Hall, D.T. (2002), 'The protean career: a quarter-century journey', Everett Hughes Distinguished Speakers Address, presented at the Academy of Management annual meeting, Denver, CO.

Hall, D.T. & Associates (1986), *Career Development in Organizations*, San Francisco, CA: Jossey Bass.

Harris, H. (2004), 'Global careers: work–life issues and the adjustment of women international managers', *Journal of Management Development*, **23** (9), 818–33.

Harris-Bowlsbey, J. (2002), 'Career planning and technology in the 21st century', in S.G. Niles (ed.), *Adult Career Development: Concepts, Issues and Practices, (3rd edn)*, Columbus, OH: National Career Development Association, pp. 157–65.

Heilman, M.E. (2001), 'Description and prescription: how gender stereotypes prevent women's ascent up the organizational ladder', *Journal of Social Issues*, **57** (4), 657–74.

Hite, L.M. and K.S. McDonald (2003), 'Career aspirations of non-managerial women: adjustment and adaptation', *Journal of Career Development*, **29** (4), 221–35.

Holland, J.L. (1966), *The Psychology of Vocational Choice: A Theory of Personality Types and Model Environments*, Waltham, MA: Blaisdell.

Holland, J.L. (1973), *Making Vocational Choices: A Theory of Careers*, Englewood Cliffs, NJ: Prentice Hall.

Holland, J.L. (1985), *Making Vocational Choices: A Theory of Vocational Personalities and Work Environments*, (2nd edn), Englewood Cliffs, NJ: Prentice Hall.

Huang, T.C. (1999), 'Gender differences in company training: the case of Taiwanese high-tech firms', *Employee Relations*, **21** (5), 500–508.

Inkson, K. and M.B. Arthur (2002), 'Career development: extending the "organizational careers" framework', in S. Niles (ed.), *Adult Career Development: Concepts, Issues and Practices*, (3rd edn), Columbus, OH: National Career Development Association, pp. 286–306.

Jackson, L.A., C.N. Hodge and J.M. Ingram (1994), 'Gender and self-concept: A reexamination of stereotypic differences and the role of gender attitudes,' *Sex Roles*, **30**, 615–30.

Jackson, S.E., M.A. Hitt and A.S. DeNisi (eds) (2003), *Managing Knowledge for Sustained Competitive Advantage*, San Francisco, CA: Jossey Bass.

Jain, H.C., P.J. Sloan and F.M. Horowitz, with S. Tagger and N. Weiner (2003), *Employment Equity and Affirmative Action: An International Comparison*, Armonk, NY: M.E. Sharpe.

Jung, C. (1921), *Psychological Types*, Princeton, NJ: Princeton University Press.

Jung, C. (1971), 'Psychological types', *Collected Works*, Vol. 6, Princeton, NJ: Princeton University Press.

Kupferberg, F. (2003), 'The established and the newcomers: what makes immigrant and women entrepreneurs so special?', *International Review of Sociology*, **13** (1), 89–104.

Larwood, L. and B.A. Gutek (1987), 'Working towards a theory of women's career development', in L. Larwood and B.A. Gutek (eds), *Women's Career Development*, Newbury Park, CA: Sage, pp. 170–83.

Law, B., F. Meijers and G. Wijers (2002), 'New perspectives on career and identity in the contemporary world', *Journal of Guidance and Counseling*, **30** (4), 431–49.

Lemelle, A. (2002), 'The effects of the intersection of race, gender and educational class on occupational prestige', *Western Journal of Black Studies*, **26** (2), 89–97.

Lim, Y.C. (1982), 'Women in the Singapore economy', Economic Research Centre, National University of Singapore occasional paper, Singapore: Chopmen Publishers.

Linehan, M. and J.S. Walsh (2001), 'Key issues in the senior female international career move: a qualitative study in a European context', *British Journal of Management*, **12** (1), 85–95.

Lo, S. (2003), 'Perceptions of work–family conflict among married female professionals in Hong Kong', *Personnel Review*, **32** (3), 376–90.

Lyness, K. and D. Thompson (1997), 'Above the glass ceiling? A comparison of matched samples of female and male executives', *Journal of Applied Psychology*, **82** (3), 359–75.

Lyness, K.S. and M.B. Kropf (2005), 'The relationships of national gender equality and organizational support with work–family balance: a study of European managers', *Human Relations*, **58** (1), 33–60.

Marini, M.M., P. Fan, E. Finley and A.M. Beutel (1996), 'Gender and job values', *Sociology of Education*, **69** (1), 49–66.

Mayrhofer, W., A. Iellatchitch and M. Meyer (2004), 'Going beyond the individual: some potential contributions from a career field and habitus perspective for global career research and practice', *Journal of Management Development*, **23** (9), 870–84.

McBrier, D.B. (2003), 'Gender and career dynamics within a segmented professional labor market: the case of law academia', *Social Forces*, **81** (4), 1201–66.

McNabb, R. and G. Psacharopoulos (1981), 'Further evidence on the relevance of the dual labor market hypothesis for the UK', *Journal of Human Resources*, **16** (3), 442–9.

Mennino, S.F. and A. Brayfield (2002), 'Job–family trade-offs', *Work and Occupations*, **29** (2), 226–56.

Meyerson, D.E. and J.K. Fletcher (2000), 'A modest manifesto for shattering the glass ceiling', *Harvard Business Review*, **78** (1), 127–36.

Mincer, J. (1962), 'Labor force participation of married women', in H.G. Lewis, (ed.), *Aspects of Labor Economics*, Princeton, NJ: Princeton University Press, pp. 63–97.

Muryn-Kaminiski, J.A. and A.H. Reilly (1984), 'Career development of women in information technology', *SAM Advanced Management Journal*, **69** (4), 20–31.

Nachum, L. (2003), 'Does nationality of ownership make any difference and if so under what circumstances? Professional service MNEs in global competition', *Journal of International Management*, **9**, 1–32.

Ngo, H., S. Foley, A. Wong and R. Loi (2003), 'Who gets more of the pie? Predictors of perceived gender inequality at work', *Journal of Business Ethics*, **45** (3), 227–43.

Ngo, H., C.S. Tang and W.W. Au (2002), 'Behavioral responses to employment discrimination: A study of Hong Kong workers', *International Journal of Human Resource Management*, **13** (8), 1206–23.

Noor, N.M. (2004), 'Work–family conflict, work- and family-role salience, and women's well-being', *Journal of Social Psychology*, **144** (4), 389–405.

O'Leary, V.E. (1977), *Towards Understanding Women*, Monterey, CA: Brooks/Cole.

Parson, F. (1909), *Choosing a Vocation*, Boston, MA: Houghton-Mifflin.

Petersen, T. and I. Saporta (2004), 'The opportunity structure for discrimination', *American Journal of Sociology*, **109** (4), 852–901.

Pleck, J.H. (1985), *Working Wives/Working Husbands*, Beverly Hills, CA: Sage Publications.

Porter, M. (1990), *The Competitive Advantage of Nations*, New York: Basic Books.

Rapoport, R. and R.N. Rapoport (1980), 'Balancing work, family and leisure: a triple helix model', in C.B. Derr (ed.), *Work Family and Career*, New York: Praeger, pp. 318–28.

Reitzes, D.C. and E.J. Mutran (2002), 'Self-concept as the organization of roles: importance, centrality, and balance', *Sociology Quarterly*, **43** (4), 647–67.

Rothbard, N.P. (2001), 'Enriching or depleting? The dynamics of engagement in work and family roles', *Administrative Science Quarterly*, **46** (4), 655–84.

Rothman, N.B. (2005), 'Complex occupational identities: integrating multiple distinct occupational identities', presentation to the Academy of Management annual meeting, Honolulu, HI.

Rousseau, D.M. (1995), *Psychological Contracts in Organizations: Understanding Written and Unwritten Agreements*, Thousand Oaks, CA: Sage.

Rowbotham, S. (1973), *Woman's Consciousness, Man's World*, Harmondsworth: Penguin Books.

Sassen, S. (1990), *The Mobility of Labour and Capital: A Study in International Investment and Labor Flow*, Cambridge: Cambridge University Press.

Schmitt, M.T., N.R. Branscome and T. Postmes (2003), 'Women's emotional responses to the pervasiveness of gender-discrimination', *European Journal of Social Psychology*, **33** (3), 297–312.

Selmer, J. and A.S.M. Leung (2003), 'International adjustment of female vs. male business expatriates', *International Journal of Human Resource Management*, **14** (7), 1117–31.

Sen, B. (2003), 'Why do women feel the way they do about market work: the role of familial, social and economic factors', *Review of Social Economy*, **61** (2), 211–34.

Shore, L.M. and J.A.M. Coyle-Shapiro (2003), 'New developments in the employee–organization relationship', *Journal of Organizational Behavior*, **24**, 443–50.

Shu, X. and Y. Bian (2003), 'Market transition and gender gap in earnings in urban China', *Social Forces*, **81** (4), 1107–45.

Simpson, Patricia A. and L.K. Stroh (2002), 'Revisiting gender variation in training', *Feminist Economics*, **8** (3), 21–54.

Steensma, H.K., L. Marino and K.M. Weaver (2000), 'The influence of national culture on the formation of technology alliances by entrepreneurial firms', *Academy of Management Journal*, **43** (5), 951–73.

Stier, H. and N. Lewin-Epstein (2001), 'Welfare regimes, family-supportive policies, and women's employment along the life-course', *American Journal of Sociology*, **106** (6), 1731–60.

Sullerot, E. (1971), *Women, Society and Change*, London: Weidenfeld and Nicolson.

Super, D.E. (1957), *The Psychology of Careers: An Introduction to Vocational Development*, New York: Harper & Row.

Super, D.E. (1970), *The Work Values Inventory*, Boston, MA: Houghton Mifflin.

Swim, J. and L.J. Sanna (1996), 'He's skilled, she's lucky: are attributions for others' successes and failures gender biased?', *Personality and Social Psychology Bulletin*, **22**, 507–19.

Tam, T. (1997), 'Sex segregation and occupational gender inequality in the United States: devaluation or specialized training?', *American Journal of Sociology*, **102**, 1652–92.

Tam, T. (2000), 'Occupational wage inequality and devaluation: a cautionary tale of measurement error', *American Journal of Sociology*, **105**, 1752–61.

Tharenou, P. (2001), 'Going up? Do traits and informal social processes predict advancing in management?', *Academy of Management Journal*, **44** (5), 1005–17.

Tomaskovic-Devey, D. and S. Skaggs (2002), 'Sex segregation, labor process organization, and gender earnings inequality', *American Journal of Sociology*, **108** (1), 102–29.

Valcour, P.M. and P.S. Tolbert (2003), 'Gender, family and career in the era of boundarylessness: Determinants and effects of intra-and inter-organizational mobility', *International Journal of Human Resource Management*, **14** (5), 768–87.

Verdier, D. and R. Breen (2001), 'Europeanization and globalization: Politics against markets in the European Union', *Comparative Political Studies*, **34** (3), 227–62.

Williamson, E.G. (1939), *How to Counsel Students*, New York: McGraw Hill.

Williamson, E.G. (1965), *Vocational Counselling: Some Historical, Philosophical, and Theoretical Perspectives*, New York: McGraw Hill.

Williamson, E.G. (1972), 'Trait and factor theory and individual differences', in B. Stefflre and W.H. Grants (eds), *Theories of Counseling*, New York: McGraw Hill, pp. 136–76.

Wong, O.M.H. (2003), 'Postponement or abandonment of marriage? Evidence from Hong Kong', *Journal of Comparative Family Studies*, **34** (4), 531–55.

Yoo, G.J. (2003), 'Women in the workplace: gender and wage differentials', *Social Indicators Research*, **62–63** (1–3), 367–85.

Zhou, L.Y., M.L. Dawson and C.L. Herr (2004), 'American and Chinese college student's predictions of people's occupations, housework responsibilities, and hobbies as a function of cultural and gender influences', *Sex Roles*, **50** (7–8), 547–63.

Zuo, Jiping (2003), 'From revolutionary comrades to gendered partners', *Journal of Family Issues*, **24** (3), 314–38.

Zytowski, D.G. (1969), 'Toward a theory of career development of women', *Personnel and Guidance Journal*, **47**, 660–64.

2. Images of women and government in the Chinese cultural heritage: a brief overview

Cherlyn Skromme Granrose

During the ancient dynasties that ruled various groups of Chinese people before the twentieth century, a feudalistic, patriarchal tradition influenced by the teachings of Lao Tse, Confucius, Buddha and the Legalist scholars dominated the lives of most women (Stockwell, 1993). This tradition spread with the migration of Chinese Han and non-Han people throughout many countries in Asia and became the controlling cultural force in Hong Kong, Singapore, Taiwan and the People's Republic of China (PRC). This brief chapter explores the legacy of Chinese Taoist, Confucian, Buddhist and Legalist traditions for the role of government and the status of women in Chinese society. It focuses on the common cultural heritage of the people so that the effects of specific governmental structure and policies can be seen more clearly in the following chapters addressing the status of women in Taiwan, Singapore, Hong Kong and PRC. Since there are many sects or forms of each of these traditions, only the shared most central teachings will be described, supplemented by quotes when they are available from a primary source.

THE ROLE OF GOVERNMENT AND THE ROLE OF WOMEN IN TAOISM

The animist principle of emphasizing harmony with the natural order of Mother Earth has been extant in China from earliest recorded time. This tradition also includes ideas that spirits inhabit places and things, and that spirits of the deceased could influence daily life among the living. These ideas were formalized into a more structured and widespread religious system about the end of the Spring and Autumn Period when a master–slave social system was beginning to change into feudalism.

The formalization of these beliefs was organized by a man called Lao

Tse or possibly by some of his contemporaries and followers. The life of Lao Tse is almost completely unknown today. He may have been an official in a remote dukedom (Mitchell, 1988). Most think he could have lived about 552 to 497 BCE but others claim 403 BCE, or some scholars even see influences in writings that might have appeared as recently as 221 BCE (Ren, 1993). Although the religious beliefs were systematized by a loose network of teachers and followers, the structure was deliberately decentralized since one of the principles of the philosophy was to free people from the bonds of traditional organized religion and government.

Government

The book attributed to Lao Tse, the *Tao Te Ching*, conceived of society as the interaction between human beings and nature or 'the way things are', rather than as a function of formal government. The central belief is that followers should come to understand the eternal, natural law, or 'heaven's way', rather than the mortal, fallible 'way of the law' (Ren, 1993). The ideal state was perhaps a small state with a sparse population and few laws, since according to the contemporary social conditions, he may have seen law as a tool of the emerging wealthy class. This text preferred to focus on the methods an individual might use to develop his or her relationship to the natural and spiritual world:

> Let the state be small, and let the population be sparse.
> Though there are various kinds of instruments let them not be used;
>   ... The neighboring states are within sight of each other, and the cries of roosters and dogs can be heard by one another,
> But the people do not have any contact with each other until they die of old age.
>   (Ch. 80, trans. Ren, 1993)

He does speak about 'the Master' and some might interpret this as guidelines for a sound governor, although in most translations, it seems to refer more to a learned spiritual leader or sage. There are a few passages that seem to be translated as if they speak more directly about government or rulers:

> The best rulers are those about whom people know nothing but their existence.
> The next best are those whom people love and praise.
> The next are those whom people fear.
> The next are those whom people despise.
> Only when one is not faith-worthy will faithless events take place!
> So idle, [the best rulers] seldom issue any orders.
> When some affairs are accomplished,
> All common people will say 'We are in [did it] ourselves.' (Ch. 17, trans. Ren, 1993)

. . . Therefore the government of the sage [under heaven or the kingdom] lies in:
Simplifying the people's minds,
Filling their bellies,
Weakening their ambitions,
Strengthening their bones,
and always keeping people innocent of knowledge and desires.
[Thus] anyone who thinks himself clever is afraid of meddling.
By handling affairs on the principle of non-action everyone will do well. (Ch. 3,
    trans. Ren, 1993)

The sage [idealized ruler] has no fixed personal will,
He regards the people's will as his own.
I take the people's will if it is good, as good.
I take the people's will, if it is not good, as good too.
Thus goodness is attained.
I believe in the people's will if it is believable,
I also believe in the people's will even if it is not believable,
Thus faith is attained.
The sage dwells under heaven, harmoniously keeping all the people under heaven
    in confusion,
[While all the people concentrate upon their own eyes and ears].
Thus the sage treats them all as ignorant infants without desires. (Ch. 49, trans.
    Ren, 1993)

Thus the role of government according to Taoist principles was noteworthy for its absence, and alignment with the will of the people: governors should keep people ignorant and ready to focus on human spiritual life, rather than having citizens be concerned with government as something to study or to influence or to follow.

Women

The main ideals of Taoism persisting into the twenty-first century include a widespread acknowledgement of the principle of dualism of opposites: Yang–yin, male–female, light–dark, active–passive and good–evil. In this philosophy, part of the natural order is that the male is stronger and more active and more dominant than the female, and the male is related to light, good and other positive characteristics. The female is honored as central to the natural process of reproductive capacity, but also seen either as passive or as a source of powerful warrior-spirits who may be useful or dangerous:

The spirit of the valley [Tao, or Great Emptiness] is an immortal being.
It is called subtle and profound female.
The gate of the subtle and profound female is the root of Heaven and Earth.
It exists formlessly,
But its utility is never worn out. (Ch. 6, trans. Ren, 1993)

All things in the world have their origin in something, which is their foundation [mother].
Having grasped the Mother as the foundation of all things, one can know her children as all things.
Having grasped the children as the thing, one must hold to the Mother as the foundation of all things.
Thus one will never encounter danger all his life . . .
(Ch. 52, trans. Ren, 1993)

He who knows the masculine but keeps to the feminine is ready to be the ravine under heaven.
Being the ravine under heaven he is not parted from constant 'De' [Virtue],
He returns to the simple state like an infant . . .
(Ch. 28, trans. Ren, 1993)

True to the tradition of opposites that is central to this philosophy, the essential feminine characteristics are at once the most profound mysterious core of all being, also the dark, fearful opposite of men and perhaps the infantile. These ideas are exemplified in contemporary Chinese societies when women are seen as both gentle maternal nurturing creatures and as powerful, fierce warriors to be feared by men.

CONFUCIANISM

The philosophy most often associated with Chinese culture is Confucianism. Kong Qiu, Zhong Ni, Kong Fu Zhi or Confucius as he has been called at various times, lived in what is now Shandong province in Southeastern China from 549 BCE to 479 BCE, during the Spring and Autumn dynastic period (Legge, 1893; Brooks and Brooks, 1998). His father was a warrior who died when Confucius was three. The impoverished son was minimally trained in the traditional gentlemanly arts of music, archery, mathematics, calligraphy, ceremonial rites, horsemanship and in the classical writings.

Confucius did not create any original manuscripts that have survived. His students and later followers compiled *The Analects* as a set of dialogues, sayings, questions and answers that have been much revised and interpreted in later years. Thus what we have today represents the collected wisdom of Confucius, his students and later editorial scholars.

Confucian teaching disdained religious and spiritual thought central to Taoism and advocated development of an ideal society based on the model of the social relationships existing in a Chinese family and the ideal of gentlemanly conduct.

Government

Good government is a central objective of Confucianism and, according to Confucius, the goal of every good citizen. Rulers, like all good men, should be exemplary persons. The government should rule by appropriate ritual that demonstrates this good conduct.

One key principle of Confucian thought values hierarchical interpersonal relationships of obligation of the superior to protect and sustain the subordinate in exchange for loyalty and obedience from the subordinate:

> The Master said 'lead the people with administrative injunctions and keep them orderly with penal law, and they will avoid punishments but will be without a sense of shame. Lead them with excellence and keep them orderly through observing ritual propriety and they will develop a sense of shame and moreover will order themselves.' (2.3, trans. Ames and Rosemont, 1998)
>
> Zizhang inquired, 'What does the scholar apprentice have to do to be described as being "prominent"?'
> 'What can you possibly mean by being prominent?' replied the Master.
> 'One who is sure to be known, whether serving in public office or in the house of a ruling family,' answered Zizhang.
> 'That is being known,' said the Master, 'it is not being "prominent". Those who are prominent are true in their basic disposition, and seek after what is most appropriate. They examine what is said, are keen observers of demeanor, and are thoughtful in deferring to others. They are sure to be prominent whether serving in public office or in the house of the ruling family. As for being merely known, they put on appearances to win a reputation for being authoritative [virtuous] while their conduct belies it. They are wholly confident that they are authoritative, and sure to be known, whether serving in public office or in the house of a ruling family.' (12.20, trans. Ames and Rosemont, 1998)

In Book 13 of *The Analects* several verses give advice to a ruler:

> Set an example yourself for those in office, pardon minor offenses and promote those with superior character and ability. (13.2)
>
> If people are proper in personal conduct, others will follow suit without need of command, but if they are not proper, even when they command, others will not obey. (13.6)
>
> When people are already so numerous, what more can be done for them?
> The Master said 'Make them prosperous.'
> 'When the people are already prosperous,' asked Ranyou 'what more can be done for them?'
> 'Teach them' replied the Master.' (13.9)
> . . . Don't try to rush things and don't get distracted by small opportunities. If you try to rush things, you won't achieve your ends; if you get distracted by small opportunities, you won't succeed in the more important matters of government. (13.17, trans. Ames and Rosemont, 1998)

The Confucian gentleman should seek constant self-improvement, follow rituals, and exhibit patriotic loyalty to the ruler:

> The Master remarked that Zichan accorded with the way of the exemplary person in four respects: he was gracious in deporting himself, he was deferential in serving his superiors, he was generous in attending to the needs of the common people, he was appropriate in employing their services. (5.16, trans. Ames and Rosemont, 1998)

Women

In each of the dyadic hierarchical relationships based on benevolence and loyalty (with the exception of friendship), the female is subordinate to a male, first to her father, then to her husband and later to her adult son. Several times *The Analects* mentions the role of women as a useless or a negative influence on a gentleman's household:

> . . . King Wu also said, 'I have ten ministers who bring proper order to the world.' Confucius said: 'As the saying has it "human talent is hard to come by." Isn't it indeed the case? And it was at the transition from Yao's Tang dynasty to Shun's Yu dynasty, that talented ministers were in the greatest abundance. In King Wu's case with a woman, perhaps his wife, among them, perhaps there were really only nine ministers' . . . (8.20, trans. Ames and Rosemont, 1998)

> The Master said 'It is only women and petty persons who are difficult to provide for. Drawing them close, they are immodest, and keeping them at a distance, they complain.' (17.25, trans. Ames and Rosemont, 1998)

The central message from the Confucian doctrine that permeates contemporary Chinese culture is the subservient role of women and their uselessness in important matters of government, the most important employment institution of his era. In fact women are seen as a nuisance. All important norms, roles and official positions are given to men.

BUDDHISM

The legendary human who became Buddha is supposed to have lived about 563 to 483 BCE and was of royal lineage. He began a normal married life and was later called to a special divine task (Campbell, 1962). There are two great streams of Buddhism – Theravada, which posited nirvana for only a few enlightened individuals, and Mahayana, which emphasized personal salvation and acknowledgment of a world of senses (Fisher, 1993). Regardless of the branch of Buddhism, the central beliefs of the religion are that from ignorance arise actions, senses, desire, attachments to the world, pain and death. One can, by meritorious deeds on earth, attain reincarnation in a state closer to painless perfection. In the ultimate pain-less existence, which one must recognize as having always existed inside oneself, one enters the state of lack of attachment or nirvana, a state of perfect wisdom and recognition of non-being (Bechert and Gombrich, 1984).

The entrance of Buddhism from India into China (100 BCE to AD 200) contributed to the Chinese culture a formal system of religious deities dis-tinct from natural spirits. Buddhism advocated entering a state of enlight-enment and urged people to gain understanding of the mysterious perfection of the oneness of all things and eternal transitoriness. The aspects of Buddhism that were adopted by the Chinese were ones that could be seen as similar to the existing Confucian or Taoist traditions. Thus the need to accumulate merit and good deeds was seen as similar to some aspects of ancestor worship, and the mystical aspects of Buddhism were seen as similar to the magical aspects of Taoism (Fisher, 1993).

Government

While this religion advocates acceptance of one's fate, and unremitting tol-erance, it also preaches that benefits in a future life might be earned by living a virtuous present life. The governmental forms in place in India during the rise of this religious system were created by the Brahmins of Hinduism: a highly developed system of inherited castes that dictated a social position to each member of society. The Buddhist response to this system was for each individual to rise through and above this hierarchy through various reincarnations to the perfect state of being unattached to this worldly system. The Chinese did not adopt the Hindu-related caste system, however they did recognize a very clear hierarchy formerly based on social or imperial power. The Law in the Buddhist sense however was religious law, not the law of material government, and it described the system of laws and processes for the universe existence. In this religious system, the self does not exist, all is a mirage:

> 'Everything subject to causation' said the Buddha to Mitreya [Future Buddha] and to those around him, 'is like a mirage, a dream, the moon beheld in water, an echo: neither removable nor self-subsistent and the Wheel of Law is described neither "it is" nor "it is not." For this, Sirs, is the Mahayana, set forth by all Buddhas. By worshiping the Buddhas, the Bodhisattvas [those souls who have attained Nirvana], the Pratyeka Buddhas [those who do not teach] and the Arhats [illuminated sages], a man will generate in his mind the idea of Buddha-hood and

proclaim the Law in good works.' (Asyaghosa (n.d.), 16, 57–128 as quoted in Campbell, 1962)

The practical outcome of this philosophy was that, according to Buddhist principles, rulers and important government officials as well as common people were governed by duty to do good deeds and show respect and aid to those more enlightened than oneself – monks, Arhats and the other Buddhist deities illustrating various states of enlightenment. If the real world including government was painful, unjust or exploitative, it was actually an illusion to be risen above meditatively.

Women

The position of men in relation to women is not central to Buddhist thought. However Gautama Buddha gave up his wife and family for the meditative state of being one with the universe, nirvana:

> Ananda said 'Lord how should we behave toward women?'
> The Master: 'Not see them.'
> Ananda: 'And if we have to see them?'
> The Master: 'Not speak to them.'
> Ananda: 'And if we have to speak to them?'
> The Master: 'Keep your thought tightly controlled.' (Conze, n.d.)

Some of the more prominent forms of the Buddhist divine figure Guan Yin are seen as dark, powerful and dangerous males. Other forms of Guan Yin are depicted as a benevolent, protective and nurturing goddess. Shri Lakshmi, as the primary female deity is called in India, appears on a lotus and sometimes appears naked, or in erotic poses with the erotic aspects of female nature emphasized. Especially in Tibet, the Tantric Buddhist practices sometimes used sexual union as a meditative way to approach the state of non-being. This form of Buddhism was repressed in Han and Manchu parts of China. The female Buddhist deity sometimes also appears as the Goddess of the Tree of Life or the life force. Thus women in Buddhism are seen as temptations of worldly pain and something to be avoided, or as a source of life, as a partner in a perfect union in Tantric sexual experience, one route to approaching nirvana.

This attitude of reserve from worldly (and governmental) concerns may be the most pervasive influence of government on women arising from Buddhism. But the virtue of endurance of worldly troubles also may contribute to a reluctance of women to protest a lower status or unequal treatment.

LEGALISM

Perhaps the clearest influence on employment of both men and women in China comes from the Legalist tradition. Most of the Chinese bureaucratic system emerged and was codified when the empire became united in the Qin (221 to 206 BCE) and Han (206 BCE to AD 220) dynasties during the influence of the Legalist school.

Government

The Legalist school declared that government authority is a right granted by law and obedience should be enforced by harsh punishment. In this way of thinking, the law is the legitimization of government. The government is administered through a hierarchical system of positions attained by examination through a civil service system. The civil service examination system started around AD 650. The first establishment of a centralized personnel system for government offices occurred during this period. The system provided the major mechanism for civilian people to gain status, power and positions in government organizations through passing successive hurdles of examinations. Usually only boys and men had access to the schools that prepared one for the civil service examinations, and only men took the examination and were appointed to the important civil service ranks with government authority over specific geographic areas.

Although the system was banned 100 years ago, at the end of the Qing dynasty, many remnants continue. For instances in many Chinese societies today, quite a few occupations and positions in both public and private sectors require a certificate, which is awarded mostly through examination.

Under legalism, because the law is seen as establishing the right to rule and is less influential in dispute resolution and enforcement of social norms in China than in Western nations, cultural practices enforced through social approval are a more common form of social control than adjudication based on law. The practical consequence is that, although there may be laws protecting women, laws may be the least effective way that Chinese governments control the status of women. Prohibitions against women studying for and taking qualifying examinations were also codified under this philosophy and persist in customs, if not in laws, today.

Women

According to the Legalist codes, women were seen as the property of men and had few legal rights of their own. They could not own property or appear in courts as a legal petitioner. They had no access to the schools that prepared individuals for government positions, although some were taught to read and write in wealthy homes of indulgent fathers. According to this system, women became powerful or attained status via the status of their fathers or husbands. In a few rare cases, women became prominent by taking over the position of their dead husband, but the more common fate would be to become reduced to the lowest servant of the husband's family or in some cases to be returned in disgrace to her father, if the husband was not dead but the wife proved barren.

SUMMARY OF BELIEFS FROM CHINESE HERITAGE

If we think in chronological terms, the animist spiritual foundations of Taoism are the oldest beliefs against which the a-religious principles of Confucianism argued for a virtuous worldly society. Buddhism then brought the focus back to ordering the spiritual world and finally Legalism focused on ordering the temporal affairs of men. Each of these philosophies persisted even as new beliefs were adopted. The result is a culture with some opposing or contradictory and other complementary aspects selected from each of these systems.

In sum, the combined cultural heritage of these four traditional sources of values reveals mixed attitudes about the role of government in influencing citizens' lives. Government is administered by men who have earned the right to their position through examination on academic subjects. Good government is either invisible and based on the will of the people, or it is formal, bureaucratic and hierarchical in structure. It should provide benevolence for citizens, and has the right to demand obligatory loyalty of its male subjects. If government is painful or unjust, one may as a gentleman try to influence the ruler to become a virtuous man, or if this is not possible, ignore the government as a painful illustration of worldly illusion.

Although women have the capacity to be powerful creators, the life force, and the foundation of all existence, they might also be powerful and dangerous warriors and something to fear. In a world controlled by men, they should be subservient, invisible, domestic, uneducated, loyal to the men in their lives and tolerant of worldly injustice.

Certainly these are not an auspicious set of norms for a modern era in which Chinese women may want or need to seek employment outside of the home. There is little in any of these traditions to lead us to expect that the power of government would be an active force in supporting women as independent economic entities. Yet in the contemporary world of the twenty-first century, we see many women in leadership positions in Chinese societies. The following chapters describe how these changes have occurred and how some of these traditions persist.

REFERENCES

Ames, R.T. and H. Rosemont (1998), *The Analects of Confucius: A Philosophical Translation*, New York: Ballantine Books.

Asyaghosa (n.d.), *Buddhacarita*, **16**, 57, abridged, as quoted in J. Campbell (1962), *The Masks of God: Oriental Mythology*, New York: Penguin Books, p. 129.

Bechert, H. and R. Gombrich (1984), *The World of Buddhism*, London: Thames & Hudson.

Brooks, E.B. and A.T. Brooks (1998), *The Original Analects: Sayings of Confucius and his Successors*, New York: Columbia University Press.

Campbell, J. (1962), *The Masks of God: Oriental Mythology*, New York: Penguin Books.

Conze, E. (n.d.), *Buddhism, its Essence and Development*, 'Rules of the order Vinayana', New York: Philosophical Library; later published at Oxford by B. Cassier (1975), New York and London: Harper & Row.

Fisher, R.E. (1993), 'Introduction: the subject matter of Buddhist art', in *Buddhist Art and Architecture*, London: Thames & Hudson.

Legge, J. (1893), *Confucius, Confucian Analects, The Great Learning, and the Doctrine of the Mean: Translated with Critical and Exegetical Notes, Prolegomena, Copious Indexes, and Dictionary of all Characters*, Oxford: Clarendon Press (reprinted 1971, New York: Dover Books).

Mitchell, S. (1988), *Tao Te Ching: A New English Version*, New York: Harper & Row.

Ren, Jiyu (1993), *A Taoist Classic: The Book of Lao Zi*, English translation by He Guanhu, Gao Shining, Song Lidao and Xu Junyao, Beijing: Foreign Language Press, from Lao Tse, *Book of Lao Zi – A Modern Chinese Translation*, (1985), translated by Ren Jiyu, Shanghai: The Shanghai Chinese Classics Publishing House.

Stockwell, F. (1993), *Religion in China Today*, Beijing: New World Press.

PART II

Government policies and the employment
status of Chinese women

3. National policy influence on women's careers in the People's Republic of China

Yong-Qing Fang, Cherlyn Skromme Granrose and Rita V. Kong (Mei Hui Jiang)

The People's Republic of China (PRC) is the ancient motherland of Chinese people throughout the world, and as such, plays a particular cultural role in shaping careers of Chinese women in many other nations. However PRC also is unique because it alone bears the history of a socialist government for the past half-century. This chapter outlines the characteristics of PRC as they influence particularly the women who live within its borders. The description, following the theoretical outline for international study of careers (Granrose, 1997), examines the national level of analysis. The chapter begins with an overview of the general situation that affects careers in China, then describes the particular aspects of Chinese legislation and policy that pertain to women.

NATIONAL CAREER FACTORS

China has 9.6 million sq km of land area that slopes toward the east from the Tibet high plateau and lower western deserts across the interior loess plateau and lower mountain ranges to the broad coastal river deltas. Only 108 million hectares are cultivatable, mainly in the northern plains and interior river valleys, however some uncultivated land contains deposits of the world's third-largest mineral resources. The total human resources of China are over 1.26 billion people (see Table 3.1), most of them living an agricultural life in rural areas (National Bureau of Statistics of China, 2001). The way China allocates these human and natural resources has the potential to influence global business strategy and practice.

The authors wish to thank Yueh Ting Cheong, Lay Chin Lim, and Kwan Theng Ngan, for their valuable contributions to an early version of this chapter.

Table 3.1   *Composition of the population of the PRC by gender (in thousands)*

Year	Total	Male	Female
1990	1 143 330	589 040	554 290
1995	1 211 210	618 080	593 130
2000	1 265 830	653 550	612 280

Source: National Bureau of Statistics of China (1991, 1996, 2001).

National Economic Conditions

In the time between 1949 and 1979 the Chinese economy evolved from a landlord-dominated, agrarian economy into a socialist centrally planned state where production and distribution of goods and services were controlled by the government and employment was accomplished by government assignment to a state-owned industry based on needs of the state. Since 1979 the government has taken several steps to reform. It has (1) instituted a population control policy; (2) reformed agriculture to motivate peasants to produce more goods; (3) opened import–export trade and encouraged foreign investment; (4) initiated a limited market economy with private enterprises, joint ventures, stock markets and production and distribution based on competition; (5) decentralized administration of most of the remaining state-owned enterprises and state-controlled key industries; and (6) reduced support of failing state-owned enterprises (SOEs) to promote mergers, bankruptcies and dissolution of non-competitive businesses.

These reform policies have fueled overall economic growth and avoided the economic collapse suffered by other Asian nations during the 1990s, but serious problems remain. The government is struggling to continue to transform or close faltering SOEs, to define a market-appropriate legal system and to find jobs for a large population with limited education.

China's gross national product (GNP) growth rate averaged about 4.5 percent between 1949 and 1978; it accelerated to an average of 9 percent for the next two decades but has been growing at a slower rate in recent years (Perkins, 1997; Itoh, 1997; National Bureau of Statistics of China, 2001). The gross domestic product (GDP) increased from RMB$ 451.78 billion in 1980 to RMB$ 7477.2 billion in 1997, although the rate of increase shows signs of declining.

The distribution of economic growth has varied in different sectors of the economy and also in different geographical regions, and this has had a strong impact on the availability of jobs. Employment in the primary agricultural sector has continued to decline, however because of population growth the absolute number employed in every sector, including agriculture, has continued to grow (National Bureau of Statistics of China, 1996, 2001). While each geographic region presents unique economic challenges, the most striking differences occur between the coastal and the central and western inland regions (Guo, 1999). In general, the levels of economic development and job opportunities decline as one travels from the coastal region through the center to the western interior. The coastal region is more developed due to its proximity to the western shores of the Pacific Ocean and a long history of doing business with a trade and export orientation. A market economy was established in this region prior to the revolution of 1949 and the first reopenings to international trade began on the Pacific coast in the 1980s.

Employment opportunities also vary by ethnic group and gender. There are 56 ethnic groups in China. The Hans make up 93 percent of the population. Other minority groups have great linguistic and cultural difficulty integrating into the Han Chinese majority society in spite of official policies outlawing discrimination against them. Educational limits provide substantial barriers to many minority members participating in the economy in jobs other than agriculture or manual labor (World Bank, 1992).

On 1 October 1949 the government of the People's Republic of China abolished the feudal system that fettered women. In the new PRC constitution, equality between men and women was supported. At the founding of PRC, employed women accounted for only 7 percent of the total workforce (*Beijing Review*, 1995). In 2000, there were 44,113,000 women employed in the PRC, which was 39.2 percent of the total working population, according to the National Bureau of Statistics (see Table 3.4). Chinese women are found in almost every industry and trade, from industrial sectors to technological sectors.

National Career Processes

Before 1998 placement of individuals into an organization occurred primarily through official government personnel offices. Employees were usually placed in the work units of their parents if they did not receive higher education. After graduation from secondary school or university, the government assigned students to jobs in SOEs or collective enterprises (COEs) according to state quotas. People's professions were chosen for them either by parental guidance into specific educational options or by official placement resulting from educational or employment examinations. Nepotism complemented ideology as selection and placement criteria because of the general belief that family members can be trusted and should be helped.

If a person wanted to move from one SOE to another, university graduates and others with special reasons could request alternative placements with good recommendations from their advisors or from their former work unit personnel directors. Change was difficult unless the old and new work unit and the individual all agreed on the change (Gao and Chi, 1997; Ignatius, 1988). A person could also, on his/her own, find another person mutually willing to swap units. The majority of this type of exchange involved people from their own household who were working in different cities.

Beginning in the 1990s, individuals had the option to seek their own jobs and then had to arrange releases from their former work unit to take a new offer. If they were good workers however, this permission might not be granted. Limitations on individual movement were also complicated by increasing unemployment and competition for a limited number of jobs.

Official unemployment increased dramatically when China shifted from a planned economy to a market-oriented one. Although the government seeks to keep as many people employed as possible, Beijing central government authorities no longer guarantee each person a job placement in a state-owned enterprise. Regulations permit organizations to close enterprises or to lay off, fire, retire or separate workers from their work units, but there may be local government pressure to keep poorly performing SOEs alive so that their members do not become officially unemployed (Fang, 1999).

Now the responsibility for finding work rests heavily on the individual worker's own shoulders with some help from state institutions charged with addressing these labor problems. Some who lack mobility try to establish tiny private enterprises, offer to perform some menial service for money, rely on the support of family members who still have jobs, or as a last resort, beg or protest in the street. Those with the ability to migrate flock to the cities and coastal areas seeking construction, crafts, vending, manufacturing or service jobs created by the growing private enterprises and joint ventures.

With the growth in technology and growing change in distribution of jobs from primary agriculture to tertiary technical industries, there is a substantial mismatch between the skills of the population and the tasks that need to be performed. Not only is there skepticism about whether China can provide enough skilled workers for developing companies, there is also a serious question of whether China can provide jobs for all of its workers.

WOMEN'S CAREER PROCESSES

In 1949 when the PRC was founded under the ideology of Communism, the official status of women began to improve and they gained a legal status previously denied them. In order to promote women's employment the state has intervened through legislative, administrative, economic and media educational mechanisms. The Constitution of the PRC was written with several provisions that aimed to protect women's rights and define their economic role. Legislation enhancing the legal rights of women was strengthened in 1992 by Order Number 58 of the President of the PRC. Unfortunately, legal rights do not match the daily reality of women's lives.

Today while the market economy being built in China has unleashed productivity to a great extent, it has also posed uncertainty for most Chinese people's lives, and women are the most challenged by the changing society. The PRC recognizes and respects the principle of sexual equality affirmed in the United Nations Charter (Chapter VIII Active Participation in International Women's Activities). Even so, the perceptions of employers and the lack of proper implementation of laws and regulations stand in the way of realization of this equality.

Legal Structures

During the 1990s legislation was passed and amended to improve women's equality with men. While many regulations are now in place, the fairness of these regulations and the effectiveness of their implementation are highly debatable. Although the formulation of laws is only one factor in the struggle for equality, it is of great importance because it provides a legal basis for action. This review will describe two major laws passed in 1992 and in 1994.

Law on the Protection of Women's Rights and Interests (1992)
On 3 April 1992, the Law on the Protection of the Rights and Interests of Women was passed by the National People's Congress (NPC), providing a legal basis for women's awareness of their rights, operation of organizations devoted to protection of women's rights and interests, and social efforts in this regard (Jiang, 1997). In spite of the guarantee of equal rights for women that was included in the Constitution of the PRC, this law revealed the extent to which problems in education, employment and discrimination against women were widespread and continued after the social reforms that increased the market economy. The most revealing articles of this law are reproduced in Appendix 3.1. This Women's Law was implemented 1 October 1992.

This comprehensive women's law provides a systematic and full-scale legislative regime for protecting women's equality. There are many aspects of equality included in this law – the right to healthcare, and the right to education and political rights. The law also provides for equality in employment, especially in career opportunities, hiring, working conditions, education, training and lay-offs.

The Women's Law and many of the province-level implementation regulations for the law contain programmatic provisions prohibiting discrimination against women in employment and prohibitions of dismissal on grounds of pregnancy, childbirth or lactation. Some regulations require that an enterprise consult with the trade union before terminating a woman employee's contract. Such provisions may provide additional protection to women employees if they are actually implemented and if union leaders are committed to ensuring equal opportunities for women (HRIC, 1999).

The Labor Act (1994)
This law, passed in 1994 and implemented on 1 January 1995, has requirements that focus on the physical safety and protection of women (please refer to Appendix 3.2 for details of Sections 59 to 63). These sections provide a legal basis on which female workers can act if employers fail to adhere to the constitutional requirements for equality in protection of workers' physical safety. Female workers are entitled to additional benefits because they are physically weaker, experience menstrual inconvenience and are responsible for childbearing. This law also includes requirements for a paid maternity leave of 90 days. In addition to these stipulations, Article 13 prescribes that women shall have equal rights to employment as men (Chen, 1999).

Administrative Measures

The guiding stipulation in the Constitution about protection of equality between men and women, the Women's Law, the Labor Act and other relevant laws and regulations have formed a Chinese legal system safeguarding women's rights. In reality however, legal equality does not amount to true equality (Chen, 1999). While seemingly progressive laws have been passed, necessary enforcement mechanisms have not been attached. Equal rights to employment may not be carried out effectively because employers have to provide more protections and benefits to female workers. Such regulations deter employers from seeking and hiring female workers because the provision of these incentives will increase their costs. Recognizing this limitation, administrative measures have been taken to assist women in attaining their rights.

The PRC government has formulated a program to further promote the development of Chinese women. The Program for the Development of Chinese Women (1995–2000), known as The Program for short, has a general aim to improve the equality of the women as a whole and implement the rights of equality of women. A full description of The Program is attached in Appendix 3.3. Articles of this program provide women with opportunities for employment, especially in rural and underdeveloped regions of the country, and also support efforts and services to help women find these jobs. It holds work unit leaders responsible for protecting women from harmful work settings, for providing equal pay for equal labor, and prohibits employment of girls under age 16. The education provisions strive to remove illiteracy and to provide opportunities for women in technical and higher education.

Based on the section on Legal Protection in Appendix 3.3, The Program has its emphasis placed on promoting existing laws. Moreover it states that sanctions will be imposed on those who violate the laws. This enforcement is made possible through strict supervision of government officials. Thus discrimination against women is not actionable under the law, but subject only to administrative sanctions.

A number of factors contribute to serious weakness in the implementation of these laws and the use of the administrative dispute procedures. Although legislation exists, female workers may not be aware of their entitlements. Even with the laws and regulations in place, workers have to cover any costs of bringing a case and there are very few institutions in the country providing legal assistance or advice to workers. A few local efforts have had some success (see Chapter 7 in this volume for examples of local efforts).

Economic Policy Efforts to Create Jobs for Women

The government of the PRC has made a variety of policies to change the economy toward a market orientation, and some of these policies have helped and some have hindered employment of women. Those policies include general policies of economic development, educational policies and policies to support retraining and re-employment of workers displaced by industrialization and market economy restructuring.

Economic development programs

A major state intervention to increase the scale of female employment has been conducted through continuing adjustment of the economic structure. In order to balance the proportion of men and women in employment, the state has made some specific efforts to create jobs for women. Economic policy to support creation of firms in the suburbs near large cities, such as the Nanhai area near Guangzhou and Wuxi near Shanghai, has been most successful in creating jobs in the agricultural and non-agricultural sectors. Many of these firms are engaged in export processing and tend to be female intensive. For example women comprised 51.2 percent of the workers in non-state rural firms in a sample taken in Nanhai and Shangrao (Byrd and

Lin, 1990, pp. 101, 406). Similarly, the Special Economic Zones have hired women from adjacent rural areas to do approximately 80 percent of the assembly work (*Beijing Review*, 1988). Joint ventures frequently locate on the outskirts of cities because their jobs are more attractive to rural women than those in the city proper, for example Smart Garments Ltd in the Chao Yang District of Beijing (Summerfield, 1994).

Most of the economic development projects to support women's employment focus on the rural areas and are agricultural in nature, in line with The Program (Appendix 3.3) however this may not meet the long-term needs of many women. Agriculture is a large sector in China's economy and it creates job opportunities for women, however with industrialization, machinery has replaced manual labor. There was a 38.6 percent drop in the total number of employees registered in farming, forestry, animal husbandry and fishery between 1990 and 2000; however the larger drop occurred in men leaving this agricultural sector to seek industrial jobs (see Table 3.2). A large proportion of females are involved in agriculture, but with the advent of science and technology, modernization has been displacing their jobs. While at present the agricultural projects create more job openings, women need to be educated sufficiently to work in industrial settings if they are to be able to safeguard themselves from being laid off the farms as agricultural work becomes a smaller segment of the economy.

Development of human capital: education and training
There is a high correlation between education and employment (Zhan, 1995), and having the necessary education is a way to safeguard against being laid off. Women are far from equal to men in getting education for jobs, especially in rural areas. While the market economy will be demanding more talented, better-educated people, girls continue to receive little schooling, being forced to quit school at an early age. Thus they cannot compete for the better jobs. The PRC government has recognized this problem and instituted several policies and programs to counteract this deficit.

The Women's Institute survey, conducted more than a decade ago, found disparities in the education of the sexes at all levels, with women having 4.75 years of schooling on the average and men 6.63 years. While only 9.7 percent of the men had no schooling at all, this was true for 27 percent of the women. Only 34.6 percent of women and 51 percent of men finished middle school education, while 1.7 percent of women and 3.4 percent of men received college education (*Women's International Network News*, 1993). In 1990, female students comprised 45.4 percent of students in specialized secondary schools and 33.7 percent in institutions of higher education. In 2000, the proportion increased to 56.6 and 41.0 respectively (see Table 3.3).

Table 3.2 Number of registered employees in the PRC by gender and sector (in thousands)

Sector	1990			1995			2000		
	Total	Male	Female	Total	Male	Female	Total	Male	Female
Farming, forestry, animal husbandry and fishery	8 399	5 361	3 038	6 601	4 118	2 483	5 161	3 205	1 956
Manufacturing	63 777	37 348	26 429	54 389	29 810	24 579	32 993	18 740	14 253
Construction	9 274	7 347	1 927	10 529	8 488	2 041	7 784	6 344	1 440
Financial and insurance	1 956	1 254	702	2 732	1 638	1 094	3 269	1 857	1 412
Health, sport and welfare	3 918	1 819	2 099	4 381	1 944	2 437	4 881	2 099	2 782
Education, culture and arts, radio, film, television	11 436	7 212	4 224	12 910	7 690	5 220	12 666	5 773	6 893

Source: National Bureau of Statistics of China (1991, 1996, 2001). The figures for male were calculated based on the available figures for total number of people and females.

Table 3.3   Women and education in the PRC

(a) Female students in schools (Unit: 1000)

Year	Colleges and universities		Polytechnic schools		Ordinary middle schools		Vocational middle schools		Primary schools		Total	
	No.	%	No.	%	No.	%	No.	%	No.	%	No.	%
1995	1 029	35.4	1 871	50.3	24 075	44.8	2 182	48.7	62 411	47.3	91 568	46.5
1998	1 306	39.3	2 727	54.7	28 777	45.7	2 597	47.9	66 456	47.6	101 863	47.1
1999	1 621	39.2	2 875	55.8	31 092	45.9	2 547	47.7	64 549	47.6	102 684	47.1
2000	2 279	41.0	2 773	56.6	34 024	46.2	2 374	47.2	61 946	47.6	103 396	47.1

(b) Female teachers in schools (Unit: 1000)

Year	Colleges and universities		Polytechnic schools		Ordinary middle schools		Vocational middle schools		Primary schools		Total	
	No.	%	No.	%	No.	%	No.	%	No.	%	No.	%
1995	132	32.9	107	41.6	1 192	35.8	108	37.0	2 640	46.6	4 179	42.0
1998	148	36.3	123	44.0	1 454	39.3	138	41.1	2 846	48.9	4 709	44.7
1999	159	37.6	122	46.6	1 550	40.4	142	42.3	2 910	49.7	4 883	45.5
2000	177	38.2	115	44.9	1 657	41.4	137	42.9	2 967	50.6	5 053	46.3

Source: All China Women's Federation.

In 2000, the net primary school attendance rate of female students was 99.07 percent, while the rate of female dropouts from primary schools was reduced by 0.88 percent between 1995 and 2000. The proportion of female students in polytechnic schools increased to over 50 percent and for the first time the proportion of female students in colleges exceeded 40 percent in 2000. Also, women's vocational education advanced. In 2000, the number of female students in vocational middle schools increased 8.7 percent compared with that in 1995, and the number of female students receiving adult higher education increased 37.6 percent.

The Women's Institute survey showed that nearly half of the girls who dropped out of school did so because of poverty. But women have become more conscious of the importance of education and among the poorly educated, 26.2 percent were in adult education such as technical training and literacy classes (*Women's International Network News*, 1993).

In the 1990s, the State Council promulgated the Program for China's Educational Reform and Development, which clearly defined specific goals for the next five years to devote major efforts to developing women's education and improving generally the standard of women's cultural and scientific knowledge (*Women's International Network News*, 1996). For those who had minimal education, the government sought to provide vocational training and retraining programs.

Vocational retraining for laid-off women workers
Generally speaking, China's reform and liberalization have accelerated economic growth and created more jobs and opportunities for women. However because of government attempts to revamp enterprises and restructure the economy, some workers have become redundant while others have been laid off because their technical skills were not up to the needs of modernized production and a changing market. As a result of their disadvantaged educational and technical background, women make up a larger share of those laid off. This poses a serious challenge to the Chinese government.

In urban areas, over 30 million female workers have taken part in various vocational skills training, and over 1 million of these workers were re-employed (*China Daily*, 2001). The problem may not be solved by re-education programs alone however. First, only 3.3 percent of those who took part in vocational skill training were re-employed. Second, as 30 rural women from farm families in Cangxian County, Hebei Province stated, as women they have to shoulder responsibilities both at home and on the job, which often restricts their ability to improve themselves through further training or education (*China Daily*, 2002).

Government projects for re-employment of workers

To help workers who have lost their jobs to become re-employed and thereby ensure that the reform process progresses smoothly, the Ministry of Labor launched the Re-Employment Project in 1993. Its central task was to help laid-off workers find jobs as soon as possible by making use of policy support and other employment services. This project focused on giving full play to government, enterprise and community initiatives, combining enterprise recruitment, self-employment and community-based placement schemes. This project provides job orientation, job introduction, cross-training and other services.

More specifically, the project has worked out plans to assist women in the following ways. First, women enjoy free instruction in professional skills. Second, women are taught up-to-date technical skills to enable them to keep pace with technical advancement. This not only makes it easier for them to find new jobs, but also helps women keep the work they have. The training expenses are paid by the unemployment relief fund. Third, labor departments pay the application fee and most of the women's salaries during their trial period. Finally, an unemployed woman can use money from the relief fund as starting expenses if she becomes self-employed (*Women's International Network News*, 1997).

Policy efforts continued into the late 1990s, when the Ministry of Labor, the All-China Women's Federation and other national institutions jointly issued several policies aiming to promote re-employment of laid-off female workers by providing them with retraining, employment services and favorable taxation and loans or funding for those who wished to set up their own business.

The regulations concerning the Arrangement of Surplus Workers of the State Owned Enterprises (State Council, 1998; Ministry of Labor, 1998; Ministry of Labor and Social Assurance, 2002) were enacted to require SOEs to locate new jobs for their laid-off employees. These regulations still fail to address the issue of discrimination against women in lay-offs. In addition, they legitimize certain types of disguised retrenchment of women workers allowing for 'fixed-term vacations', two-year-long maternity leaves and early retirement for women as young as 35. Such effective lay-offs are presented as voluntary, but in practice women workers are given little choice.

In September 1997, the State Council issued a directive ordering all cities to set up minimum living standards for *xiagang* (laid-off) workers by the end of 1999. Under these provisions, local governments are required to set up re-employment centers and workers are to be provided with a living allowance and outpatient medical care for two to three years. Although the officially unemployed are theoretically entitled to benefits, what is allocated cannot meet demand. Laid-off workers may be pushed out of company housing, lose their entitlement to some free medical care and may even be forced to pay for their children's education.

Authorities have launched various retraining programs to accompany efforts of enterprises to deal with their displaced workers. However even China's official press has published criticism of such programs' lack of coordination and poor planning. Few training courses are provided free of charge. Many programs for women are aimed at getting them into occupations such as domestic service or childcare, or encourage them to set up businesses, all of which do not have benefits attached. Furthermore even if they have completed retraining programs, urban women may still not be able to find work due to discrimination in favor of younger peasant workers who are willing to work for less, with no benefits (HRIC, 1999).

Many women employees who were laid off have turned their sense of crisis into a motivating force, and are seeking to reshape themselves and to create self-employment. While creating and running business, they are not only resolving their own employment problem, they are also opening up new channels for increasing state tax revenues.

Local government incentives for enterprises

The 31 provinces, autonomous regions and municipalities directly under the central government have all put in place, in accordance with their respective conditions, preferential policies to promote re-employment schemes for laid-off female workers. For instance according to Hebei Province, any employer that recruits one laid-off female worker and signs a labor contract with her for over one year will get a subsidy of RMB$ 1000 from the local labor department (Feng, 2000). The example of one set of provincial efforts are described and evaluated in Chapter 7 of this volume.

POLICY RESULTS: CAREER OUTCOMES OF WOMEN IN THE PRC LABOR FORCE

In spite of the legal, administrative and policy efforts that have extended through the past half-century, women still face difficulties in all aspects of employment in the PRC. Research indicates gender discrimination still exists in all aspects of the Chinese labor market. Women are more likely to be in lower-paid and more casual jobs, less likely to be promoted and more prone to be laid off (Riley, 1996). The policy focus has been on protecting women's labor rights and increasing their share in employment quantitatively, whereas little provision exists which aims to ensure and improve the quality of women's employment prospects (Cooke, 2001).

Industrial Distribution of Jobs

The industrial structure reflects economic development and also reveals the extent to which past policy efforts have been effective. The analyses in this section are based on statistics obtained from the *China Statistical Yearbooks*. All calculations are based on the figures found in Tables 3.1, 3.2 and 3.4. The industrial classification of economic activities was made according to the nature or purpose of the goods produced, economic activities engaged or services rendered by the units. There are a total of 13 major industrial divisions but this analysis focuses on six divisions for comparison. The six divisions were selected based on the nature of their work scope; jobs that are physically demanding versus those that are not.

The six selected divisions
The categories of jobs that are physically demanding include farming, forestry, animal husbandry and fishery; manufacturing; and construction. As for those that do not require manual work, we have selected financial intermediation and insurance; healthcare, sporting and social welfare; and education, culture and arts, radio, film and television.

The two periods
The analysis compares two time periods: 1990 to 1995, and 1995 to 2000. This is due to the economic downturn in the second half of the 1990s, which resulted in an overall decline in employment in Asia. Discussing gender equality without taking this issue into account would be inappropriate.

Results: 1990 to 1995
In Table 3.4, we see that from 1990 to 1995, total employment increased by 8.486 million workers. There was an increase of 8.7 percent (an increment of 4 604 000 persons in absolute terms) in the number of registered female employees. This increase was more than the increase in the population of females (7 percent). The number of registered male employees increased by only 4.4 percent (an increment of 388,200 persons in absolute terms) when the increase in the male population was 4.9 percent. In general, there was a rise in the overall number of female employees and an increase in the percent of the labor force that was female from 37.6 percent to 38.6 percent.

Results: 1995 to 2000
As shown in Table 3.1, employment in general has fallen from 149 080 000 to 112 585 000 (24.5 percent). However from Table 3.2 we can see that employment in the service sectors of financial intermediation and insurance; healthcare, sporting and social welfare; and education, culture and

Table 3.4 The total number of employees in the PRC by gender and by type of unit in all units (in thousands)

Type of Unit	1990			1995			2000		
	Total	Male	Female	Total	Male	Female	Total	Male	Female
State-owned units	103 464	68 064	35 399	109 550	69 977	39 573	78 775	49 250	29 525
Urban collective-owned units	35 492	18 792	16 700	30 760	17 028	13 732	14 465	8 407	6 058
Other ownerships units	1 638	796	842	8 770	4 530	4 240	19 345	10 815	8 530
GRAND TOTAL	140 594	87 653	52 941	149 080	91 535	57 545	112 585	68 472	44 113

Source: National Bureau of Statistics of China (1991, 1996, 2001).

64

arts, radio, film and television has actually increased for both genders while farming, manufacturing and construction, those occupations demanding high physical labor and requiring fewer educational skills, declined. This put women with lower educational preparation at a large disadvantage while job hunting at the end of the twentieth century and bodes ill for these less-educated women in the future.

In both periods, in almost every sector, males dominate the workforce; however females constitute the larger proportion of the workforce in healthcare, sporting and social welfare. This trend is consistent throughout the years from 1990 to 2000. We cannot conclude that males dominate in physically demanding industrial sectors and females in non-physically demanding sectors from these data, since the percentage of females in manufacturing and farming is not less than the percentage of females in education, culture and arts. The sector with least female representation in all times is construction however, and the sector with the most consistent gains in female employment is education, culture and arts.

Although this analysis does not cover all economic sectors, from examination of the same data sources we can see that women are present in virtually all parts of the labor force. About two-thirds of urban women in China work outside the home, as do more than three-quarters of rural women. Nevertheless Chinese women do not participate fully and equally with men in economic, political and social life. Women constitute a very small percentage of the senior government officials at all levels and are generally under-represented in the political arena and in higher managerial positions. One study found that at all government levels, only 4.1 percent of top leaders were women ('Development of Female Human Resources', 2003).

A survey of 1184 village councils in 2000 found that (1) only 2.3 percent were headed by a woman, which is 3.1 percent down from the previous councils; and (2) in Communist Party branch committees, only 2.5 percent of general secretaries (top leaders) were women, down by 1.9 percent from the previous committee ('Development of Female Human Resources', 2003). Although many rural women have taken non-agricultural jobs or joined the flow of migrants seeking jobs in towns, surveys have found that a smaller proportion of the female rural labor force (20.7 percent) than of males (42.6 percent) have done so (Khan and Riskin, 2001).

Although more employment opportunities have been created for women, the occupational levels of women are still lower than those of men. The proportion of jobs available for women is still small and occupational fields where women have superiority are restricted (Li, 1995). In part this is a result of restriction of educational opportunities for women, and in part this is due to discrimination in hiring and promotions.

Recruitment and Selection

Even with the opening of more jobs for women, female workers seeking employment face discrimination. This is partly because the task of hiring has been left to the discretion of employers in private enterprises since market reforms. During the 1950s, workers were assigned to jobs by administrative measures and wages were centrally regulated in wage scales. After leaving school, almost all women entered the labor force and their number of working hours was similar to men (Gustafsson and Li, 2000).

Market economy reform has given existing enterprises more freedom to maneuver, including autonomy in how to remunerate workers and whom to hire (Cooke, 2001). Employers value employees who are relatively inexpensive to keep. Legal regulations requiring employers to provide maternity benefits or on-site nurseries or restricted working hours for women generally make female employees more expensive than male employees. This leads employers to prefer to hire men rather than women. In addition, employers' preferred traits for workers tend to be more prevalent among stereotypes of men than of women and this turns queues for rural off-farm labor from labor queues to 'gender queues' (Reskin and Roos, 1990) where men are overwhelmingly preferred as employees over women. Management often ignores the protective policies and regulations previously applied to women who were working in SOEs. Many factories and other business enterprises prefer to recruit men because of women's traditional responsibilities of bearing and rearing children and maintaining households, and because of the extra costs when they do attend to legal protections for women.

Wages

Earnings for women tend to be below those for men. On average, women earn only 60 percent of what men earn. Women are thinly represented at the top end of the salary continuum; a disproportionate share of women work in low-paying light industry, handicraft, service and less-skilled occupations, while in managerial positions men outnumber women by more than ten to one (Riley, 1996). Table 3.5 shows the breakdown of total labor force, percentage female, and salary by sector.

There are several possible causes of these differentials, other than gender discrimination in hiring and firing. One cause is differential educational attainment. Women make up a large majority of those still illiterate, and women generally receive less education than men. Another reason for lower earnings is women are less well represented in senior ranks of their occupations, and they have been compelled to retire earlier

Table 3.5 Wages in the PRC in 1999 by gender and sector

	Wage				Female (%)				Average Salary in RMB			
	People (1000)	Total wages (RMB1000)	Average/ (1000)	Ave. wage	Weighted average	State-owned units	Collective	Others	Weighted average	State-owned units	Collective	Others
National total, grouped by sector	83 361	716 079 750	83 824	8 543	38.0	36.5	41.1	42.4	8 346	8 543	5 774	9 829
Farming, forestry, animal husbandry and fishery	4 999	24 284 074	5 045	4 813	37.6	37.9	25.9	34.1	4 832	4 813	4 878	6 740
Mining and quarrying	5 251	41 300 602	5 341	7 732	26.5	26.4	37.4	21.6	7 521	7 732	4 545	7 651
Manufacturing	16 482	128 360 820	16 865	7 611	43.4	39.5	49.3	45.6	7 794	7 611	5 327	9 316
Production and supply of electricity, gas and water	2 388	26 675 227	2 373	11 239	32.1	32.3	32.4	31.1	11 513	11 239	9 834	13 856
Construction	3 985	36 072 165	4 130	8 734	18.5	20.1	17.4	15.0	7 982	8 734	6 296	9 540
Geological prospecting and water conservancy	1 083	9 589 157	1 084	8 843	26.4	26.3	30.1	22.2	8 821	8 843	7 636	8 439
Transport, storage, post and telecommunications	5 681	64 726 473	5 705	11 345	28.0	27.4	30.4	31.7	10 991	11 345	5 707	14 241
Wholesale and retail trade and catering services	6 080	41 067 831	6 150	6 678	46.3	44.6	46.1	52.9	6 417	6 678	4 802	9 001
Finance and insurance	2 053	24 987 792	2 040	12 249	42.7	41.9	42.0	50.9	12 046	12 249	9 088	18 648
Real estate trade	612	6 345 209	606	10 475	33.8	34.6	33.9	31.6	11 505	10 475	10 516	14 693

Table 3.5 (continued)

	Wage				Female (%)				Average Salary in RMB			
	People (1 000)	Total wages (RMB1 000)	Average/ (1 000)	Ave. wage	Weighted average	State-owned units	Collective	Others	Weighted average	State-owned units	Collective	Others
Social services	3 188	28 794 434	3 180	9 054	44.4	44.4	47.2	42.1	9 263	9 054	6 621	12 785
Healthcare, sporting and social welfare	4 154	40 771 783	4 119	9 899	56.9	57.7	51.4	49.0	9 664	9 899	7 826	16 618
Education, culture and arts, radio, film, TV	14 325	121 705 830	14 169	8 590	43.4	43.4	43.8	39.9	8 510	8 590	5 750	12 871
Scientific research and polytechnical services	1 525	17 748 338	1 538	11 543	32.9	33.7	25.8	25.7	11 601	11 543	8 771	15 671
Government agencies, party agencies and social organizations	10 837	96 718 583	10 768	8 982	24.1	24.1	40.7		8 978	8 982	7 985	
Others	718	6 931 432	710	9 762	36.3	34.6	42.7	36.8	10 068	9 762	8 135	20 548

Source: Ministry of Labor and Social Assurance.

than men. Although the Chinese constitution and laws guarantee equal employment rights, the official retirement age is 60 for men, 50 for women and 55 for female cadre and officers (Ministry of Labor and Social Assurance, 2000). Moreover with their 'triple burden' of childcare, eldercare and housework, as well as their paid employment, women are in a weaker position to exploit opportunities for second paid jobs (Khan and Riskin, 2001).

When comparing the wages the males and females receive, usually only earnings rather than total benefits are taken into account. Although females receive lower earnings than their male counterparts, they sometimes receive more allowances and paid leave for childbearing. If we take all these economic benefits into account, what the males and the females receive from a job might be closer to par. Unfortunately no reliable study taking into account all fringe benefits as well as wages is available, so this explanation will await further evidence. For at least one expensive benefit – housing – however, women are not receiving preference.

Housing Rights

The Women's Law states that women should enjoy equal rights with men regarding housing and other benefits. However work units, which have been primarily responsible for allocating housing for urban dwellers, typically discriminate against women. Males are considered to be the 'head of the household' and are given higher weight in housing allocation equations. While some work units blatantly pass over women in favor of men, others exercise disguised forms of discrimination, such as setting higher standards for seniority required for eligibility for unit housing that apply to women. As housing reform now enables people to purchase their own house, new forms of discrimination have appeared. Some work units have refused to sell housing to women outright, while others have charged women workers more than men for apartments (HRIC, 1999).

Working Conditions

The results of a 1993 survey of labor protections for women workers in 475 factories in Ningbo, Zhejiang Province, a coastal city in a highly developed region of the country, found that most factories were violating national regulations on the protection of workers. Although working conditions might be poor, it does not necessarily mean that these poor conditions are due to gender discrimination if they are in existence in a male working environment as well. However there was evidence that protections mandated under regulations on conditions for female workers were not applied.

More than 50 percent of the factories surveyed had no protections for pregnant employees. Women workers in 38.1 percent of the factories were not given leave for childbirth and in another 39 percent such leave was less than 56 days. More than 50 percent did not pay women's salaries or bonuses during time off for childbirth, nor cover their maternity care expenses.

Examinations of the health status of the more than 40 000 workers in these enterprises found that 375 suffered from gynecological disorders, a rate 4.6 percent higher than that in the female population as a whole, while their rate of premature birth was 1.34 times the normal incidence (HRIC, 1995).

Sexual Abuse and Harassment at Work

Women not only face discrimination in employment, but also are subjected to sexual abuse and harassment in the workplace. Such occurrences are not uncommon, but there appears to be a limit to the kinds of help that is being given to victims. Sexual harassment has been little reported in the media; however, some reports and an occasional study on the subject have appeared. An investigation by one Chinese scholar found that 84 percent of the women surveyed had experienced some form of sexual harassment, 47.9 percent reported that they had been the subject of sexual jokes, discussions or insults by male colleagues or superiors at work, while the men had offered some sort of professional advantage in exchange for sexual favors to over 13 percent of the respondents (*China Rights Forum*, 1995). The problem affects women of all social strata, including those who work in government offices. However it is particularly severe in private businesses, where employers may feel freer (than in government-related businesses), to act as they please (HRIC, 1995).

From the victim's point of view, the decision not to make a report might be due to the fact that if the accused has to be questioned, it might be difficult to present evidence, she might be further embarrassed, as well as concerned for being pressured by her social surroundings (Tang, 2001). As enterprise autonomy has grown, managers have much greater power than before, so they can easily punish workers who make complaints. For example managers determine workers' level of compensation and bonuses and evaluate their job performance (Gustafsson and Li, 2000). Due to lack of legal protection and to women's increasing economic vulnerability, many victims of sexual harassment do not report it, for fear of losing their jobs (Canadian International Development Agency, 2001). Other reasons why not much has been done to reduce the occurrence of such behavior include red tape on the part of the government and lack of specific laws forbidding sexual harassment.

The urgency of the need for legal reform was further emphasized in a sexual harassment case that occurred in December 2001 (Appendix 3.4). Because it is not easy to gather evidence of the crime, government officials find it a waste of time to handle such cases so the problem is ignored by the legal system and often by society. The difficulty of tracking sexual harassment cases is especially high in rural areas where control is even more difficult. Complaints from victims are not taken seriously and they usually suffer in silence.

Worker Lay-offs

Women have suffered disproportionately from lay-offs in the economic turmoil of social reconstruction and the Asian financial crisis. In a 1987 survey by the Women Workers Committee of the All China Federation of Trade Unions (ACFTU), women accounted for 64 percent of laid-off workers. Later surveys by the ACFTU found similar figures for the 1990s, demonstrating clearly that the situation has not improved during the 1990s. By 2000, official statistics indicate that women make up more than 51 percent of all laid-off workers in China (*China Daily*, 2000).

As far as the market enterprises are concerned, the female labor force only plays a role as a regulator in the labor market. Whenever the supply of labor exceeds demand, women workers are the first to be removed. The state policy mandates that it will help enterprises recruit some of its surplus labor force by developing tertiary industries. As a result, 'only a fraction of the women in state-run enterprises will be left without jobs' according to government proclamations (*Women's International Network News*, 1995) but these proclamations have not matched reality.

Because news of discrimination was so widespread, the Internal and Judicial Affairs Committee from the National People's Congress set this problem as a target of an investigation and looked into how local governments responded to the problem. The inspection found that government at each level is the major force contributing to opening new ways for laid-off women workers (*Beijing Review*, 1995). Government action has not solved all problems however. For example the Hebei General Trade Union carried out a survey on 259 laid-off women workers in eight cities in the province. Few had found new jobs and most were suffering serious psychological problems. At least 58 percent blamed the disappearance of their jobs on poor management. The workers were also furious that officials were forcing re-employed workers to accept 'special difficulty certificates' to pay 'administration fees'. The certificates were supposed to entitle recipients to reductions in rent, school fees and special tax breaks (*South China Morning Post*, 1997).

CONCLUSIONS

In the PRC, as in many other societies, the tasks of childbearing and child-rearing rest disproportionately on the shoulders of women, and the task of supporting the family lies with the men. To minimize gender inequality the government of the PRC has taken many proactive steps. These measures include legal and administrative policies to combat problems relating to employment. Although the government cannot completely solve the problem, the gap of gender inequality has been narrowed, but substantial challenge remains. The current labor market in the PRC is suffering from high levels of unemployment, especially among those with less education in rural areas of the country. When competition is fierce for jobs in the face of the massive restructuring of the economy of the PRC, women may suffer disproportionately when they have been unable to gain advanced education. As of 2000, PRC women are systematically under-represented in graduates of educational institutions and in jobs with greater responsibility, and they are over-represented in agriculture, health and education, and among the ranks of the unemployed. They face discrimination in hiring, wages and fringe benefits such as housing, but have legal access to special benefits when pregnant or nursing, although these extra benefits are not always provided.

The legal basis for equality in employment that exists in the PRC provides ample opportunity for improvements in the future if adequate implementation is enforced. Since much Chinese tradition rests on implementation via cultural norms rather than legal enforcement, perhaps the most optimistic hints lie in the exemplary local programs that inform women of their rights, provide them with legal recourse and educate employers regarding their social duty to treat women fairly. While steps have been taken to solve current problems and difficulties faced by women, the future is not being neglected. Programs are planned with a long-term perspective such that women in PRC will become more capable of competing with their fellow counterparts in the workplace in future.

Current data indicate that managerial autonomy for purposes of market competition poses a threat to the protection of women's rights to equal employment opportunity even as it poses opportunities for women to become entrepreneurs. Women in the rural segments of the country need more help from the government, but problems of urban women clearly indicate that all programs should not be targeted solely toward rural areas. Instead a more holistic approach should be adopted to counter gender differences in employment in the PRC. Continuous efforts to maintain and monitor these measures and programs are required to ensure that the situation will not be further aggravated. Gender equality is a goal that many will hope to achieve eventually in the PRC.

REFERENCES

Beijing Review (1988),'New challenges to women's employment', 31 October, 18.
Beijing Review (1995),'Historic liberation of Chinese women', **38** (36), 4–10 September.
Byrd, W. and Q. Lin (eds) (1990), *China's Rural Industry: Structure, Development, and Reform*, New York: Oxford University Press.
Canadian International Development Agency (2001), *Gender Profile in China*, May, http://www.acdicida.gc.ca/cida_ind.nsf/0/cc2a244620ba0e5785256af5005a1518.
Chen, M.X. (1999), 'From legal to substantive equality: realizing women's rights by action', *Violence Against Women*, **5** (12), 1394.
China Daily (2000),'Program to help women make money', 18 October, http://www.china.org.cn/english/2937.htm.
China Daily (2001), 'Chinese women hold up half the sky', 24 August, http://www.china.org.cn/english/2001/Aug/18032.htm.
China Daily (2002),'Rural women still face inequality', 1 February, http://www.china.org.cn/english/2002/Feb/26285.htm.
Cooke, F.L. (2001), 'Equal opportunities? The role of legislation and public policies in women's employment in China', *Women in Management Review*, **16** (7), 334–48.
'Development of Female Human Resources', (2003), http://news.inhe.net/job/case/2003-4/46671/46671_0.html.
Fang, Y. (1999). 'Two challenges facing the Bohai area', in J.J. Williams, S.B. Chew, Y. Cao and A.M. Low (eds), *Business Opportunities in Northeastern China*, Singapore: Prentice Hall, pp. 125–32.
Feng, C. (2000), 'Chinese women in the economic reform', *All-China Women's Federation*, 1 November, http://www.women.org.cn/allnews/02/04.html.
Gao, S. and F. Chi (1997). *The Development of China's Non-governmentally and Privately Operated Economy*, Beijing: Foreign Languages Press.
Granrose, C.S. (ed.) (1997), *The Careers of Business Managers in East Asia*, Westport, CT: Quorum.
Guo, R. (1999), *How the Chinese Economy Works: A Multi-regional Overview*, New York: St. Martin's Press.
Gustafsson, B. and S. Li (2000),'Economic transformation and the gender earnings gap in urban China', *Journal of Population Economics*, **13** (2), 305.
Human Rights in China (HRIC)(1995), 'Protective exclusion or excluded from protections: working conditions and discrimination against women in employment', in 'Caught Between Tradition and the State', *China Rights Forum*, August, p. 117.
HRIC (1999), 'Definition of discrimination and measures to combat it', *China Rights Forum*, (Spring), 40–42.
Ignatius, A. (1988), 'Foreign firms hiring workers in China hit catch-22', *Wall Street Journal*, p. 15.
Itoh, F. (ed.) (1997), *China in the Twenty-first Century: Politics, Economy, and Society*, Tokyo: United Nations University Press.
Jiang, W. (1997),'Protection of women's rights progressing', *Beijing Review*, **40** (33), 18–24.
Khan, A.R. and C. Riskin (2001), *Inequality and Poverty in China in the Age of Globalization*, New York and Oxford: Oxford University Press.
Li, S.Q. (1995). 'The occupational levels of women and appraisal of their work quality', *Women's Status in Contemporary China*, Beijing: Beijing University Press.

Ministry of Labor (1998), 'Directives on social assurance and basic livelihood of SOE *xiagang* workers', serial no 1998–10, Beijing: Ministry of Labor of PRC.

Ministry of Labor and Social Assurance (2000),'What is the legal retirement age?' serial no 1999–08, http://www.molss.gov.cn/index_zcwj.htm.

Ministry of Labor and Social Assurance (2002), 'On further implementing the State Council directives on re-employment of *xiagang* workers', serial no 2002–20, Beijing: Ministry of Labor and Social Assurance PRC.

National Bureau of Statistics of China (1991), *China Statistical Yearbook*, Beijing: China Statistics Press.

National Bureau of Statistics of China (1996), *China Statistical Yearbook*, Beijing: China Statistics Press.

National Bureau of Statistics of China (2001), *China Statistical Yearbook*, Beijing: China Statistics Press.

People's Daily Online (2000), 20 November http://english.peopledaily.com.cn/200010/20/eng 20001020_53162.html

Perkins, D. (1997), 'History, politics, and the sources of economic growth: China and the East Asian way of growth', in F. Itoh (ed.), *China in the Twenty-first Century: Politics, Economy, and Society*, Tokyo: United Nations University Press, pp. 25–41.

Reskin, B.F. and P.A. Roos (1990), *Job Queues, Gender Queues: Explaining Women's Inroads Into Male Occupations*, Philadelphia, PA: Temple University Press.

Riley, N.E. (1996),'Holding up half the economy', *China Business Review*, January–February, 22–24.

Schauble, J. (2001), 'Failed sex harassment case reveals need for law reform', *Sydney Morning Herald Online*, 24 December, http://www.smh.com.au/news/0112/24/world/world11.html.

South China Morning Post (1997), 'China Worker's Daily defends laid off women workers in Hebei', 18 November.

State Council (1998), 'Directives on social-welfare and re-employment of SOE's *xiagang* workers', serial no. 1998–10, Beijing: PRC State Council.

Summerfield, G. (1994), 'Economic reform and the employment of Chinese women', *Journal of Economic Issues*, **28** (3), 715.

Tang, C. (2001), 'Sexual harassment in the workplace and ways to control it', *Journal of Research on Women, (Funu Yanjiu Congkan)*, **5**, 26–31 (in Chinese).

Women's International Network News (1993), 'A survey of the status of women in China', Summer, **19** (3), 59.

Women's International Network News (1995), 'China: Women's Changing Employment', Autumn, **21** (4), 64.

Women's International Network News (1996), 'Program for the development of Chinese women', Autumn, **22** (4), 68.

Women's International Network News (1997), 'China: women facing unemployment – the re-employment project', Spring, **23** (2), 71.

World Bank (1992), *China: Strategies for Reducing Poverty in the 1990s*, World Bank Country Study, Washington, DC: World Bank.

Xinmin Evening News (2001), 'Sexual harassment: tough for office lady to fight back', 23 December, http://photo.eastday.com/epublish/gb/paper148/20011223/class 014800009/hwz564913.htm.

Zhan, J. (1995), 'The effects of gender differential on females' status', *Women's Status in Contemporary China*, Beijing: Beijing University Press.

APPENDIX 3.1   THE PROTECTION OF THE RIGHTS AND INTERESTS OF WOMEN

Excerpts from the Law of the People's Republic of China on the Protection of the Rights and Interests of Women adopted at the 5th Session of the Seventh National People's Congress on 3 April 1992 (Woman's Law of 1992).

   Source: http://www.unescap.org/esid/psis/population/database/poplaws/law_china/ch_record002.htm.

Discrimination in Educational Preparation for Careers

Article 17. Parents or other guardians must perform their duty of ensuring that female school aged children or adolescents receive compulsory education. Where parents or other guardians fail to send female children or adolescents to school, the local people's government shall admonish and criticize them and by adopting effective measures order them to send their female school aged children or adolescents to school, with the exception of those who on account of illness or other special circumstances are allowed by the government not to go to school. The governments, society and schools shall, in the light of the actual difficulties of female school aged children or adolescents in schooling, take effective measures to ensure that female school aged children or adolescents receive compulsory schooling for the number of years locally prescribed.

Discrimination in Employment

Article 21. The state shall guarantee that women enjoy the equal right with men to work.
Article 22. With the exception of the special types of work or posts unsuitable to women, no unit may, in employing staff and workers, refuse to employ women by reason of sex or raise the employment standards for women.
Article 25. All units shall, in line with women's characteristics and according to law, protect women's safety and health during their work or physical labor, and shall not assign them to any work or physical labor not suitable for women. Women shall be under special protection during menstrual period, pregnancy, obstetrical periods and nursing periods.

Discrimination because of Gender

Article 35. Women's right of life and health shall be inviolable. Drowning, abandoning, or cruel infanticide in any manner of female babies shall be prohibited; Discrimination against or maltreatment of women who give birth to female babies or women who are sterile shall be prohibited; Cruel treatment causing injury even death of women by superstition or violence shall be prohibited; Maltreatment or abandonment of aged women shall be prohibited.

APPENDIX 3.2 THE LABOR ACT (1994)

Source: http://www.unescap.org/esid/psis/population/database/poplaws/law_china/ch_record005.htm.

The following is extracted from Chapter VII Special Protection for Female and Juvenile Workers, The Labor Act (1994):

Section 59. It is prohibited to arrange female workers to engage in work down the pit of mines, or work with Grade IV physical labor intensity as stipulated by the State, or other work that female workers should avoid.

Section 60. Female workers during their menstrual period shall not be arranged to engage in work high above the ground, under low temperature, or in cold water or work with Grade III physical labor intensity as stipulated by the State.

Section 61. Female workers during their pregnancy shall not be arranged to engage in work with Grade III physical labor intensity as stipulated by the State or other work that they should avoid in pregnancy. Female workers pregnant for seven months or more shall not be arranged to extend their working hours or to work night shifts.

Section 62. After childbirth, female workers shall be entitled to no less than 90 days of maternity leave with pay.

Section 63. Female workers during the period of breast-feeding their babies less than one year old shall not be arranged to engage in work with Grade III physical labor intensity as stipulated by the State or other labor that they should avoid during their breast-feeding period, or to extend their working hours or to work night shifts.

APPENDIX 3.3   THE PROGRAM FOR THE DEVELOPMENT OF CHINESE WOMEN (1995–2000)

Source: http://www.unescap.org/esid/psis/population/database/poplaws/ law_china/ch_record016.htm. (Following are excerpts from the program).

Introduction

The women are a great force in creating the human civilization and promoting social development. The development level of women is an important index for social development as well as an important yardstick to measure social progress. To promote the progress and development of Chinese women is the common task of the governments at all levels, the relevant departments, social organizations and the Chinese people as a whole. With a view to further promoting the development of Chinese women, the Program for the Development of the Chinese Women (1995–2000) is stipulated.

The concrete targets for the development of women are:

1.   Improve the participation of women in the decision-making and management of state and social affairs.
2.   Organize women to take an active part in the open-and-reform and modernization efforts so as to promote the development of social productive forces.
3.   Guarantee the labor rights of women.
4.   Work hard to develop women's education and raise the scientific and technical level of the women.
5.   Further improve the health of women and guarantee their right over family planning.
6.   Encourage establishment of civil, harmonious and stable families with equality between the husband and the wife.
7.   Effectively contain violence on women and the criminal acts of abducting and trading women and prostitution.
8.   Pay great attention to and try to help in the development of the women in border and remote areas, poverty-stricken areas and areas inhabited by ethnic minorities. The problem of subsistence for the women in the poverty-stricken areas will be basically solved by the end of this century.
9.   Improve the social environment for the development of women and raise their quality in life.
10. Expand the friendly exchanges of Chinese women with women of the various countries to promote world peace.

11. Establish a mechanism of dynamic studies of women's status, data gathering and information communiations.

Policies and measures
There are specific policies and measures to reach the targets as mentioned above. As the areas that the Program touched on is very wide, this report shall put the emphasis on the policies and measures taken in the legal protection of women, in the employment and labor protection and in education and vocational training.

Legal Protection

1. Formulate practical and operational administrative decrees or corresponding policies and measures, in light of the Constitution of PRC and the Law on Guaranteeing Women's Rights and Interests of PRC, to make the laws regarding the safeguard of women's rights and interests more feasible.
2. Improve the quality and strengthen the contingent of the legal and administrative law enforcement personnel and enhance leadership and strict supervision to ensure that the laws and decrees in the safeguard of the women's rights and interests are implemented in an all-round way. The acts that are not in strict observance of the law or in violation of the law and the rights and interests of women will be legally prosecuted and punished.
3. The Marriage Law of PRC and relevant other laws and decrees will be continuously publicized in a deep-going and sustained way all over the country, in the rural areas and border and remote areas and poverty-stricken areas in particular. Strengthen the registration and management of marriages and adopt effective measures to curb such illegal marriages as early, mercenary or consanguineous ones.
4. Protect the personal rights of women and their rights over legal property and investigate and punish in time the civil cases that are in violation of the rights and interests of women.
5. Deal severe blows to such criminal acts as abduction, trade, abandonment, maltreatment, persecution and insult of women and safeguard women's personal safety and dignity. Resolutely ban prostitution and eliminate evil social phenomena.
6. Seriously investigate and deal accordingly with such criminal acts as killing, trading and cruelly injuring newborn baby girls. Strictly forbid fetus sex appraisal with modern medical means for non-medical purposes and deal heavy blows to such criminal acts as violating birth control.

7. Make use of various channels and forms to carry out in a broad and deep-going way the campaign of publicity about legality and strengthen the awareness of legality of the whole people; it is especially necessary to guide and help the broad masses of women to foster solid awareness of legality and consciously use the law as a weapon to safeguard their legitimate rights and interests.
8. Protect the rights of women to prosecute and appeal. Improve the work to receive and handle the complaints filed by women and guard against shifting responsibility to others and long delay and indecision. Open legal consultancy and agency services to help women to solve their legal difficulties and those women who are wronged to have justice upheld (UN ESCAP, 1995).

Employment and Labor Protection

1. Actively develop areas and means of employment suitable to women's characteristics and provide more job opportunities for women.
2. Develop services in job hunting and relevant consultancy services to guide women in their hunting for jobs.
3. Actively develop diversified rural economies and rural industries to create more job opportunities for women and organize in a planned way the flux of the labor service of women from poor-stricken areas to other areas.
4. Improve the working conditions of women workers in private, rural industrial and foreign-funded Wrms and strengthen labor protection. It is forbidden to assign women to do jobs that are not suitable for the female sex. Establish and improve labor protection for women workers; establish a system of regular general physical and gynecological check-ups for women workers; strengthen scientific research in goods relating to women's labor protection to constantly raise the level of labor protection.
5. Actively carry out labor supervision and ferret out and punish those acts that are in violation of women's labor legitimate rights. Resolutely curb the firms from terminating the labor contracts with women in pregnancy, lying-in and breastfeeding, from forcing women workers to engage in super-intensity labor and from violating the principle of equal pay for equal labor for both sexes and guarantee that women workers work in environments that do not bring harms to their body and mind and are safe. The units and individuals that employ girls under 16 years of age will be punished legally.
6. Make labor protection of women workers as part of the responsibility of the leaders of a unit for safe production and part of the important

content to assess their work. Strengthen the publicity work among the women workers of the decrees and policies relating to labor protection and raise their awareness of self-protection.

7. Reform the social security system for the childbearing workers. Steps will be taken to cover the childbearing insurance fees with socially coordinated funds instead of with funds from each firm. This reform will spread from state-owned firms to all firms.

Education and Vocational Training

1. The governments at all levels must implement conscientiously the Rules for the Elimination of Illiteracy promulgated by the State Council. The focus will be laid on young and middle-aged illiterate women in remote and border areas, poverty-stricken areas and areas inhabited by ethnic minority groups. The work will be conducted in light of the practical situation of uneven economic and cultural development in each locality and guidance will be offered according to each classified category.

2. The governments at all levels must conscientiously implement the Law on Compulsory Education of PRC and popularize compulsory education as part of the efforts to develop the productive forces and overcome old habits and ideas and create a favorable social environment for girls to accept formal education. Assistance in terms of policy and funds will be rendered to those remote and borders areas, poverty-stricken areas and areas inhabited by ethnic minority groups. All forms of education such as special girls' training classes will be run to facilitate the attendance to school by girls in poverty-stricken areas. The governments at all levels should actively help solve the practical difficulties the girls of poor families face in their education.

3. Raise step by step the percentage of the female sex in receiving intermediate technical and specialized education and higher education. In enrolment of students, the intermediate technical schools and institutions of higher learning must abide by the principle of equality for both sexes, except for the specialties the state has otherwise defined.

4. Make full use of all kinds of existing adult educational and vocational schools and, in light of the need for social development and the characteristics of women, carry out vocational education or training in a variety of forms and at different levels among the women in the city and the countryside.

Organizaion and Implemtation

1. The Women's and Children's Working Committee of the State Council is responsible for the implementation of this Program. The relevant State Council departments and the various social organizations, in accordance with the requirements set in this Program and in light of the responsibilities of each, formulate detailed plans and are held responsible for their implementation.
2. Implementation of this Program is the bounden and important duty of the governments at all levels. The people's government in each province (autonomous region and municipality) must, under the guidance of this Program and in light of local concrete conditions, formulate its own plan for the development of women in each locality and incorporate it into the local general plan for economic and social development and have it arranged and implemented in a unified and coordinated way. It is necessary to establish a system of targeted responsibility and make the implementation of the Program as part of the content to appraise the work of the main leaders of the government and relevant departments of a province (autonomous region, municipality), prefecture (city), county and township.
3. The governments at all levels must increase step by step the funds for the cause of the women. Strengthen and perfect the construction of the socialized service system and support the women in their economic activities in terms of materials, information, technique and loans. Encourage people in all walks of life to sponsor the cause of the women.

APPENDIX 3.4 A CASE STUDY OF SEXUAL HARASSMENT

This case study was reported by John Schauble, a correspondent in Beijing. A Chinese court has thrown out the country's first sexual harassment case on the grounds of insufficient evidence and lack of legal foundation. A closed hearing at the Lianhu District Court in the provincial capital of Xi'an ruled against the 30-year-old female plaintiff who complained that her boss repeatedly groped her in the office and pressured her to have sex with him.

The woman, identified only as Ms Tong, lodged a civil suit against her employer on 26 October 2001. Ms Tong, who worked in a state-owned enterprise, complained of repeated unwanted touching by her manager since 1994. Her writ also complained that he had asked her to accompany him to a hotel for sex on one occasion. The manager was reprimanded when Ms Tong complained, but he then made her presence in the workplace untenable, withholding bonus payments and allowances.

The court ruled that it was difficult to obtain direct evidence in the case and to confirm independently the alleged victim's story. In addition, the official Xinhua news agency reported that the court noted that there was no law on sexual harassment in China (*Xinmin Evening News*, 2001).

Forced to stay at home after making the complaint, Ms Tong then found it impossible to return to work as no work was assigned to her.

The 1992 Law on the Protection of the Rights and Interests of Women guarantees equal rights in theory. Sexual harassment at work has yet to receive the attention given to domestic violence and bigamy. The fact that the Xi'an court even accepted the case was seen as breaking new ground.

'Under our Constitution and labor law, equal protection is stipulated,' said Ms Wang Simei, deputy director of the Women's Studies Institute at the All China Women's Federation. 'But what we need are some concrete policies to bring these into force.'

About the only recourse a woman has in such cases is through the criminal law which stipulates the offence of 'hooliganism', but this refers to harassment and assault in a public place (Schauble, 2001).

4. Women in Taiwan: social status, education and employment

T.K. Peng and Tsai-Wei Wang

On 20 May 2000, a new administration was inaugurated in Taiwan after a close presidential campaign. One unusually impressive fact about the new government was its personnel composition: 14 Cabinet members were female, more than a quarter of the total. They were sworn into such high-profile positions as Vice-President, Minister of Interior Affairs as well as Minister of Transportation and Communications and Chairperson of Labor Affairs. Observers of feminism hailed it as a milestone for women in Taiwanese history.

Women in Taiwan have come a long way to be what they are and to do what they do. Historically and culturally their ancestresses suffered far more structural gender inequality. Concepts such as 'A woman without capability is virtuous' and 'Education is unnecessary for women' were pervasive in Mainland China by 1600 (late Ming Dynasty) and were transferred to Taiwan during repeated migrations to the island. Canadian missionary George L. Mackay founded the first girls' school in Taiwan in 1884 (the Ching Dynasty). In 2000 the first female vice-president of Taiwan took office. Today women's status is obviously on the rise but there is still a long way to go before the society can be considered gender equal.

This chapter presents a broad picture of the employment patterns, educational and vocational opportunities and work–family concerns of the women in Taiwan. These dimensions are central to understanding women's social status and the utilization of their potential. While studies of gender issues with a focus on females in the West are quite common, research focusing on Taiwanese women is rare in Western literature. As the business world has shifted quickly towards globalization and Taiwan was admitted into the World Trade Organization (WTO) effective 2001, a study of Taiwan's women is not only necessary but also timely.

SOCIO-CULTURAL BACKGROUND

An island 193 km from Fukien province of the People's Republic of China, with an area of 36 000 sq km and a population of about 23 million (49 percent female), Taiwan is among the most densely populated economies in the world. In the eyes of many Westerners, Taiwan's economic development in the past decades has been impressive. Generally speaking, Taiwan was a post-war ruin and a 'white terror' society in the 1950s. It experienced an economic take-off in the 1960s, high growth in the 1970s and steady growth in the 1980s and finally emerged as a relatively democratic and prosperous society in the 1990s. Meanwhile it faced critical challenges to upgrade its competitive edge from traditional manufacturing to high value-added technological advantage.

Of the total population, about 2 percent are aborigines who are linguistically and racially related to Austronesian people. About 85 percent are descendants of settlers from the coastal provinces of Mainland China who traversed the Taiwan straits about four hundred years ago, while 13 percent consist of those who fled Communist rule in the late 1940s and their descendants. These latecomers were from all areas of China.

Therefore culturally the people of Taiwan are predominately Chinese. Being immigrants or descendants of immigrants from the China Mainland, Taiwanese share much cultural heritage with other Chinese in Mainland China, Hong Kong and Singapore. They speak the same languages (Mandarin and provincial dialects), celebrate the same folklore festivals (Chinese New Year and Dragon Boat Festival), and observe the same traditional values (for example respect for their elders and reciprocation of favors and greetings), among other things. The power of Confucian traditionalism is widespread in these communities, but has different effects in each individual context (Redding, 1990). Over the years, Taiwan has developed a Confucian culture of its own. Nonetheless as one studies the people on Taiwan it is impossible to limit the focus on the context of Taiwan's 'here and now' without taking into account its Chinese roots. Although the Chinese societies may have shared similar traditional values, each has evolved some distinct practices in the workplace.

Taiwan's Work Values

Hofstede's large-scale survey (1980, 1983), probably the most frequently cited cross-national analysis, identified four work-related value patterns: power distance (PD), uncertainty avoidance (UA), individualism (IND) and masculinity (MAS). Taiwan appeared to be somewhat average on both PD (19th out of 40 nations) and UA (20th), quite low on IND (36th) and relatively low on MAS (27th). This suggests Taiwan is a collective society. On the cluster plot of pairs of these values, the Taiwanese put relatively strong emphasis on social status and group conformity, were collectively minded and not very comfortable with ambiguity, but did not show much concern for control and decisiveness.

Michael Bond and his associates initiated a 22-nation research on 40 items fundamental to Chinese culture (Chinese Culture Connection, 1987). These items include humbleness, filial piety and self-cultivation, among others. Ecological factor analysis yielded four indices: integration, Confucian work dynamism, human heartedness and moral discipline. The result indicated Taiwan was relatively low on integration (19th out of 22 nations), moderately high on moral discipline (8th), moderate on human heartedness (13th), and among the highest on Confucian work dynamism (second after Hong Kong). They argued that this last cultural dimension was what made the 'Asian Tigers' (that is, Hong Kong, Singapore, South Korea and Taiwan) achieve high economic development. However they did not foresee that the Tigers and other so-called 'newly industrialized countries' in Southeast Asia were weakened after the regional financial crisis in 1997 (see the cover story of *Time*, 7 July 2003).

The meaning of work research was carried out by a group of 14 scholars in eight industrialized nations (including Japan, the US, the Netherlands and the UK). A key construct is termed 'work centrality', defined as 'the degree of general importance that working has in life of an individual at any given point in time' (MOW International Research Team, 1987, p. 81). With two questions combined to measure the construct and some scale conversion, a range from 2 to 10 was developed for the indicator, the mean and standard deviation of the eight-nation data were 6.98 and 1.83, respectively.

From a replication study with samples from Taiwan as well as Hong Kong and PRC, Taiwan (8.22) (and PRC, 7.98) appears to have amazingly high work centrality, whereas Hong Kong (6.95) stands very close to the US and Belgium, the average group (Peng, 1996). While there is possibility of a great overlap between individual distributions among the 11-nation samples, the mean score of Taiwan is greater than that of the UK by over one standard deviation. This high work centrality may be a reflection of the commonality among Taiwanese of diligent and pragmatic personality traits (Whitley, 1992).

Women's Values

A 2001 issue of *Reader's Digest* (2001, Chinese edition) reported a telephone survey that compared values, social status and other experiences of 1550 Chinese women aged 15 to 45 in Taipei, Hong Kong and Shanghai.

In spite of the fact that they all inherited traditional Chinese culture, these females expressed different value orientations due to their respective backgrounds and experiences. It appeared that relatively more Taipei women (32 percent) experienced serious social discrimination compared to their counterparts in Hong Kong (25 percent) and in Shanghai (19 percent). In response to the question 'How important are family, career, and money to happiness?', while all of them considered family indispensable, more Taipei women (71 percent) than those in Hong Kong (61 percent) and in Shanghai (58 percent) perceived the importance of money. In contrast, Shanghai women (81 percent) seemed to have emphasized careers more than did their sisters in Taipei (66 percent) and in Hong Kong (61 percent).

Psychologist C.K. Wang (1993) investigated work values of college graduates of both genders from three 'generations', meaning the research subjects were controlled by the year they graduated from college as three independent groups: class of 1967, class of 1977 and class of 1987, respectively. Out of 567 respondents, usable female responses of the three generations were 11, 82 and 93, respectively (not too many women went to college in the 1960s and might already be retired; many of the class of 1987 went abroad for graduate education). Following the Rokeach framework (1973), work values were dichotomized as instrumental values and terminal values. Factor analyses generated five dimensions out of 45 items for instrumental values: perseverance and ability, politeness and open-mindedness, respecting tradition, self-discipline and justice, and practicality. A similar procedure derived four factors from 25 items for terminal values: intrinsic reward, extrinsic reward, collective interest, and safety and harmony.

All of the instrumental values were perceived as substantially more important now than they had been before for all generations except for the class of 1987's value of self-discipline and justice. Furthermore the order of importance did not change significantly over time within groups, but it varied more obviously between the subgroups. For the youngest generation (that is, the class of 1987), perseverance and ability had been most valued when they got out of the school but politeness and open-mindedness became the number one instrumental values later in life. Furthermore self-discipline and justice had been placed on top by the class of 1967 but was viewed as the last by the class of 1987.

Regardless of these generation discrepancies, there is a pattern about their instrumental values. Perseverance and ability were never ignored whereas politeness and open-mindedness was valued even more highly now then before. In contrast, self-discipline and justice became less important over time, while practicality and respecting tradition were not perceived as extremely helpful in reaching their ultimate career goals.

All four terminal values were thought to be significantly more important now than before. The overall pattern seemed to be quite clear: safety and harmony became the number one terminal value over time, followed by intrinsic rewards. In contrast, extrinsic rewards and collective interest were never on top. However it is noteworthy that the youngest generation, unlike their senior sisters, altered their priority to place extrinsic reward before collective interest for 'now'.

Women's Education and Vocational Preparation

Over the past few decades, the proportion of female students involved in elementary-, middle- and high-school education as well as higher education has increased steadily to represent nearly half of the total students in each educational level (*Indicators of Educational Statistics*, 2000, p. 33). The change is particularly pronounced among women attending colleges (see Table 4.1). The proportion of women in higher education has soared: 10.9 percent (junior colleges, four-year colleges and universities) in the academic year of 1950, 36.5 percent (four-year colleges and universities) in 1971 and 47.8 percent in 2001.

Based on a variety of sources, a key report (*National Information Statistics*, 2003) summarized women's educational opportunities in Taiwan relative to those in other countries. Specifically, there were 55.8 female and 52.5 male students in higher education per 1000 people in Taiwan in 2001, while the corresponding numbers in Japan and US during 1992–97 were on average 27.2 and 35.8, and 58.4 and 48.2, respectively. Moreover there were 49 percent female students in high school and 50.5 percent in higher education in Taiwan in the year 2001. In contrast the percentages in 1997 were 48.4 for high school and 37 for college in Japan, and 48.8 for high school and 55.5 for college in the US. It appears that women in Taiwan enjoyed equal opportunity with men in attending high schools and college, and that their chance of receiving higher education seemed much better than their sisters in Japan, but not quite as good as those in the US.

Table 4.2 reports the percentage distribution of female and male students by college major completing undergraduate, master's and doctoral degrees for the period of 1991–2001. Some patterns of gender segregation can be found. For example women were outnumbered by men in the areas of science and engineering at all three levels throughout the years. On the other hand, there were about twice as many women as men graduating with a bachelor's degree in humanities than in management or business. The picture altered at the graduate levels as more men completed a master's or a doctoral degree in management and a doctoral degree in humanities. In contrast, the distribution in medical schools reflected a different but quite

Table 4.1 Percentage of female students at all educational levels in Taiwan

Academic year	Total	Kinder-garten	Elementary school	Middle school	High school	Vocational school	Junior college	College/University
1950	37.52	43.52	38.99	28.66	27.09	15.51		10.89
1961	44.60	45.07	47.07	36.53	32.08	31.80		23.39
1971	45.78	44.77	48.41	42.33	36.97	44.06	37.27	36.45
1980	48.05	46.85	48.59	47.43	43.87	50.27	41.82	39.42
1981	48.25	46.80	48.60	47.68	44.63	50.41	42.45	40.00
1990	49.15	47.72	48.45	48.62	46.85	54.05	47.86	44.08
1991	49.11	47.81	48.48	48.57	46.57	53.97	48.67	43.30
1992	49.12	47.82	48.42	48.69	46.92	53.60	49.56	42.86
1993	49.09	47.68	48.40	48.65	46.74	53.34	50.13	42.57
1994	49.22	47.49	48.31	48.67	46.95	53.28	51.11	43.23
1995	49.21	47.18	48.23	48.59	47.38	53.03	52.30	44.40
1996	49.21	47.16	48.12	48.57	48.05	52.28	52.80	45.60
1997	49.32	47.47	47.96	48.57	48.76	51.54	53.51	46.48
1998	49.30	47.18	47.87	48.54	49.31	50.62	53.81	46.90
1999	49.16	47.48	47.82	48.47	49.55	49.99	53.70	46.96
2000	49.03	47.68	47.81	48.25	49.54	49.52	53.42	47.17
2001	48.95	48.23	47.83	48.12	49.78	48.44	53.71	47.78

Source: *Indicators of Educational Statistics* (2000), p. 33; *Education Statistics of the Republic of China* (2002), pp. 26–7.

Table 4.2 Gender of Taiwanese students by college major and by year (% graduating with a certain degree in a year)

Year	Degree	Science		Medicine		Humanities		Business		Engineering		Others		Total by Degree	
		M	F	M	F	M	F	M	F	M	F	M	F	M	F
1991	Bachelor	3.95	1.69	4.34	2.63	12.77	23.26	8.01	13.19	18.78	2.72	4.35	4.31	0.52	0.48
	Master	7.06	2.25	4.90	3.12	8.35	7.87	8.78	4.34	41.48	2.54	5.94	3.36	0.77	0.23
	Doctoral	9.38	0.82	6.41	4.11	11.51	5.26	3.62	0.82	49.01	2.14	5.26	1.64	0.85	0.15
1995	Bachelor	3.45	1.12	3.53	3.26	11.19	20.94	10.26	12.11	20.67	2.93	5.34	5.20	0.54	0.46
	Master	6.06	1.40	4.29	3.50	8.79	8.92	10.14	4.74	40.08	3.01	6.00	3.08	0.75	0.25
	Doctoral	9.50	1.52	6.55	3.42	11.68	6.08	4.46	1.33	46.34	1.71	4.65	2.75	0.83	0.17
1999	Bachelor	2.72	1.31	2.86	5.14	7.53	18.14	9.05	15.17	21.50	4.87	5.09	6.64	0.49	0.51
	Master	4.97	1.94	3.69	4.36	8.28	9.94	9.26	5.68	38.36	4.60	5.25	3.70	0.70	0.30
	Doctoral	7.15	1.37	7.70	3.64	13.06	7.70	5.84	2.20	41.10	1.99	5.91	2.34	0.81	0.19
2000	Bachelor	2.33	1.06	3.12	5.90	6.97	16.33	8.71	14.60	24.56	5.21	4.63	6.58	0.50	0.50
	Master	4.37	1.81	3.89	4.30	8.76	10.47	10.46	6.05	36.12	4.93	5.19	3.68	0.69	0.31
	Doctoral	6.22	1.57	6.90	4.78	14.29	9.02	4.44	2.26	41.29	1.50	5.33	2.39	0.78	0.22
2001	Bachelor	2.10	0.86	2.80	5.80	6.17	14.42	9.04	16.44	26.20	5.70	4.15	6.33	0.50	0.50
	Master	4.23	1.75	3.72	4.25	9.32	11.79	11.86	6.48	33.71	4.59	4.78	3.51	0.68	0.32
	Doctoral	7.53	1.07	9.19	4.33	10.06	8.53	5.06	2.20	39.64	2.53	6.93	2.93	0.78	0.22

Source: Computed from the website of the Ministry of Education, Republic of China, http://www.edu.tw/statistics/service/g 80_90b.xls

interesting pattern. At the undergraduate level, there were less women completing healthcare education than men from 1991 to 1995, but the trend has reversed since 1996. At the master's level the female graduates became the majority two years later in 1998. However a lot more men than women earned a doctoral degree in medical-related areas throughout 1991–2001. Since medicine is still a male-dominated profession, it appeared that a lot of women attended medical schools with a major in life or health sciences or pharmacy (rather than in the more mainstream career goal of doctor of medicine) and many of them moved on to the master's programs after finishing their undergraduate education. However they did not further their learning because their male counterparts were the majority of those graduating with a doctoral degree over the 11-year time period.

In general, the statistics in Table 4.2 sketched a clear picture regarding the preferences and educational opportunities of women in Taiwan. Consistent with stereotypes, most of the females completing higher education in the 1990s majored in areas other than science and engineering, and there seems to be no sign of change in the near future. Nonetheless female students in the science and technology departments were often among the top students in their classes. In terms of opportunities, women had equal chances with men to attend undergraduate programs, but somehow fewer of them continued their education at the graduate level regardless of major. Nonetheless as indicated in the far right column of Table 4.2, the trend was that more and more women went for a graduate degree over the time span. Specifically, of those earning a master's degree in 1991 only 23 percent were female, whereas 32 percent were female in 2001. At the doctoral level, only 15 percent of the PhD holders were women in 1991 and the number increased to 22 percent ten years later. Since all these trends are very stable, it should be reasonable to contend that women's education opportunities are increasing and they are better prepared to join the workforce now than before.

LEGAL AND POLICY EFFORTS THAT SUPPORT WOMEN'S EMPLOYMENT

The right to work is guaranteed by the Republic of China Constitution. Article 153 of ROC Constitution reads: 'women and children engaged in labor shall, according to their age and physical condition, be accorded special protection'. Female workers' welfare such as maternity leave before and after childbirth has long been granted (Article 50 of Labor Standards Law, see the English language website of the Ministry of Justice, www.law.moj.gov.tw/Eng/Fnews) (Labor Standards Law). However women face discrimination in gaining access to employment.

Many women in both the public and the private sector are forced to quit their jobs after marriage or when giving birth to their children. For example in June 1987 the female employees of the Sun Yat Sen Memorial in Taipei and of the Kaohsiung Municipal Cultural Center experienced just such a deep-rooted bias. Both of these organizations are government agencies that sponsor cultural activities such as exhibiting fine arts and antiques. Employers demanded that 101 females sign an agreement that upon getting married or pregnant, or reaching the age of 30, they should resign voluntarily or be fired. The rationale behind this agreement was that, according to these two agencies, women over 30 were no longer suitable for introducing the beauty of Chinese culture (The Awakening, 2003).

In addition, female workers are more likely to encounter sexual harassment in the workplace. According to a survey of women in the paid labor force by the Council of Labor Affairs, Executive Yuan in 2000, working women did experience different pay for equal work, different treatment for promotion practices, job assignments and evaluation. They also faced unequal treatment during job interviews and lay-off processes (*The Survey Reports of Women in Employment, Taiwan Area, ROC*, 2000, p. 4).

In July 1994, the idea of gender equality was finally enacted and written into the 'Additional Articles of the Constitution of the Republic of China' (*Republic of China Yearbook*, 1995, p. 769). A part of the Article specifies that 'the State shall protect the dignity of women, safeguard their personal safety, eliminate sex discrimination, and further substantiate equality between the sexes' (*Republic of China Yearbook*, 1994, p. 708).

In December 1996, the Democratic Progressive Party, then an opposition party, formally adopted a new motion mandating one-quater of the candidates for election for government positions to be females. That is 15 percent more than what had been promulgated in the ROC Constitution of 1947. In May 2000, 14 female Cabinet members were sworn into the new administration.

Finally on 21 December 2001, after 11 years of hot debates and political wrestling, the Equal Employment Opportunity Act was enacted in Taiwan and became effective on Women's Day – 8 March 2002. This act mandates a watchdog role on the part of the government to ensure gender equality in employment practices. More specifically, it states that the governments, from local to central, shall establish an Equal Employment Committee to handle relevant issues. The committee should consist of five to 11 professionals experienced in labor relationship and/or gender matters, all tenured for two years. More than half of the committee members shall be female.

As for corporate responsibilities, any in-house regulations or policies implying sex discrimination shall be terminated. An employer hiring more than 30 individuals should observe provisions such as: (1) Female workers may ask for a day of menstrual leave per month, to be included in the sick leave. (2) Pregnant workers are entitled to have an eight-week leave before, during and after giving birth or a five-day to four-week sick leave in case of miscarriage. Male workers are entitled to have a two-day leave when their spouse gives birth. (3) Female workers may have two 30-minute feeding sessions daily for children less than one year old. (4) An employee, upon being hired for more than a year, is entitled to a childrearing leave up to two years for each child younger than three years old. During the leave, the employee keeps the job but ceases to receive a salary. Furthermore any employer hiring more than 250 employees should establish adequate childcare facilities. The government will subsidize the employer for such an effort. An employee feeling unfairly treated in the workplace may file a grievance to the local government, and the latter should exercise jurisdiction within seven days. If unsettled, either the employee or the employer may appeal the case to the central government. The employer is held accountable and should compensate the victimized employee if the employer is found to have violated the provisions.

However the actual situation does not necessarily match the expectation (*China Times*, 2002). First, employers found some of the regulations difficult to implement. For instance, what should be done if enough qualified nursing staff are not available to meet the high demand generated by three-shift factories? If two nursing sessions each day are not enough for feeding infants can mothers take them to the workplace, or shall the employer hire nannies? Second, while employers may not fully endorse the Act, many employees welcomed the Act but reacted to it with apparent reservations. They had reason to worry that taking a long leave (while not getting paid) may eventually result in 'voluntarily' job quitting as the employer could somehow manage to evade legal disputes. In addition some workers simply cannot sustain a long leave without any income. In fact, since the Act inevitably boosts operating costs, a survey reported that some companies tended to hire fewer women in order to offset expense increase.

Nonetheless practices are not all that pessimistic. In general, government agencies follow the equality regulations more thoroughly than do the private organizations, and some multinational companies do a better job, sometimes beyond what is required, than the domestic ones. For instance Taiwan Hewlett-Packard established a broad and flexible benefit program covering childcare, insurance, real estate purchase and the like to let their employees take whatever best meets their individual needs. Some 'new parents' may choose to work from home. Accton, a domestic hi-tech company, has reserved parking spaces for pregnant employees and allows two months' paid leave following childbirth and 10 months' childrearing leave (without pay) if asked (*China Times*, 2003).

WOMEN'S EMPLOYMENT PATTERNS

Gains in educational attainment as well as Taiwan's economic growth have opened up new employment opportunities for women. As revealed in Table 4.3, the proportion of women in Taiwan in the paid labor force has increased from 39.3 percent in 1980 to 46.6 percent in 2002, while male labor force participation has declined from 77.1 percent in 1980 to 68.2 percent in 2002 (compiled from *Statistical Yearbook of the Republic of China*, 1994, p. 50; *Yearbook of Manpower Survey Statistics, Taiwan Area, ROC*, 1999, pp. 4–5; *Monthly Bulletin of Statistics of the Republic of China*, 2001, p. 6; and the website of the Directorate-General of Budget, Accounting and Statistics, Executive Yuan, ROC). In fact the number of women in the paid labor force may be underestimated since many more housewives are doing piecework at home and/or are involved in volunteer work that improves the lives of members of their families and communities. Yet they are not formally included in the statistical data.

Recently 82 percent of women were in the labor force before their marriage and about 30 percent quit after marriage. The top two reasons for quitting were 'preparing for giving birth' and 'distance between worksite and home'. Among those who quit, only 31 percent returned to work,

Table 4.3   Taiwanese labor force participation rate and unemployment rate

Year	Labor force participation rate		Unemployment rate	
	Male	Female	Male	Female
1980	77.1	39.3	1.11	1.47
1985	75.5	43.5	2.90	2.92
1990	74.0	44.5	1.68	1.64
1995	72.0	45.3	1.79	1.80
1996	71.1	45.8	2.72	2.42
1997	71.1	45.6	2.94	2.37
1998	70.6	45.6	2.93	2.33
1999	69.9	46.0	3.23	2.46
2000	69.4	46.0	3.36	2.44
2001	68.4	46.1	5.16	3.71
2002	68.2	46.6	5.91	4.10

Sources: Statistical Yearbook of the Republic of China (1994), p. 50; *Yearbook of Manpower Survey Statistics, Taiwan Area, ROC* (1999), pp. 4, 5; *Monthly Bulletin of Statistics of the Republic of China* (2001), February, p. 6; (2003) August, pp. 2, 11; *Social Indicators of the Republic of China* (2003), pp. 284–5.

particularly those who had held supervisory positions previously (*China Times*, 2003). These statistics suggest that housework is still women's work and that those who are more competitive are more likely to resume working, perhaps due to better education and/or higher income to enable them hire someone to take care of the housework. The relatively low percentage of women returning to work after marriage or giving birth also suggested that the 'M'-form pattern (twin peaks) of women participating in the labor market before and after marriage in Western nations (for example Hantrais and Letablier, 1996) does not seem to occur in Taiwan. In an empirical analysis of 2401 women with spouse present and some work experience, Chuang and Lee (2003) found that a husband's negative attitude toward a working wife discourages his wife more strongly than the presence of young children from returning to the labor market. However in a separate survey of over 800 unmarried career women aged 28 to 45, the majority planned to retire by age 55; only 4 percent wanted to retire at age 65. Those who planned to retire early also planned well in terms of individual financial investments (*China Times*, 2004).

Table 4.4 reports employment patterns by demographics. Several points are noteworthy. First, among the women employed, as young girls stay in school for a longer period, the labor force participation rate for women aged 15 and 24 dropped from 50.2 percent in 1980 to 37.6 percent in 2002 (*The Survey Reports of Women in Employment, Taiwan Area, Republic of China*, 2000, Appendix, 18). Second, women who are married are as likely to be employed as women who are single. In 1980 the labor force participation rate for women between 25 and 44 years old was 41.6 percent; in 2000 the rate was 66.3 percent. Although we do not know how many of them are married, it is estimated that nearly half of the married women were in the labor market in 2000 (ibid., p. 21). Finally, women who complete high school and college are more likely to be employed than those who graduate from middle school (ibid., p. 20). In 2000 labor force participation rates for middle school graduates and college graduates were 33.9 percent and 63.4 percent, respectively.

Sex segregation in occupational distribution still prevails. As shown in Tables 4.5 and 4.6, most women work within a narrow range of occupations. They tend to hold low-paying jobs and positions of less prestige. For example in 2002 the great majority (85.4 percent) of legislators, government administrators, business executives and managers were male. In contrast, a very high proportion (77.3 percent) of clerks were female. In addition, men were more likely to be employers or to hold executive or managerial positions, while women were more likely to be employees or simply unpaid family workers. Only 15.9 percent of employers in 2002 were women.

Table 4.4 Taiwanese women's labor force participation rate by age, educational attainment and marital status

Year	Total	Age				Educational attainment			Marital status		
		15–24	25–44	45–64	65+	Middle school	High school	College/University	Single	Married	Divorced, etc.
1980	39.3	50.2	41.6	28.6	1.8	36.7	44.3	53.0	59.5	32.2	18.2
1985	43.5	49.2	50.6	34.5	3.4	40.0	47.6	58.4	57.8	39.7	23.6
1990	44.5	45.4	55.4	35.6	4.0	38.7	50.2	59.3	55.3	42.3	26.1
1995	45.3	38.9	60.4	38.1	4.2	36.9	50.8	62.6	52.1	45.2	26.9
1996	45.8	38.3	61.6	39.0	4.0	36.2	51.4	63.5	52.0	46.0	27.2
1997	45.6	37.6	62.0	39.3	3.9	35.8	51.0	63.2	51.3	46.1	26.9
1998	45.6	37.0	63.0	38.9	3.9	34.8	51.1	63.2	51.5	46.1	26.7
1999	46.0	37.7	63.7	39.7	3.8	34.6	51.5	63.2	52.4	46.3	26.5
2000	46.0	37.1	64.5	39.6	3.7	33.9	51.3	63.4	52.5	46.1	26.6
2001	46.1	37.2	65.3	39.4	3.5	n/a	n/a	n/a	53.0	46.3	26.6
2002	46.6	37.6	66.3	39.9	3.8	n/a	n/a	n/a	n/a	n/a	n/a

Source: The Survey Reports of Women in Employment, Taiwan Area, Republic of China (in Chinese), (2000), pp. 18–21; *Monthly Bulletin of Manpower Statistics*, (2003), July, pp. 14–15; *Social Indicators of the Republic of China* (2003), p. 194.

Table 4.5   Percentage of Taiwanese females employed by occupational category

Year	Legislators, government admin, business executives and mgrs	Professional	Technicians and associate professionals	Clerks	Service workers and sales	Agriculture, animal husbandry, forestry, fishing	Prod. machine operators etc.
1980	9.4	41.5	32.7	57.9	37.8	31.4	30.1
1985	13.2	44.5	38.4	61.4	45.8	31.0	33.4
1990	15.1	47.8	41.8	66.1	44.2	29.8	31.7
1995	13.1	51.0	39.4	74.7	52.4	28.3	27.4
1996	13.1	51.3	39.6	75.8	53.3	29.1	26.9
1997	14.5	51.1	38.9	76.0	53.3	28.9	27.0
1998	14.1	51.7	40.1	76.4	53.0	28.5	26.5
1999	14.0	51.7	40.1	76.1	53.7	28.1	26.3
2000	14.3	50.0	40.4	76.8	54.0	27.8	26.4
2001	14.8	49.3	40.6	77.3	54.8	27.5	26.5
2002	14.6	49.2	41.5	77.3	55.1	27.2	26.9

Source: Computed from *Yearbook of Manpower Survey Statistics, Taiwan Area, Republic of China* (1999), pp. 56–7 and from www.stat.gov.tw/bs2/ (the website of the Directorate-General of Budget, Accounting and Statistics, Executive Yuan, ROC).

Table 4.6   Percentage of employed Taiwanese females by work location

Year	Employers	Self-employed Workers	Paid Employees	
			Private	Government
1980	10.0	17.0	36.3	28.5
1985	11.0	17.4	40.0	32.3
1990	11.5	18.1	41.0	35.3
1995	13.3	19.1	41.3	39.8
1996	13.2	19.7	41.9	41.1
1997	14.2	19.9	42.1	41.3
1998	13.8	20.0	42.3	41.9
1999	14.7	20.8	42.6	42.9
2000	14.6	20.8	43.0	42.7
2001	16.1	20.9	43.7	42.4
2002	15.9	21.4	44.1	43.8

Notes: 'Employer' refers to those who hire employees to run a business owned by themselves. 'Own-account worker' refers to those who operate a business by themselves or with partners without hiring any employees.

Source: Computed from *Yearbook of Manpower Survey Statistics, Taiwan Area, Republic of China* (1999), pp. 60–61 and from www.stat.gov.tw/bs2/ (the website of the Directorate-General of Budget, Accounting and Statistics, Executive Yuan, ROC)

Taking the educational profession as an example, in the 2000 school year, 65.5 percent of the faculty in four-year colleges and universities were male (*Education Statistics of the Republic of China*, 2002). In terms of job ranks (teaching assistant, lecturer, assistant professor, associate professor and full professor), a lower proportion of females worked in the higher echelon. Specifically, 66.4 percent of the teaching assistants (defined as those who work as staff members doing routine departmental work) were female, while only 28.9 percent of the assistant professors, 24.5 percent of the associate professors and 13.4 percent of full professors were female (*Education Statistics of the Republic of China*, 2002; *Humanities and Social Sciences Newsletter Quarterly*, 2003).

In international comparisons, there were 59.5 percent female teachers in high schools and 34.7 percent in colleges in Taiwan in 2001, compared to corresponding percentages for Japan of 32.7 and 21.8, while those for the US were 55.6 and 38.6 in 1997 (*National Information Statistics*, 2003). Women in Taiwan appeared to have much better opportunity than their counterparts in Japan, but the females in all three nations were obviously the minority on college campuses.

Wages

Partly due to the fact that females often hold positions at the lower ranks within a job category, women in the labor force persistently receive lower wages than men. Although the female-to-male average income ratios have improved over the years, the disparity still exists. As clearly shown in Table 4.7, the pay gap remains substantial (*Report on the Manpower Utilization Survey, Taiwan Area, Republic of China*, 1994, p.146; 1995, p. 146; 1996, p. 152; 1997, p. 152; 1998, p. 152; 1999, p. 152; 2000, p. 152). For example within the category of legislators, government administrators, business executives and managers, the females on average earned a monthly income of NT$58 595 in 2000 whereas their male counterparts made NT$70 980 per month.

This disparity was consistent with the findings of an analysis by Zveglich et al. (1997) of gender earnings in Taiwan during 1978–92. They examined household survey data from Taiwan's Manpower Survey and concluded that gender earnings inequality remained persistent in that women continued to earn 65 percent of what men earned despite their relative gains in education.

WORK–FAMILY CONCERNS

The balance between work and home is always an issue that attracts much attention from academics and practitioners alike (for example Friedman and Greenhaus, 2000; Martins et al., 2002; Kossek and Ozeki, 1998; Wiersma, 1990). In Cheng and Liao's study (1985), 540 career women in Taiwan were asked to recommend research topics on female issues that reflected their major concerns. Not surprisingly, the topic that most of the interviewees (58 percent) chose was the conflict between family and work roles and obligations.

Women are expected to be dutiful wives and devoted mothers. Two incomes have become a must for many families in Taiwan. In families where both husbands and wives have careers, the husband's career generally receives priority because raising children and doing housework are still widely considered to be a woman's job, although she is sharing financial responsibilities. Thus women may have to sacrifice their career opportunities in favor of their husband. A survey indicates that if there were sufficient daycare services and nursing homes, women would re-enter the job market (*The Survey Reports of Female Labor Force, Taiwan Area, ROC*, 1998, pp. 29–32).

Bianchi and Cohen (1999) argued that most modern career women in the West were torn between employment, marriage and children, just like their mothers and even grandmothers before them. Such also seems to be the case

Table 4.7 Average monthly income in Taiwan by gender and occupational category (in New Taiwan Dollars (NT$); 32 NT$ = 1 US$)

Year		Total	Legal, government and business managers	Professionals	Technical and associate professionals	Clerks	Service sales workers	Agriculture, animal husbandry, forestry, and fishing	Production machine operators etc.
	Male	31 336	52 075	44 437	35 441	29 783	27 565	22 570	27 822
1993	Female	20 698	38 739	32 538	25 057	21 402	17 430	11 097	15 992
	Male	35 058	59 512	48 051	39 217	32 922	31 718	24 703	31 232
1995	Female	23 784	41 613	35 959	28 867	24 072	20 353	14 670	18 401
	Male	36 323	60 202	53 486	41 118	35 115	32 833	25 467	31 439
1997	Female	26 009	52 069	39 276	31 683	25 854	21 011	17 386	19 716
	Male	37 881	68 841	55 052	42 878	37 318	34 705	27 557	31 662
1999	Female	28 120	55 908	41 519	33 667	27 071	23 640	16 668	21 220
	Male	38 636	70 980	57 230	43 715	38 060	34 800	26 661	32 198
2000	Female	28 153	58 595	42 623	34 801	27 431	22 352	16 295	21 081

Sources: Computed from Report on the Manpower Utilization Survey, Taiwan Area, Republic of China (1994), p. 146; (1995), p. 146; (1996), p. 152; (1997), p. 152; (1998), p. 152; (1999), p. 152; (2000), p. 152.

in Taiwan. In a qualitative study of four female executives (Yu, 2000), it was revealed that the managers spent an average 12 hours a day at work and, naturally, their time for family and leisure was compressed. Nonetheless that did not suggest the family was being ignored. One of the subjects who had no children had more leeway to pursue personal interest and pace her life pattern. For the other three, family was inevitably the central element in their non-work life. As they were not able to stay with relatives as often as they wanted to, they tried to make quality time at home. As evidenced in some other research (Friedman and Greenhaus, 2000), it was their high psychological involvement, rather than the time spent in both family and work, that led to their satisfying work life. In any case, all four managers enjoyed full support from the family. For instance some had elderly parents help taking care of their schoolchildren, and some obtained professional advice from their husbands with regard to office matters. It is clear that family support, physical and mental, was a key factor behind the success of these female executives.

Another study examined the moderating effects of different gender combinations between supervisors and subordinates on the relationship between supervisory support and work–family conflict (Hsu et al., 2001). They found that more supervisory work support than family support was provided in the male–male, male–female and female–male sub-samples while the opposite only existed in female–female groups. It is particularly interesting when women and men worked together that female subordinates expected more work support from their female supervisor but received more family support instead, and they hoped to get more family support from their male leader but experienced more work support. The implication from these findings is that work–family conflict may be effectively reduced if male leaders had expressed more family concern and the female supervisor had showed more work support to their female colleagues.

DISCUSSION AND CONCLUSIONS

The society of Taiwan is in transition and, as the above information suggests, so are its women. Mainly using the Taiwanese literature on men and women at work, the authors, as residents of Taiwan for decades, would like to address the role the government has taken toward gender matters and the characteristics of today's women in Taiwan.

Government's Role: Facilitator or Bystander?

There has been a gradual increase in the proportion of women working in the paid labor force over the last few decades. Women's high career aspirations, the economic needs of the family and demands for national economic development all have a large impact on the increase in labor participation. Nonetheless the women in Taiwan hold an 'equal but different' social status. Career women are very much under-represented in prestigious and controlling positions and many of them are underpaid compared to their male colleagues. Therefore members of feminist groups and political parties have increasingly become concerned about efforts to minimize discrimination in the workplace and to protect employment rights for both sexes, particularly through legal means. Gradually, the government has begun to act and react to such demands.

The 1987 incident where two government organizations made it clear that they did not want their female employees to continue to work when getting pregnant or reaching 30 years old, was a triggering event that touched a central nerve of the society and the government began to feel the pressure for gender equality. In a Cabinet reshuffle in 1988, the first female Cabinet member of the government, Dr Shirley W.Y. Kuo, was appointed as the chairperson of the Council of Economic Development (*Republic of China Yearbook*, 1989, p. 193).

The first edition of the Equal Employment Opportunities Act drafted by a female legislator was introduced into the Legislative Yuan in March of 1990. Unfortunately it did not receive enough support from the legislators to become law. In March 1994, the Council of Labor Affairs jumped on the bandwagon, proposing its own version of an equal employment bill for both sexes. Again the whole issue of equal employment legislation was left pending in the Legislative Yuan due to lack of consensus on such issues such as whether a husband's paternity leave should be paid or unpaid.

In 1994, the idea of gender equality was enacted and written into the Additional Articles of the Constitution of the Republic of China (*Republic of China Yearbook*, 1995, p. 769). Later in 2001, the Equal Employment Opportunity Act was enacted in Taiwan. This enactment is, by any account, a milestone in Taiwan's movement for gender equality that will have a tremendous impact on the society in general and the workplace culture in particular. While advocates of gender equality hailed the Act to be a victory for the society, most of the corporate executives see it as a serious blow to national competitiveness.

Although it is sometimes due to the pressure from the outside, this legal procession indicates that the government is becoming more sensitive to gender issues. Quite slowly but surely, a few steps have been taken to make the society a fairer one. For occupational segregation to decline and women's qualifications improve, the government has the mandate to further its policy to strengthen equal employment, to ensure a harassment-free work environment and to encourage better daycare services for minors and the elderly. Given the past record, the society will need to continue placing pressure on the government to take a more active role in taking care of women's well-being.

Women in Taiwan: Becoming more Individualistic and Independent?

For thousands of years, Chinese women were viewed as inferior to men, and all believed a woman should be submissive in male–female relationships. Women were expected to marry, and married women had to give birth and take care of children as well as parents-in-law. Over the past few decades, women in Taiwan have had more opportunities to receive higher education, are joining the workforce more actively and have become financially more competent than before. Nonetheless even when they are wage earners, women are still expected to fulfill traditional roles as good mothers as well as dutiful wives and daughters-in-law. A curious reader may ask: just how different are today's Taiwanese women from those of the last generation?

Hofstede's (1980) study of employee attitudes from IBM subsidiaries (1980) categorized Taiwan as a society of high power distance and collectivism in the later 1960s and early 1970s. That was a time when Taiwan's economy had not even started to take off. Politically, the society was still under the autocratic rule of the late President Chiang Kai-Shek. Over the last decades however, Taiwan has been transformed to a much more dynamic society in terms of almost any indicators, be it per capita income, diversified political ideology, industrial technology or educational opportunities. With all these transitions in progress, we have reasons to believe that Taiwan's power distance is shortened and collectivism is weakened empirically; some scholars have argued that Taiwan is much more individualistic today than was suggested by Hofstede (Yeh, 1989; Yeh and Lawrence, 1995). Logically, Taiwanese women today are likely to be more independent, confident and individualistic than their senior sisters in the earlier days.

C.K. Wang's study of three generations of women (1993) revealed interesting value changes. Our interpretation is that these females had stronger career interests as they grew more mature. With the reality they were facing, they knew what they wanted and knew what to do to make it. Also the order of importance of certain values altered, a sign of changes in value – for example both politeness and open-mindedness became more important over time.

The discussion so far suggests some attributes of the women in Taiwan today. They are confident and autonomous in that they appear more eager to be competent in the workplace and to take hold of their work life themselves. They are more interested in being open and polite than self-disciplined when seeking life goals. They seem more individualistic because they care less about their group's well-being. Yet they are not naive and shallow because they believe perseverance and ability to be the necessary trait in reaching their goals, and because they are more satisfied when rewarded intrinsically rather than extrinsically. The emergence of numerous feminist groups in the 1990s further indicates that they are more aware that they need to let their voice heard and, ultimately, to keep a firm hand on their future themselves.

Future Research Possibilities

The study presents a general profile of the social status and work life of women in Taiwan. The authors in the enquiry process have identified a number of phenomena that warrant further examination. For example while the high ratio of female Cabinet members is impressive, several of these women are unmarried. What does this imply? Does it suggest that a woman is doomed to have a tough experience trying to maintain a successful family and career? Where is a married woman's place in politics and in other professions? Can or should the government do something about it?

What about women in non-professional careers? Do their attitudes reflect those of the educated women reported in most studies? How do they manage with balancing work and family responsibilities? Is the government doing enough to help? Are employers? What about employment policies that discriminate against women? Are employers bringing their practices into line with the new legislation?

These and other related issues need to be examined in future research. As Taiwan changes, this future research can be used to document the movement of women into positions more equal to those of men.

REFERENCES

Bianchi, S.M. and P.N. Cohen (1999), 'Marriage, children and women's employment: what do we know?', *Monthly Labor Review*, **122** (12), 22–31.

Cheng, W.Y. and L.L. Liao (1985), *Changing Women in Taiwan*, Taipei: Ta Yang, (in Chinese).

China Times (2002), 'Equal Employment and Opportunity Act: effective tomorrow', 7 March (in Chinese).

China Times (2003), 'Equal Employment and Opportunity Act: A Year After', 8 March (in Chinese).

China Times (2004), 'Unmarried career women plan to retire early', 21 February, (in Chinese).

Chinese Culture Connection (1987), 'Chinese values and the search for culture-free dimensions of culture', *Journal of Cross-cultural Psychology*, **18** (2), 143–64.

Chuang, H.L. and H.Y. Lee (2003), 'The return on women's capital and the role of male attitudes toward working wives: gender roles, work interruption, and women's earnings in Taiwan', *American Journal of Economics and Sociology*, **62** (2), 435–59.

Education Statistics of the Republic of China, 1992–2002 (2002), Taipei: Ministry of Education (in Chinese).

Friedman, S.D. and J.H. Greenhaus (2000), *Work and family – Allies or Enemies?*, New York: Oxford University Press.

Hantrais, L. and M.T. Letablier (1996), *Families and Family Policy in Europe*, London: Longman.

Hofstede, G. (1980), *Culture's Consequences: International Differences in Work-Related Values*, Thousand Oaks, CA: Sage.

Hofstede, G. (1983), 'The cultural relativity of organizational practices and theories', *Journal of International Business Studies*, **14** (3), 75–89.

Hsu, B.F., C.P. Chou and W.L. Wu (2001), 'Moderating effect of gender combinations on supervisory support – work–family relations', annual meeting of the ROC Technology Management Association, Taipei (in Chinese).

Humanities and Social Sciences Newsletter Quarterly (2003), 'Gender issues and academic work environment', **4** (4), 10–17 (in Chinese).

Indicators of Educational Statistics (2000), Taipei: Ministry of Education (in Chinese).

Kossek, E. and C. Ozeki (1998), 'Work–family conflict, policies, and the job–life satisfaction relationship: a review and directions for OB/HR research', *Journal of Applied Psychology*, **83**, 139–49.

Labor Standards Law, www.law.moj.gov.tw/Eng/Fnews.

Martins, L.L., K.A. Eddleston and J.F. Veiga (2002), 'Moderators of the relationship between work–family conflict and career satisfaction', *Academy of Management Journal*, **45** (2), 399–409.

Monthly Bulletin of Manpower Statistics, Taiwan Area, Republic of China (2003), July, Taipei: Directorate-General of Budget, Accounting and Statistics, Executive Yuan (in Chinese).

Monthly Bulletin of Statistics of the Republic of China (2001), February, Taipei: Directorate-General of Budget, Accounting and Statistics, Executive Yuan (in Chinese).

Monthly Bulletin of Statistics of the Republic of China (2003), August, Taipei: Directorate-General of Budget, Accounting and Statistics, Executive Yuan (in Chinese).

MOW International Research Team (1987), *The Meaning of Working*, London: Academic Press.

National Information Statistics (2003), March, Directorate-General of Budget, Accounting and Statistics, ROC: Executive Yuan (in Chinese).

Peng, T.K. (1996), 'Modern work cultures and traditional values', presented at the annual meeting of the Academy of International Business (SE Chapter), Otago, New Zealand.

Reader's Digest (2001), 'What are the differences and why in the mindsets of the women in Shanghai, Hong Kong and Taipei?' April (Chinese edition).

Redding, G.S. (1990), *The Spirit of Chinese Capitalism*, Berlin: Walter de Gruyter.

Report on the Manpower Utilization Survey, Taiwan Area, Republic of China (1994–2000) Taipei: Directorate-General of Budget, Accounting and Statistics, Executive Yuan (in Chinese).

Republic of China Yearbook (1989, 1994, 1995), Taipei: Hilt Publishing Company.

Rokeach, M. (1973), *The Nature of Human Values*, New York: Free Press.

Social Indicators of the Republic of China (2003), Taipei: Directorate-General of Budget, Accounting and Statistics, Executive Yuan (in Chinese).

Statistical Yearbook of the Republic of China (1994), Taipei: Directorate-General of Budget, Accounting and Statistics, Executive Yuan (in Chinese).

The Survey Reports of Female Labor Force, Taiwan Area, Republic of China (1998), Taipei: Council of Labor Affairs, Executive Yuan (in Chinese).

The Survey Reports of Women in Employment, Taiwan Area, Republic of China (2000), Taipei: Council of Labor Affairs, Executive Yuan (in Chinese).

The Awakening (2003) http://taiwan.yam.org.tw/womenweb/workright (the website of The Awakening, a renowned women's foundation in Taiwan), 13 May.

Time (2003), 'Tigers no more', cover story, 7 July, 24–36.

Wang, C.K. (1993), 'The values of college-educated workers of three generations', *Indigenous Psychology Research*, **2**, 206–50 (in Chinese).

Whitley, R. (1992), *Business Systems in Asia*, Thousand Oaks, CA: Sage.

Wiersma, U.J. (1990), 'Gender differences in job attribute preferences: work–home role conflict and job level as mediating variables', *Journal of Occupational Psychology*, **63**, 231–43.

Yearbook of Manpower Survey Statistics, Taiwan Area, Republic of China (1999), Taipei: Directorate-General of Budget, Accounting and Statistics, Executive Yuan (in Chinese).

Yeh, R.S. (1989), 'On Hofstede's treatment of Chinese and Japanese values', *Asia Pacific Journal of Management*, **6** (1), 149–60.

Yeh, R.S. and J. Lawrence (1995), 'Individualism and Confucian dynamism: a note on Hofstede's cultural root to economic growth', *Journal of International Business Studies*, **26**(3), 655–69.

Yu, H.J. (2000), 'A study of female managers' coping behavior with work–family conflicts in terms of sex-role attitudes, life style and job involvement', Taiwan: Graduate School of Human Resource Management, National Sun Yat Sen University, unpublished master's thesis (in Chinese).

Zveglich, J.E., Y. Rodgers and W. Rodgers (1997), 'The persistence of gender earnings inequality in Taiwan, 1978–1992,' *Industrial and Labor Relations*, **50**(4), 594–609.

5. The impact of government policy on working women in Hong Kong

Irene Hau-Siu Chow

Hong Kong women compared favorably in employment with their counterparts in other Chinese societies. In Hong Kong, a modern capitalist economy, there is no doubt that the social status of women has improved significantly in recent times. Individualism, achievement orientation and equality of opportunity have led to reduced inequality between men and women. In a large cross-cultural research project, Global Leadership and Organizational Behavior Effectiveness (GLOBE), headed by House, Hong Kong ranked number one in gender egalitarianism and third in performance orientation among the 61 countries surveyed (House et al., 1999).

Hong Kong represents an interesting case to examine the topic of the impact of government on women. On the one hand, experience as a British colony with rapid economic development in the past few decades has generated many employment opportunities for women. On the other hand, being a Chinese society recently returned to People's Republic of China (PRC) control, Hong Kong has been characterized by a marked sexual division of labor both inside and outside the family (Ngo, 1992). A powerful traditional Chinese culture, stereotypical socialization practices, together with a history of women's oppression, subjugation and subordination, provide interesting cultural components that affect the status of women in Hong Kong. This economic and cultural combination raises many of the issues this volume seeks to address.

GENERAL GEOGRAPHIC, ECONOMIC AND CULTURAL BACKGROUND

Hong Kong (HK) is composed of about 1070 sq km, of land surrounding the mouth of the Pearl River, including one major and several outlying islands plus Kowloon and the New Territories. Formerly a part of the feudal empire in southeastern China, following the second opium war in 1898, HK was governed by the British as a capitalist economy until 1997 when government was returned to the communist and socialist People's Republic of China as a Special Administrative Region with a pledge to maintain the free enterprise economy for at least 50 years.

The 6.7 million inhabitants are mostly of Chinese ethnicity, primarily Cantonese-speaking people from neighboring Guang Dong province. About 95 percent are ethnic Chinese. Other ethnic groups consist of 2.1 percent Filipino, 0.8 percent Indonesian and 0.4 percent British respectively. American, Canadian, Japanese, Indian, Pakistani, Thai and Nepalese consist of 0.2 percent each. According to the latest official statistics, the female life expectancy is 82.5 years, 5.2 years longer than men. Women make up half of the population (48.7 percent males and 51.3 percent female according to the 2000 Hong Kong Census and Statistics Department). The city has become trilingual for many purposes, since English is used for many international business transactions, Cantonese is the home language of the majority of the ethnic Chinese who have migrated from the PRC coastal regions, and Mandarin is required for government transactions and communications with PRC.

Economic Development

Many believe that economic development and industrialization would bring gender equality by freeing women from the domestic role. However industrialization in Hong Kong has not significantly changed the patriarchal family and its values; it has only led the family to work out a new strategy to adapt to the changing society (Salaff, 1981; Ng, 1991). Women have to make major sacrifices for both family and society, according to local norms, and their contribution may not be fully recognized.

Industrialization, Westernization and modernization have brought about a drastic transformation of local social institutions and practices. However not all women have benefited equally, since rapid industrialization relies heavily on using cheap female labor in manufacturing. Low wages as well as increases in the number of single parents, unemployed women and aged women with no pensions are significant factors contributing to women's poverty despite increased modernization.

Economic growth has had peaks and valleys in the 1980s and 1990s with the per capita GDP climbing from HK$5567 in 1970, to HK$27 014 in 1980, HK$97 968 in 1990 and HK$193 299 (US$24 782) in 2000 (HK Census and Statistics Department, 2000), a sevenfold increase in two decades. Fear of the political transition from British to PRC control caused many individuals, firms and their capital to flee the island; however by the turn of the twentieth century, a sense of stability was returning and Hong Kong was serving as a major trade route between the PRC and the rest of the world.

EMPLOYMENT OF WOMEN

As part of a response to modernization, lower birth rate, later marriage and the predominance of the nuclear family form enhanced the female labor force participation rate in the second half of the twentieth century. However in the 1980s, Hong Kong manufacturing firms captured the advantages of lower operating costs by relocating to Mainland China when China opened its market to outsiders. As a result most of the working women were laid off. The manufacturing industry had shed over 30 percent of its employment and 13 percent of the entire labor force in less than a decade. Unemployment has ranged from 3.9 percent in 1980 to 1.3 percent in 1990 and 5.6 percent in 2000 for men, and 3.4 percent in 1980, 1.3 percent in 1990 and 4.1 percent in 2000 for women (HK Census and Statistics Department, 2000). Some workers successfully transferred to the service sector. Others were reluctantly forced to exit from full-time employment or involuntarily retreated to domesticity if they could not find a permanent job. Many women were caught up in fluid and unstable jobs.

The economic restructuring has also deteriorated the social position of working women (Chiu and Lee, 1997). The lack of power to find alternative employment may be one factor that accounts for the increase of sexual harassment in the workplace. Little formal research has been conducted on harassment in Hong Kong. Sexual harassment of students is growing in Hong Kong schools and universities. Between September 1996 and April 2003, the Equal Opportunities Commission received 27 complaints of sexual harassment in schools and universities. No one knows how many cases go unreported because students are too scared to or unwilling to talk about their experience. Less than 5 percent have officially complained. An article in the *South China Morning Post* reported that 28.3 percent of the 2495 full-time students across disciplines and years admitted to having experienced sexual harassment from other students, while 11 percent said they had been sexually harassed by their teachers (Yip, 2003). Maybe the issue of sexual harassment in Hong Kong is serious. In addition the mass media promoting sexist images leads some women to wear provocative clothing and enhance their attractive appearance in ways that men use to justify sexual harassment at work.

Trends in the Labor Force Participation of Women

In 2000 the female labor force participation rate was 49.2 percent. The median monthly income for males and females was HK$12 000 and HK$8800 respectively. Women on average earned 73 percent of a man's wage (HK Census and Statistics Department, 2000). The ways this changed between 1985 and 2000 can be seen in Table 5.1.

Table 5.1   Labor force participation and wages in Hong Kong 1980–2000

	1980	1985	1990	1995	2000
Women in LF (%)					
15–19	39.0	31.5	26.1	18.7	15.7
20–29	n/a	76.3	80.3	80.3	81.1
30–39	n/a	52.4	53.9	60.9	68.7
40–49	n/a	53.3	53.0	52.1	56.1
50 and over	n/a	24.2	18.0	15.4	18.0
Average wages (median monthly employment earnings (HK$)*					
Men	n/a	3 000	5 500	10 000	12 000
Women	n/a	2 000	4 000	7 500	8 800
Unemployment rate					
Men	3.9	3.5	1.3	3.4	5.6
Women	3.4	2.6	1.3	2.9	4.1
Part-time employment rate (underemployment rate)					
Men	n/a	2.0	0.9	2.8	3.4
Women	n/a	1.7	0.8	1.0	1.8

Note: *US$1 = HK$7.8

Source: Hong Kong Census and Statistics Department, Hong Kong Special Administrative Region.

The drop in female labor participation for the age group 15–19 was due to increases in educational opportunity. Young women joined the workforce later. Female labor force participation had a steady increase in the 1990s, particularly for women in the age group 30–39. Female labor force participation rate reaches a peak in the mid-40s. Thereafter women gradually leave the workforce for retirement. The median monthly earnings ratio between women and men improved from 66 percent in 1985 to 75 percent in 1995.

The distribution of women in the labor force in Hong Kong is partly the result of social forces that require women to do the majority of household labor, and partly the result of stereotyped assumptions about the kind of work that is proper for women to do. Most of the economically active women are concentrated in wholesale, retail, etc. (46 percent) and community, social and personal services (21 percent). In terms of occupation, more than half (56.6 percent) of working women are concentrated in clerical and elementary occupations, with only 8.3 percent in the managerial, administrative and professional ranks. Strong evidence of vertical gender segregation seen in the small numbers of women in management is supplemented by strong evidence of horizontal gender segregation by industry seen in Table 5.2.

Table 5.2   Distribution of Hong Kong men and women by industry (%)

	1980		1990		2000	
Industry	Men	Women	Men	Women	Men	Women
Manufacturing	35.9	54.7	26.9	31.5	10.4	9.3
Electricity and gas	0.9	0.2	1.0	0.2	0.5	0.1
Construction sites	11.6	1.5	10.6	1.1	6.3	0.5
Wholesale, retail, import/export, restaurants and hotels	21.4	17.0	21.9	24.4	42.5	45.6
Transport, storage and communications	10.7	2.6	13.3	4.4	9.4	5.8
Financing, insurance, real estate and banking services	4.6	5.6	10.3	11.4	19.9	17.9
Community, social and personal services	14.9	18.4	15.9	27.0	11.0	20.8
TOTAL (%)	100.0	100.0	100.0	100.0	100.0	100.0

Source: Hong Kong Census and Statistics Department, Hong Kong Special Administrative Region.

It should be noted that there was a significant shift in employment from manufacturing to the service sector in 1980–2000. The percentage of women employed in manufacturing decreased from 55 percent in 1980 to 9.3 percent in 2000. Service sectors in retail and trade, restaurants and hotels absorbed a large share of the female labor force resulting in a dramatic increase from 17 percent in 1980 to 46 percent in 2000. Communications, finance, insurance and real estates also showed a substantial increase of two- to threefold in the female employment rate.

Organizational Support for Female Employees

The most admired corporations for women to work for are women-friendly organizations. Women-friendly organizational policies and practices – such as flexitime policies, maternity and paternity leave, sick leave benefits for family illness, childcare facilities or subsidies, and policies on dual-career couples – not only enhance women's opportunities for promotion, training and career development, but also eradicate sex discrimination. In a recent study Chiu and Ng (1999) found that women-friendly policies are not prevalent in organizations in Hong Kong. Support in the workplace is very limited. Each of 300 respondents was asked to indicate whether his or her organization currently had women-friendly policies (20 human resource management policies covering areas such as fair practices on recruitment, training, development, promotion, pay equity, sex discrimination and sexual harassment). The least-practiced policies included reduced work hours for women (1 percent), promoting women over men (2 percent), and providing childcare facilities (2 percent). Policies reported to be practiced more frequently were maternity benefits exceeding the minimum labor law requirements (35 percent), counseling for female employees (14 percent), control on gender quotas (12.7 percent), and setting up anti-sexual discrimination and harassment committees (8 percent). The presence of women-friendly policies affected only women and only their affective commitment, with no effect on continuance commitment. The value of women-friendly policies and practices served to 'win the heart and minds' of the women workers but did not turn them into stable employees.

Women Employed in the Public Sector

The Hong Kong government, the largest employer in Hong Kong, employed 182 527 civil servants in 2000, 33.3 percent of whom were female, compared with only 19 percent in 1973 (Hong Kong Civil Service Personnel Statistics, 2000). Civil servants represent 2.8 percent of the population and 5.5 percent of the Hong Kong workforce. In the Hong Kong civil service, men still hold disproportionately more elite positions in the administrative system. Among the 1269 directorate officers, 22 percent were females. The majority of the female staff are concentrated in the lower pay scale grades (see Table 5.3). Only 0.4 percent of the female civil servants were able to reach the apex of the bureaucracy, compared to 0.7 percent for their male counterparts.

Progress has been made since 1980. Women now hold high-ranking positions in government service. The number of women directorate officers in government service has increased significantly, from 35 in 1981 to 241 in 1998; the percentage of total directorate grade positions held by females shot up from 9.2 percent in 1980 to 26 percent in 2000. Women have also made dramatic token gains at the top levels. In 2000, several of the highest-ranking positions were women. Women headed the civil service (Chief Secretary for Administration's Office), judiciary (Secretary of Justice) and Security Bureau (Secretary of Security).

It is common for women to head the 'feminine' departments such as social work, public health and education; however women have now also entered traditionally 'masculine' areas successfully. With heavy emphasis on the importance of education and qualifications, good education, a university degree, fluency in English and Mandarin are the criteria for selection and promotion in the public sector. Social class rather than gender

Table 5.3   Distribution of men and women in Hong Kong civil service (%)

	1980		1990		2000	
Salary group	Men	Women	Men	Women	Men	Women
Directorate pay scale	90.8	9.2	87.9	12.1	74.1	25.9
Master pay scale						
4th quartile	90.6	9.4	80.8	19.2	74.2	25.8
3rd quartile	73.5	26.5	76.9	23.1	68.2	31.8
2nd quartile	n/a	n/a	61.8	38.2	54.7	45.3
1st quartile	64.5	35.5	51.7	48.3	58.5	41.5
Police pay scale						
High	100	n/a	95.1	4.9	89.5	10.5
Medium	89.5	10.5	83.0	17.0	79.2	20.8
Low	62.1	37.9	91.1	8.9	87.7	12.3
General disciplined services pay scale						
Constable	n/a	n/a	100	0	92.5	7.5
Officer grades	n/a	n/a	83.7	16.3	77.2	22.8
Rank and file	91.5	8.5	91.9	8.1	90.1	9.9

Source: Hong Kong Civil Service Personnel Statistics (2000).

may be the main determinant of access to the top positions in the future (Leung, 1993).

The Hong Kong Civil Service claims to adopt a policy of equal treatment of male and female employees. There is no restriction on the recruitment of female candidates. However the Hong Kong government has been slow to address the needs of women in the workforce and even as an employer has continued to use discriminatory practices, or else practices that have a disparate effect.

Following the British tradition, before 1973, female officers received approximately 80 percent of the pay of a male officer doing comparable work, and married women took a marriage gratuity and became temporary staff. Such discriminatory practices no longer exist. In 1981 equal eligibility for fringe benefits for married men and women was introduced. Despite pay parity for the sexes, men were five times more likely to attain a senior position than women were, and thus the average wage of male civil servants is still higher than that of female civil servants. Tang (1982) found that on average it took male senior officers 13.5 years to reach their present positions while it took 18 years for women to reach senior ranks, suggesting disparities in promotion opportunities. Even though it is the largest employer, the government cannot be considered as an innovative or leading model for gender equality in employment in Hong Kong while these kinds of disparities exist.

The Underdeveloped Political Potential of Women in HK

There are a number of high-profile women involved in politics. Women councilors with a business or professional background and top civil servants have become part of the power elite, mainly through government appointment or indirect election. Women comprise 26.7 percent of the Executive Council, 16.7 percent of the Legislative Council and 26 percent of the Municipal Councils (Tang et al., 2000). In the Legislative Council, women are grossly under-represented and women constituted only a small percentage of all advisory board and committee members. The non-elite or grassroots women have had no chance to participate and full-time housewives have never been well represented in elected or appointed offices. Family responsibility has taken most of the time of married women. They can spare little time for participation in public affairs.

Hong Kong Chinese women are not radical in their political or social values, but are concerned about opportunities for individual achievement and about rewards for individual efforts. In their political actions they show a determination to maintain their career opportunities, but at the same time they are very conventional about family values and childcare. Their conservatism makes them skeptical of the wider social and political aims of the women's movement as they see it. This position is better understood when we address the role of women in the family in Hong Kong and when we see how this role affects their employment.

THE IMPACT OF GOVERNMENT POLICY ON WOMEN'S EMPLOYMENT

Under the laissez-faire policy, the Hong Kong government has made little effort to encourage women to join the workforce. The government of Hong Kong does not have a comprehensive and well-defined women's policy. In the chief executive's policy address, there is a lack of concern for women. Women's issues are included as part of social welfare policy if they are addressed at all. The government does not address the wider problems of women's employment such as occupational segregation, the effect of the life cycle, childrearing responsibilities on working women and gender inequalities in job allocation.

Some women's groups have complained about the government's actions, saying they are half-hearted, aiming for too little and too late. The government's policy on women's issues is regarded by members of these groups as piecemeal, without any welfare benefits (Lui, 1990). They say that women are treated as dependents of their family unit; housework is not properly valued; casual and unemployed women are not eligible for social services; and unpaid housewives are not protected by a mandatory retirement scheme. So far there has been little response to these criticisms.

Government policies have the ability to affect women's employment both directly and indirectly through the legislation that frames employment relations, taxation, welfare provision and related matters. The government has neither adopted any policy of encouraging a higher level of women labor participation, nor has it discouraged women's participation in economic activities through its welfare policies.

Legislation and Regulations

The Equal Opportunities Commission and Bill of Rights Ordinance (1991) prohibits explicitly discriminatory practices. However this ordinance has not been enforced consistently. There are some individual pieces of legislation and regulations that in some cases hinder and in some cases help employed women.

Women as dependents
One of the most controversial laws, a continuation of the Qing Dynasty, prohibits women from the right to inherit property in the New Territories. This law remains because of the belief that it is undesirable for the government to interfere in Chinese custom and culture (Tong, 1994). Another indicator of women's dependent legal status is tax legislation. Until 1 April 1990, a married working woman had to be declared on her husband's tax return form and tax was levied on the combined income. Now working women may file their income tax separately.

Protective laws
The Women and Young Persons (Industry) Regulations were passed to regulate women's working hours, overtime and employment in shift work, and the laws also prohibit women from employment in underground work and dangerous working environments. These regulations also grant maternity leave for pregnant women. The regulations have been seen as basically protective in nature, and discriminatory as far as pay and conditions of work are concerned (Cheung, 1997).

These protective laws have been amended several times to protect women from physical hazards at work, but to permit more flexibility in employment for women and for employers. With relaxation of overtime regulations, women are now permitted to work up to a maximum of ten hours per day inclusive of overtime. Overtime for women is restricted to two hours per day and 200 hours per year maximum. Night-shift work is now permissible for women, giving enterprises greater flexibility in the employment of women and in determining shift arrangements.

Some argue that protective legislation serves to restrict women's competitiveness in the labor market and to benefit men, particularly in times of recession (Pearson, 1990, p. 119). The protective legislation encourages the assumption that women are peripheral rather than central to the workforce, to be mobilized when convenient and retired at will. The good intentions of the protective legislation have the effect of denying women certain employment opportunities and the right to choose their own time and work environment. In this regard, when such legislation applies only to women, it is discriminatory.

Training and retraining
The government-initiated Employee Retraining Scheme was established in 1992 to provide training for employees affected by the economic restructuring process. Under the Employee Retraining Ordinance, an employee retraining fund was established to finance retraining programs to enable unemployed workers to seek employment or re-enter the labor force. The Employees Retraining Board has received a capital injection of HK $1.6 billion (US$ 0.2 billion) to offer 100 000 retraining places every year. However such a government-sponsored retraining scheme has been criticized as being either irrelevant or too basic to help people secure a job after the training period (Tang et al., 2001).

There is also a gender bias in subjects offered in vocational training. For example the Apprenticeship Programs cover fewer occupations usually patronized by females, even though the potential targets are women in their mid-thirties to mid-forties. Females accounted for more than one-third (36.1 percent) of the enrollment in training courses offered by the vocational training council in 2001–2002. These failures point to a lack of women's perspective in government training policy.

Maternity benefits
Given the impact of childbearing and rearing upon female labor participation, maternity entitlements have been a controversial issue for a long time. A female employee who has worked for the same employer continuously for a period of not less than 26 weeks is entitled to ten weeks of maternity leave, generally four weeks prior to confinement and six weeks afterwards. Maternity leave pay is four-fifths of the usual monthly salary, excluding overtime pay. A relative lack of protection regarding maternity

leave and subsequent rights to return to work provide women with a greater incentive to return to work within six weeks after childbirth as the only means of securing a continued job.

In a recent court case, a senior professional IT expert in charge of the Asia Pacific region for a firm was demoted and deprived of staff support and training opportunities as a result of pregnancy. She is seeking damages for sex and family status discrimination against the internet pioneer Yahoo (Lau, 2000).

THE ROLE OF WOMEN IN THE FAMILY IN HONG KONG

A patriarchal family structure in Hong Kong stresses the importance of family relations and creates different roles and different amounts of power for men and women inside families. Traditional Chinese culture places a premium on sons. Sons are seen as investment assets to increase the family human capital. Daughters are seen as tools of current economic gain. Traditional Chinese women are expected to subordinate their individual lives to the wishes of their father as a girl, to their husband as a wife, and to their adult sons as a widow. As a mother, a woman's primary goal is to care for and protect her children, especially her sons, and to contribute in any other way she can to the economic welfare of her husband's family.

Because of this cultural heritage, when Hong Kong women began to work outside of the home, they did not make significant gains in the areas of economic power and family decision-making (Wong, 1981). They are still expected to be primary caretakers of the household and of children whether or not they are employed outside the home.

The Chinese society in Hong Kong is characterized by a cultural syndrome of 'utilitarian familism' (Lau, 1982). Utilitarian familism is 'the normative and behavioral tendency of an individual to place familial interests above the interests of society and above the interests of other individuals and groups, and to structure relationships with other individuals and groups in such a manner that the furtherance of familial interests is the overriding concern' (Lau, 1982, p. 14). In this system, all efforts go to support the family. However the current emphases on individualism, utilitarianism and materialism in Hong Kong society are believed to be instrumental in the erosion of traditional Chinese values and are seen to undermine the traditional conception of the Chinese family (Sheng, 1992).

The structure of Hong Kong families has changed during the past few decades as can be seen in Table 5.4. There are fewer multi-generational households, smaller families and more divorced single-parent families. On

Table 5.4   Hong Kong family structure

Families	1980	1990	2000
Numbers of households	1 244 738	1 582 215	2 037 000
Average number of children/household	n/a	1.0	0.7
% of nuclear family	n/a	63.6	66.2
% of one vertically extended nuclear family	n/a	10.7	8.5
Women Population	2 382 392	2 782 000	3 388 000
% of women			
Single			
never married	32.6	30.5	30.0
Widowed	10.7	12.2	9.9
Divorced	0.7	1.0	2.4
Married	56.0	56.4	57.6
Households with single parent*			
Male	n/a	11 479	13 388
		27.40%	22.90%
Female	n/a	30 402	45 072
		72.59%	77.10%

Note: *Extracted from *Women and Men in Hong Kong: Key Statistics* (2002), Hong Kong Census and Statistics Department. The surveys were conducted in 1991 and 2001.

Source: Hong Kong Census and Statistics Department, Hong Kong Special Administrative Region.

the one hand, fewer children have freed some women to work outside the home, but on the other hand, there are fewer resources in terms of extended family members to care for the children an employed woman may have.

It should be noted that the average number of children per household was 0.7 in 2000, a very low figure even compared with Western countries. Never-married women remained around 30 percent. The divorce rate increased more than threefold from 0.7 percent to 2.4 percent between 1980 and 2000. Single-parent households showed a sharp increase during the 1990s, 48 percent for women in particular.

Women are responsible for preserving the Chinese family tradition in caring for the aged and the children. Childcare remains primarily the responsibility of mothers. Caring work is undertaken by individual women in their private homes. Due to the limited subsidized childcare service available, many women are restricted to the traditional role of housewives.

Married women have to shoulder a larger share of domestic burden even when they are gainfully employed in the labor market, since their husbands have limited participation in childcare and household chores (Pearson, 1990). The husband's role in sharing household responsibility is limited. If men are involved in looking after children, it tends to be in the more enjoyable tasks such as taking children out or playing with them. Women still perform the lion's share of the childcare and household tasks (Lau and Wan, 1987; Lau et al., 1992). Neither the institutions of work nor the government wish to make changes to accommodate the dual demands of work and family.

In Hong Kong, even though they have smaller families, women's domestic family responsibilities interfere with their careers. Forty-three percent of female workers have to give up their work on giving birth to their first child (Hong Kong Federation of Trade Unions, 1989). These women of childbearing age, who potentially could work, are not available for work; 58.4 percent of the economically inactive females, compared with 4.6 percent of males, claimed the reason for leaving the labor force was because of the need to take care of housework and children at home (Hong Kong Census and Statistics Department, 1999).

When women drop out of the labor force during primary childcare years they face employment discrimination against women over aged 30 when they try to return to employment later in life. Thus professional women would not dare take a break from paid employment to take care of young children for fear of interrupting their careers. They have to rely on social networks for moral and practical support in their dual roles (Channey, 1981).

Women with low educational qualifications also find it extremely difficult to re-enter the labor force after an unemployed childrearing period. Age discrimination and lack of vocational training opportunities to prepare them to re-enter the workforce stop their re-employment. Women seeking part-time jobs are often confined to the disadvantaged secondary sector of low-paid, less secure, less skilled and less rewarding jobs – just the sort of jobs that are now being relocated to PRC.

If returning women do get a job, they also suffer from employers' policies within firms, since employers often provide less training to female employees because of gender discrimination and fear of losing a trained worker to childrearing. Women's lack of ability to keep up with technological changes in the workplace may not be due to personal choice but to discrimination in access to training for women workers. Nevertheless lower human capital reduces their chances of employment and advancement for the rest of their lives.

When women leave the labor force to care for their families they face critical family problems as well. Economic and social changes have brought increases in family disruption, sexual exploitation and violence toward women at home and at work. One unintended consequence of the increase in cross-border business dealing is that it creates opportunities for men to have 'second wives' or mistresses in China. Such extramarital affairs cause emotional and financial strain for most married women, and the divorce rate has shot up from 0.7 percent in 1980 to 2.4 percent in 2000.

Violence against women is also on the rise. The number of rape cases and indecent assault cases reported to the police were 104 and 1124 respectively for the year 2000, and the total number of female battered spouse cases rose to 2787 in 2002 from 970 in 1998 (Hong Kong Special Administrative Region Government, 2004). Immigrant wives from Mainland China are often victims of an abusive marriage, and over half of battered wives are full-time housewives who are economically dependent on their husbands. The total number of battered spouse cases reported to the Social Welfare Department rose from 1009 in 1998 to 3034 in 2002. These reported cases are only a small fraction of the true number because the Chinese tend not to reveal domestic violence for face-saving reasons. This combination of obligation to care for the family even in the face of abuse, and lack of employment opportunities due to discrimination and economic restructuring, make divorce an extremely risky economic venture. This leaves many desperate unemployed women with bleak lives and few viable alternatives.

SOCIAL WELFARE THROUGH FAMILY, NOT GOVERNMENT

Experience from European countries confirms that there is a clear link between the availability of safe, reliable childcare facilities and the continuing employment of women with young children. The availability of high-quality, reasonably priced childcare not only affects a woman's ability to stay in the job, but also influences her morale, productivity, absenteeism and health.

In Hong Kong, people are expected to take care of themselves. It is a government policy that social welfare should be avoided whenever and wherever possible. In Hong Kong, a self-help Chinese society coexists with a non-interventionist government. Familial networks, not the state, have been looked upon as the main provider of financial and social assistance in times of need. The family will continue to be the primary providers of care and welfare, and women will share the burden of the primary caretaker.

Hong Kong does not provide sufficient government support for services that might benefit families in general and working women in particular. Only 7.5 percent of the 560 000 nursery aged six and below are at government-subsidized nurseries. In 2001–2002, there were 466 privately run childcare centers providing nursery care to 54 23 children. However this is not sufficient to care for the 587 00 families with children under 12 years old. Demand for childcare facilities always outstrips supply. Few employers provide childcare either as a facility or as a benefit. Given the fact that there is little support from employers and the government concerning childcare, family responsibility, to a large extent, restricts women's full commitment to their jobs.

In Mainland China, neighborhood support is secured by sharing a common courtyard and facilities such as water taps and toilets with several families, but this is not the case in Hong Kong, where there is very weak communal support. One of the reasons for this weaker support is that as the economy develops, people have become more individualistic. Individual performance has changed work attitudes as well as the lifestyle of Chinese working women, in particular the younger generation. The change has gradually transformed social and family relationships, and created a gradual loosening of family cohesiveness. The consequence of shrinking available support resources is that the traditional emphasis on family cohesiveness and mutual support has been greatly reduced.

Social support has always been an integral and indispensable part of the lives of Chinese working mothers (Yuen-Tsang, 1997). The extent of social support depends on the frequency of contact, geographical proximity, the durability and intensity of relationships, degree of reciprocity and multiplicity. In the Hong Kong situation, housing is a serious problem. The tiny flats make it impossible to accommodate a large family. In addition, the younger generations prefer to live in their own separate household so that they can enjoy their privacy. As a result, the proportion of nuclear families is rising. Currently 66 percent of the households are one nuclear family. The average domestic household size is 3.3 people (Hong Kong Census and Statistics Department, 2000). Intergenerational support is very limited under a nuclear family structure.

Detached or complex family relationships do not necessarily imply lack of contact, but it is difficult to expect very frequent and intense support between family members. Hong Kong, being a Chinese society, still maintains the collective orientation towards family. Nuclear families are networked together into a nuclear family net – a conglomerate of separate entities. Such family networks provide the main source of support.

When family support is not available, some women pay for others to care for their children in their home. Hong Kong attracts people from other poor countries who are seeking employment, especially from the Philippines, to serve as domestic helpers with low wages. The cheap labor of maids takes up much of the time-consuming, labor-intensive domestic work and childcare responsibility of middle-class and upper-class women. While the middle class can afford to employ live-in domestic helpers, less wealthy families have to rely on mothers or mothers-in-law for childcare.

SUMMARY AND CONCLUSIONS

The status of women in Hong Kong has undergone significant changes since the 1990s. Industrialization has unquestionably contributed to the advancement of Hong Kong women's status and opportunities for career advancement. However industrialization in Hong Kong has not removed the traditional conceptions of woman as mothers and homemakers. Successful career women still have to subscribe to patriarchal values and practices that create barriers for attaining equality with men.

Nevertheless there are examples of successful women and visible role models in Hong Kong. They tend to be women of exceptional ability who have worked and struggled to reach their elite positions. Kanter (1977) refers to this phenomenon as 'tokenism'. Simply employing a few women to demonstrate non-discrimination is a strategy that fails to address the main issues.

Government policy has the potential to impose a significant impact on the sexual division of labor at work, both directly and indirectly, through the legislation that frames employment practices, taxation, welfare provision and through its actions as the largest employer. The non-interventionist approach of the HK government does not attempt to undertake active affirmative measures for the benefit of women. Given the unequal status of women and men in the family, together with women's greater household responsibilities, women are not on equal footing with men when entering the job market.

The government's protective role to safeguard and protect female workers from hazardous and dangerous working environment may restrict women's opportunity in the competitive labor market rather than promote economic opportunity for women. The lack of women-aware policy-making often puts women in a disadvantageous position.

The lack of childcare facilities, coupled with a zoning policy in new towns that separates work and home, puts women in a difficult position to accommodate domestic and work responsibilities. Middle-aged women do not necessarily seek high wages, but rather seek jobs that offer flexible work schedules allowing them to balance their work lives with their family responsibilities. An effective way to help these women is to increase job flexibility so that women can be in a better position to balance demands from these two domains of their lives. They also need effective retraining and assistance in re-entering the labor force if they have left for childbearing.

RECOMMENDATIONS FOR FUTURE DIRECTIONS

There is an urgent need to establish a Women's Commission serving an advisory function to the Hong Kong government and to increase women's representation in the political system and policy decision-making in Hong Kong. Because of the repeated appeals on the part of concerned groups and individuals, the government has responded promptly to set up a Women's Commission to advise the authorities on women's issues. The government lacks the women's perspective in designing and implementing its social policies and thus the policy makers are not aware of the problems facing women.

The Hong Kong Government has established the Equal Opportunities Commission aiming to eliminate sex discrimination and promote equal opportunities. The Equal Opportunities Commission and Bill of Rights Ordinance (1991) prohibit explicitly discriminatory practices. Yet the Equal Opportunity Commissioner has been condemned by many as having made no significant change to women's lives (Gender Research Program, 1994). Age and sex discrimination seriously deny employment and development opportunities for women. Implementation of the Bill of Rights needs to be a high priority to assist employed women in Hong Kong.

More concrete efforts are needed to address the root causes of gender injustice. Even though women's paid and unpaid labor contributes significantly to the social economy and productivity, because of power imbalances the dominant frameworks reinforce and promote existing gender hierarchies, and women do not have the opportunity to make the greatest contribution of which they are capable. There is a need for critical analysis of the political, social and institutional framework of Hong Kong.

Gender mainstreaming is an approach to advancing gender equality that involves addressing gender inequality in all aspects of development, across all sectors and programs. It is not simply about ensuring that women's position is improved within existing frameworks that are dominated by men (Taylor, 1999). Gender mainstreaming refers to a multifaceted, holistic and long-term strategy of integrating a gender perspective into all public policies in order to achieve equality between men and women in and beyond the workplace. It calls for setting up an integrated network of structure, mechanism and processes designed to arouse more gender-awareness, increase the number of women in decision-making roles, facilitate the formulation of gender-sensitive policies, plans and programs, and promote the advancement of gender equality and equity. It reviews the necessity of changing the position of women in society by addressing inequalities in employment, political participation and cultural and legal status. Establishing a program for gender mainstreaming in Hong Kong may be one way to provide access to equal employment opportunities for Hong Kong women.

Human development has two key elements: the development of human capabilities and the development of opportunities for people to use these capabilities. An important contribution to the advancement of gender within the human development paradigm has been the design of two new indices, the gender-related development index and the gender empowerment measure to measure the inequalities in key areas of political and economic decision-making structures (UNDP, 1995). There are no comprehensive data in these areas. More gender audit research that collects detailed gender statistics will provide information for future policy decisions. The Hong Kong Census and Statistics Department has compiled statistics with detailed gender focus indicators. These gender-specific indicators will provide guidance for future efforts to assist women, and information to formulate the overall strategic direction with a gender focus.

The Hong Kong government has set up an institutional structure (Women's Commission) to deal with women's issues in its policies. More effort should address the need for action to support economically deprived families (single parents, new immigrants from China, and so on) as well as to improve their disadvantaged position with respect to access to rights and resources. The planning stage involves analysing the status of women, and develops a clearly defined gender dimension in work plans. Gender issues should be integrated in the development of work plans and budget allocation. Follow-up on the implementation of the engendered work plans and reviewing key indicators on the status of women are necessary to reinforce the mission. Next, it is important to reorient the institutional process for the planning, implementation and monitoring of government policies to accommodate women's concerns. Finally, long-term strategies should be developed to build up women through the personal growth process, promote integration and equality in the workplace. It is important to ensure that women receive equal opportunities for training to ensure that they are equally competitive in their respective fields and in career advancement. Networking is a good strategy to share ideas and information. It is important to establish mutually supportive linkages.

It is rare for Hong Kong companies to provide any kind of family-friendly programs. Government should provide tax incentives for companies to set up these programs. Family-friendly programs and policies help to enhance job flexibility and reduce the household burden of working women. Employers are encouraged to allow flexibility, such as flexible or alternative work schedules, telecommuting, job-sharing and on-site childcare centers to enable working parents to spend more time to give their children better care and attention.

In general, women have fewer mentors and role models. Through mentoring programs women share their hard-earned experience and wisdom. Establishing mentoring programs is a good strategy for achieving equity and fairness in the workplace.

Hong Kong women believe that many of their problems are personal and they have attempted to find personal solutions. They are not aware of and are not encouraged to resolve many common problems and conflicts in the public arena. We need to create some means to change women's attitudes from being passive recipients of development assistance to active agents in transforming their own economic, social, political and cultural realities if Hong Kong women are to reach their full potential.

REFERENCES

Channey, J. (1981), 'Social networks and job information: the situation of women who return to work', paper presented to EOC/SSRC joint panel on equal opportunities, June, Ann Arbor, MI: SSRC.

Cheung, F.M. (ed.) (1997), *Engendering Hong Kong Society: A Gender Perspective of Women's Status*, Hong Kong: Chinese University Press.

Chiu, S.W.K. and C.K. Lee (1997), 'Withering away of the Hong Kong dream? Women workers under industrial restructuring', Hong Kong Institute of Asia-Pacific Studies, occasional paper no.61, Hong Kong: Chinese University of Hong Kong.

Chiu, W.C.K. and C.W. Ng (1999), 'Women-friendly HRM and organizational commitment: a study among women and men in organizations in Hong Kong', *Journal of Occupational and Organizational Psychology*, **72** (4), 485–502.

Gender Research Program (1994), *Survey of Public Perception on Equal Opportunity for Women and Men 1993–1994 (Main Report)*, Hong Kong: Hong Kong Government.

Hong Kong Census and Statistics Department (1999), *Hong Kong Monthly Digest of Statistics (1999)*, Hong Kong: Hong Kong Special Administrative Region, the People's Republic of China.

Hong Kong Census and Statistics Department (2000), *Hong Kong Social and Economic Trends 2000*, Hong Kong: Hong Kong Special Administrative Region, the People's Republic of China.

Hong Kong Census and Statistics Department (2002), *Women and Men in Hong Kong: Key Statistics*, Hong Kong: Hong Kong Special Administrative Region, the People's Republic of China.

Hong Kong Civil Service Personnel Statistics (2000), *Hong Kong: Civil Service Branch*, Hong Kong: Hong Kong Special Administrative Region Government Secretariat, the People's Republic of China.

Hong Kong Federation of Trade Unions (1989), *Report on a Questionnaire Survey on the Situation and Needs of Married Women*, Hong Kong: Hong Kong Federation of Trade Unions, Woman Affairs Committee, in Chinese.

Hong Kong Special Administrative Region Government (2004), *Convention on the Elimination of all Forms of Discrimination against Women: Second Report*,

Hong Kong: Hong Kong Special Administrative Region, the People's Republic of China.

House, R., P.J. Hanges, S.A. Ruiz-Quintanilla, P.W. Dorfman, M. Javidan, M. Dickson, V. Gupta and GLOBE country co-investigators (1999), 'Cultural influences on leadership and organizations', in W. H. Mobley, M. J. Gessner and V. Arnold (eds), *Advances in Global Leadership*, vol 1, Greenwich, CT: JAI Press, pp. 171–233.

Kanter, R.M. (1977), *Men and Women of the Corporation*, New York: Basic Books.

Lau, A. (2000), 'Yahoo! Discriminating', *South China Morning Post*, 7 November, p. 4.

Lau, K.S., M.K. Lee, P.S. Wan and S.L. Wong (1992), *Indicators of Social Development*, Hong Kong: Hong Kong Institute of Asia-Pacific Studies, the Chinese University of Hong Kong.

Lau, S.K. (1982), *Society and Politics in Hong Kong*, Hong Kong: the Chinese University Press.

Lau, S.K. and P.S. Wan (1987), *A Preliminary Report on Social Indicators in Hong Kong*, Hong Kong: Centre of Hong Kong Studies, the Chinese University of Hong Kong.

Leung, S.M. (1993), 'Career advancement of Hong Kong female executives in Hong Kong public sector', in M. Orhant and R.I. Westwood (eds), *Proceedings of Women in Management in Asia Conference*, Hong Kong: the Chinese University of Hong Kong, pp. 181–90.

Lui, T.L. (1990), 'The social organization of outwork: the case of Hong Kong', in E. Sim (ed.), *Between East and West*, Hong Kong: University of Hong Kong Centre of Asian Studies, pp. 185–215.

Ng, C.H. (1991), 'Women's employment and family change', in Y.S. Joseph Cheng (ed.), *Building a New Era in Hong Kong*, Hong Kong: Breakthrough Press, pp. 54–68 (in Chinese).

Ngo, H.Y. (1992), 'Employment status of married women in Hong Kong', *Sociological Perspectives*, **35**, 475–88.

Pearson, V. (1990), 'Women in Hong Kong', in B.K.P. Leung (ed.), *Social Issues in Hong Kong*, Hong Kong: Oxford University Press, pp. 114–39.

Salaff, J.W. (1981), *Working Daughters of Hong Kong*, Cambridge: Cambridge University Press.

Sheng, X.W. (1992), 'Population aging and the traditional pattern of supporting the aged', in *Proceedings of Asia-Pacific Regional Conference on Future of the Family*, Beijing: China Social Science Documentation Publishing House.

Tang, C., W.T. Au, Y.P. Chung and H.Y. Ngo (2000), 'Breaking the patriarchal paradigm: Chinese women in Hong Kong', in L. Edwards and M. Roces (eds), *Women in Asia: Tradition, Modernity and Globalization*, Ann Arbor, MI: University of Michigan Press, pp. 188–207.

Tang, C.K.D. (1982), 'An evaluation of the career patterns and attitudes of upper middle civil servants in Hong Kong', Masters of Social Science thesis, Hong Kong: University of Hong Kong.

Tang, K.L., J.T.Y. Cheung and W. Forget (2001), *An Insider View: Opinions and Assessments of Retraining Policy from Hong Kong Workers*, Hong Kong: Asia Monitor Resource Center.

Taylor, V. (1999), *Gender Mainstreaming in Development Planning: A Reference Manual for Governments and Other Stakeholders*, London: Commonwealth Secretariat.

Tong, I. (1994), 'Women', in D.H. McMillen and S.W. Man (eds), *The Other Hong Kong Report*, Hong Kong: the Chinese University Press, pp. 367–87.

United Nations Development Program (UNDP) (1995), *Human Development Report*, New York: Oxford University Press.

Wong, F.M. (1981), 'Effects of the employment of mothers on marital role and power differentiation in Hong Kong', in A.Y.C. King and R.P.L. Lee (eds), *Social Life and Development in Hong Kong*, Hong Kong: the Chinese University Press, pp. 217–34.

Yip, S. (2003), 'Teacher's pet – or victim of obsession?', *South China Morning Post*, 14 June, p. E8.

Yuen-Tsang, A.W.K. (1997), *Towards a Chinese Concept of Social Support: A Study on the Social Support Networks of Chinese Working Mothers in Beijing*, Aldershot, UK and Brookfield, VT, USA: Ashgate Publishing.

6. The impact of government and family responsibilities on the career development of working women in Singapore

Irene K.H. Chew and Naresh Khatri

Singapore, a 616 sq km island at the tip of the Malay Peninsula, gained independence from colonial Western rule and Japanese domination by declaring independence in 1959. Thrust suddenly on its own after the war, the largely Chinese population led by a paternalistic father figure, Lee Kuan Yew, evolved a democratic capitalist economy governed by a single strong leader modeled on a traditional Chinese hierarchical family with a supportive, subordinate legislative and civil service system.

In the beginning days of independence, fear of communism justified strong central control over many aspects of public and private life. Even after the immediate post-war threat of communism faded, a key assumption of the role of government in society persists that it is appropriate for the government to set important rules and policies regarding both employment and family. Civil rights laws protect the rights of all minority groups in a society with a significant number of Malays (16 percent), Indians (6.5 percent), and smaller numbers of Europeans and others (2.3 percent); however success in the large civil service and educational system depends upon performance in centralized examinations. Access to these opportunities is easier for male Chinese than for any other group in the society, in part because many families are willing to pay more money to educate sons rather than daughters.

In 1990 Lee Kuan Yew stepped down in favor of a hand-picked successor. While the public leadership was transferred, the old founder retains considerable power in a traditional Chinese social arrangement where real power and public legal power are not identical.

We would like to express our appreciation to Chan Yin Fun, Wee Lai Kuen and Tan Ching Yin for their assistance in the data collection and to all our interviewers for their contributions in the fruition of this research project.

The state of the Singaporean economy in the beginning of the twenty-first century is promising, despite a globally stagnant economy. The GDP in 1980 was S\$30 000 million in 1990, was S\$66 000 million and in 2000 was S\$157 700 million. The unemployment rate as of 2000 was 3.5 percent (Department of Statistics, 2001). In the wake of the Asian economic crisis of 1996–97 and the return of economic rival Hong Kong to the control of the People's Republic of China (PRC), Singapore has tried to assume a more important role in the regional economy. In spite of a limited geographic area, the presence of a highly educated workforce is its greatest asset and the society cannot afford to ignore the efforts and talents of half of its population. Thus the current situation in Singapore offers a particular example of whether and how a strong centralized government operating in a capitalist economic society can shape the employment and family lives of women.

Because of the increasing number of women in the labor force and the social demands put upon women to continue a primary role in the family, the government of Singapore has sought to create a balance between these two roles. Singapore has promoted various policies and initiatives to create direct and indirect long-standing impacts on the position of women and the welfare of the Singapore society at large.

Since the 1970s, we have seen a steady rise in the number of Singapore women joining the workforce as they begin to develop career mindsets and aspirations. The female labor force participation rate rose from 51.1 percent in 1997 to 53.4 percent in 2001 (Ministry of Manpower, 2002). As educational qualifications increased, women began to develop careers of their own, and simultaneously faced the pressing issue of balancing work and family. Many researchers have focused on the trade-off between work and family roles for career woman. Few actually focus on the effects of this role conflict on women's career development. This chapter examines the career development of Singapore women in their particular governmental context from the perspective of the effects of the family role demands on their careers.

The Singapore government takes a paternalistic approach to the employment of women, as it is very involved in almost every aspect of the lives of the citizens. There is a strong relationship between government initiatives and family and career development among Singapore women. Thus it is imperative for us to examine the impact of the government on women's career development, and critically to assess whether the hand of government has been positive or negative in helping women to develop their careers.

We have used literature review, interviews with government employees and interviews with employed women to analyse the government's impact on career preparedness and the availability of job opportunities in the society, as well as on the age and timing of critical life events such as marriage, pregnancy and childbirth, and career development stages. We have concluded that the government has a significant impact on the career development of Singapore women through its various initiatives in education, employment, childcare and procreation. Although the government is generally successful in making it easier for women to develop their careers in Singapore, there still remain areas for possible improvement.

To identify the factors influencing the career development of Singapore women we conducted a search of relevant literature and government documents and websites. In addition, we conducted a short survey with 30 working women aged 25 to 50, who view their job as a career. The survey was administered face-to-face with questions that relate specifically to the factors affecting women's career development. The interview questions and a tabulation of the interview results are shown in Appendix 6.1. We also interviewed the executive director of the Singapore National Employers' Federation, and the assistant divisional director of the Labor Relations and Welfare Division of the Ministry of Manpower. The objective of the interviews was to obtain updated information from persons who have relevant knowledge and experience, to provide us with a better understanding of women's experiences and of the government initiatives and the motivation behind them. The interviews are in Appendix 6.2.

WOMEN'S EDUCATIONAL OPPORTUNITIES

The government has built an unbiased, gender-blind and merit-based education system, which advocates equal opportunity access to education for both men and women, and allows for fair competition in the entrance examinations that permit entry to higher education in Singapore. This competition is fierce however, because the number of spaces in the most prestigious institutions is limited. Recognizing this problem, the Singapore government has made significant investments in education as reflected in its total recurrent expenditure on education institutions. Since 1990, its investment has increased almost fourfold.

The importance of these investments is that they made seeking an education affordable. Being Asians, a paternalistic view exists in Singapore whereby only sons will attend school if the family cannot afford to send all of their children. This was common for the older Singapore generation. However the government has heavily subsidized education and provided financial schemes, making it possible to send both sons and daughters to school. Thus scenarios whereby daughters are not able to attend schools are no longer in existence. For instance there is a scheme that allows children to withdraw from their parent's Central Provident Funds accounts to pay their tuition fees.

Singapore female students have shown that they are capable of doing well academically and thriving in this meritocracy environment. Their good performance can be shown in the number of female graduates at universities, polytechnics and institutes of technical education (ITE). There were more female than male graduates in higher education in 2001 (see Table 6.1).

As such, the statement was not unfounded when the executive director of the Singapore National Employers' Federation mentioned during our interview (see Appendix 6.2) that employers generally recognize the fact that Singaporean female employees are academically well prepared for their careers.

Graduation rates do not reveal the major gender difference in education in Singapore however: the difference in fields of study. Females, still

Table 6.1   Higher education in Singapore in 2001 and 2000

	Year 2001			Year 2000		
	Enrollment by institution	Female	Male	Enrollment by institution	Female	Male
Universities (NUS/NTU)	9 586	4 492	5 094	9 244	4 391	4 853
Polytechnics	14 936	7 695	7 241	14 059	7 349	6 710
ITEs	7 208	4 724	2 484	7 650	5 221	2 429

Courses year 2000	Enrollment by major	Female		Male	
Total	35 816	17 564		18 252	
Accountancy	2 282	1 567	(68.7%)	715	(31.3%)
Arch. & BEM2	1 337	792	(59.2%)	545	(40.8%)
Arts	6 542	4 808	(73.5%)	1 734	(26.5%)
Business	3 447	2 381	(69.1%)	1 066	(30.9%)
Computing	3 467	1 114	(32.1%)	2 353	(67.9%)
Dentistry	139	56	(40.3%)	83	(59.7%)
Engineering	13 095	3 507	(26.8%)	9 588	(73.2%)
Law	598	350	(58.5%)	248	(41.5%)
Medicine	947	336	(35.5%)	611	(64.5%)
Pharmacy	289	223	(77.2%)	66	(22.8%)
Science	3 673	2 430	(66.2%)	1 243	(33.8%)

Source: Ministry of Education (2003), Singapore website, http://www1.moe.edu.sg/esd/index.htm.

traditionally viewed as homemakers, are generally characterized as supportive, sensitive and more emotional beings compared to their male counterparts; thus occupations involving the nurturing and caring for others, such as teaching and nursing, are believed to be more suited to females (Brown and Brooks, 1990). This stereotype has influenced many women to pursue educational preparation for careers that serve others.

The percentage of women enrolled in technical subjects, such as engineering, is generally lower than that of men. This is further substantiated by studies on the social progress of Singaporean women carried out by the Department of Statistics, suggesting that female tertiary students tend to major in non-technical subjects (Chew et al., 2002) So far, business administration, accounting, and arts and social sciences courses have seen the highest number of female undergraduates (see Table 6.1).

EMPLOYMENT EXPERIENCES OF WOMEN

Gender differences in major fields of education persist in gender differences in occupations. As shown in Table 6.2, the latest labor release by the Ministry of Labor revealed that a significantly larger number of females were present in industries such as community, social and personal services and service industries, and in service occupations.

In the past, professional and senior positions were male-dominated since most females did not have the opportunity to attend school. In the present day however, education is available to both males and females, and with the meritocracy system adopted by the government, a female with the right educational qualifications, experience and willingness to work can also climb the corporate ladder.

Although occupations like managers and senior officials are still largely male-dominated, the proportion of working women in highly skilled knowledge-intensive occupations such as professional and managerial posts has seen a steady rise, registering up to a threefold increase during the 1990s (see Table 6.3).

A glass ceiling still exists for women in organizations. This is expressed by some female employees who hold senior management positions in private firms in Singapore. They reported that a 'male corporate agenda' does exist. However a contrary view is held by some women in the government sector. Hence the glass ceiling for women in Singapore varies across organizations. This bias against women was in most cases attributed to the belief that women would be bound by family commitments, and so career development opportunities would not be made available or would not be accepted when offered. The encouragement of family-friendly practices by

Table 6.2   Persons employed in Singapore by industry, occupation and gender, 2002*

Industry	June 2002		
	Total	Male	Female
Manufacturing	367 600	229 700	137 900
Construction	119 100	102 100	17 000
Wholesale and retail trade	304 400	173 800	130 600
Hotels and restaurants	125 300	62 600	62 700
Transport, storage and communications	218 800	165 300	53 500
Financial intermediation	107 900	44 700	63 200
Real estate, renting and business services	237 400	132 700	104 700
Community, social and personal services	518 700	211 900	306 700
Others	18 400	14 400	4 000

Source: Department of Statistics (2002a).

Occupation	June 2002		
	Total	Male	Female
Legislators, senior officials and managers	268 800	199 500	69 300
Professionals	231 600	140 100	91 500
Technicians and associate professionals	339 700	184 600	155 100
Clerical workers	270 900	59 800	211 100
Service workers, shop and market sales workers	228 300	130 400	97 900
Production craftsmen and related workers	130 400	120 000	10 400
Plant and machine operators and assemblers	208 500	153 700	54 800
Cleaners, laborers and related workers	265 900	77 000	188 900
Others	73 200	71 900	1 300

Note: *Age 15 and over.

Source: Department of Statistics (2002b).

*Table 6.3   Occupation of employed women in Singapore, selected years**

Occupation	1991	1992	1993	1994	1996	1997	1998	1999	2001
Total	606 521	631 818	639 726	662 199	724 523	749 446	780 135	793 531	898 014
Managers, proprietors and senior officials	21 580	25 335	28 228	31 808	43 329	50 749	48 992	50 057	67 447
Professionals	36 201	40 648	44 532	48 326	58 716	69 370	77 174	77 919	96 007
Technicians	69 799	79 922	82 610	92 596	121 232	120 366	136 020	141 747	96 007
Clerical	167 640	170 598	173 064	181 232	201 408	212 966	215 168	206 055	214 046
Service/sales	88 367	89 279	89 497	95 549	100 480	101 480	104 331	110 572	106 329
Production crafts	19 124	15 462	14 144	13 988	10 506	12 973	12 967	12 534	9 883
Machine operators	119 304	116 497	108 674	97 367	87 356	79 138	58 424	72 051	59 852
Cleaners, laborers etc.	83 513	92 377	97 372	99 671	99 921	100 821	115 327	125 740	188 281
Others	994	1 701	1 606	1 623	1 585	1 793	1 734	1 958	2 124

Note: *Age 15 and over.

Source: Ministry of Manpower (2003), Research and Statistics Department, Singapore.

the government would alleviate family commitments in some ways and would help to improve women's career development prospects. Currently there are insufficient opportunities to create equal participation of men and women in top management posts.

COMBINING EMPLOYMENT AND FAMILY ROLES

Regardless of the direction of causality, an analysis of the female labor force participation (LFP) rates and fertility rates in Singapore shows an inverse relationship between the two variables (see Table 6.4).

We examined the effects of government policy, domestic and international organizational practices, individual choices and Singaporean social customs on the way Singapore women behave to combine employment and childrearing.

Government Policies

Government initiatives aimed at reducing the impact of family events such as marriage, pregnancy and childbirth may have a positive influence on women's career development. The government has provided many family incentives,

Table 6.4   Female labor force participation rates and births in Singapore

Year	Female labor force participation rate	Fertility rates per female
1990	48.4%	1.75
1995	51.5%	1.70
1999	52.7%	1.49
2001	54.3%	1.22
2002	53.4%	1.23

Age of mother at first, second and third births in years*

	All	First	Second	Third
1980	27.1	25.3	27.6	29.4
1990	29.3	27.5	29.8	32.1
2000	30.6	28.4	31.3	33.3

Note: *Age 15 or over.

Source: The Ministry of Education (2003), Singapore website,
http://www1.moe.edu.sg/esd/index.htm.

schemes and programs beneficial for working women. The Singapore government's fertility policy has been successful in decreasing the fertility rate in Singapore during the 1980s and 1990s. However since 20 August 2001, a change in government policy to encourage women to have more children through its new pro-natalist fertility policies may be contradicting the objective of other policies to help boost women's career development and ease their dual role conflict. Table 6.4 also shows that a trade-off between lower fertility rates and higher female labor force participation rates continued to exist in the 1990s. The decreasing female participation rate could be due to the fact that with fewer children, the family responsibilities born by women are reduced, thereby encouraging more women to join the workforce.

The availability of childcare options affects a woman's desire to continue developing her career. In fact, childcare is the second most common reason why women were not working in Singapore (after not getting the job they want). As the female labor force participation rate of married women has risen from 40 to 50 percent during the 1990s in Singapore, childcare has become a more prevalent issue for working women who want to develop their careers (Ministry of Manpower, 1999).

The government allows the recent baby bonus, the incentive to encourage higher fertility, to be utilized in the payment to childcare facilities. As of 1999 however, only 1.4 percent of private establishments in Singapore are providing childcare benefits, showing that private entrepreneurial childcare organizations in Singapore are still not willing to be supportive in this area (Department of Statistics, 1999).

The government has been proactive in providing assistance in childcare. Over 440 government-supported childcare centers are available all over the island. Apart from being the provider of childcare facilities through the People's Action Party education centers, grants and tax incentives are given by the Ministry of Community Development and Sports to employers to house crèches within the organizations as a family-friendly practice. Provision of capital grants to employers who set up childcare centers at their workplace not only helps to alleviate the worries of working mothers, but also motivates a working mother to return to work sooner.

The government also has policies to encourage more available childcare at home. Priority is given to applicants of Housing and Development Board flats who want to stay with their aged parents. Together with the provision of tax relief for aged parents and grandparents under the Income Tax Act, these serve to encourage the three-generation family structure. A direct consequence of this is to present grandparents as obvious available caregivers for the children while the parents are working.

The government has also provided legislative protection for women in terms of maternity benefits and employment security, as outlined in Part IX

Maternity Protection and Benefits of the Employment Act. Mothers are entitled to eight weeks of paid maternity leave, and lay-off protection is rendered with a clause to prohibit employers from dismissing any employee who has been away from work during her eight weeks of maternity leave. This not only gives confidence to working mothers in their ability to retain their jobs, but also sets their minds at ease, allowing them to take on the role of mother without having to worry about losing their career options.

Another important childcare benefit mentioned by 30 women respondents interviewed is that in the government sector, mothers are allowed to take up to six days a year, full-pay unrecorded leave to look after a sick child who is below six years old. By easing their burden, these mothers will be less deterred from wanting to develop a career since they know that the organizations will be supportive if they need to excuse themselves from work.

Government policies that affect women's employment are not confined to childcare. The meritocracy system is reinforced in the area of employment by the existence of an anti-discriminatory recruitment environment that the government wants to create. The Penal Code provides for this by prohibiting racial and ethnic discrimination in recruitment advertisements. Although gender discrimination is not specifically prohibited, there is an implication that the government intends to prevent discriminatory employment practices (see Appendix 6.3 for the Penal Code). Perhaps adding gender as another type of prohibited discrimination is an area the government should consider improving, in order to have a greater direct impact on improving the career development opportunities of women.

The government's announcement to increase the retirement age from 60 to 62 may also have a large impact on the career plans many women have. A woman may decide to lengthen her stay in the workforce if she sees this announcement as positive news.

Organizational Policies

Some government policies influence organizational policies that assist women's career development. Organizations create employment and benefit policies that have an impact on women's careers. The government encouragement of family-friendly workplace practices to be adopted by organizations may well be a driving force behind the career development of married women.

Flexitime
Flexible work arrangements are still relatively new in Singapore, with only 3 percent of the workforce being on part-time employment while 1.5 percent are on temporary work arrangements and less than 1 percent are

on flexitime arrangements. Women who want to return to work see flexible work arrangements as a form of encouragement for them to do so (Ministry of Manpower, 1995). The respondents in our women's survey have also listed flexible work arrangements as a way to encourage more women to move up the corporate ladder. As such, this is an area of impact that the government exerts on the career development of women.

Family-friendly employment policies

Most noteworthy is the recent establishment of a government unit, the Work–Life Unit of the Ministry of Community Development and Sports (MCDS), that specializes in advocating family-friendly workplaces. The potential of this government involvement is to improve workplace environments through promoting family-friendly practices, which helps women enhance their career development. A list of the practices they advocate includes the following (Singapore Ministry of Community Development and Sports, 2002):

- maternity and paternity leave (paid or unpaid)
- leave to look after sick child/spouse/parents
- flexible benefits package
- medical coverage for dependants
- insurance for family members
- on-site childcare/other child arrangements or subsidies
- scholarships/educational assistance for dependants
- eldercare subsidies
- talks/seminars/para-counseling on family issues
- flexitime
- permanent part-time
- flexi-place
- home working
- telecommuting
- job-sharing
- gradual return from work after childbirth
- temporary work.

Globalization

Globalization is a great development opportunity for a small country like Singapore, given the size and constraints of its domestic markets. However with globalization, employees of corporations are sent abroad to oversee operations or build company foundations. When employees are sent on overseas assignments, they usually spend approximately two to five years abroad, and in most cases their families remain in Singapore either by choice or because no provisions are made for them to follow.

Corporations generally give equal opportunities for overseas assignments to both male and female employees. However more male employees accept such overseas postings. Such decisions involve more considerations when a female decides whether she should accept the opportunity. In our interviews with some employers we found that timing and family commitments are usually the common reasons why female employees decline such opportunities. This is supported in a Chew and Zhu (2002) study that found family concerns rank as the most important reason when respondents decide to accept or reject an international assignment. They are more willing to take up an international assignment if the host country provides a good environment, including educational and health facilities for themselves and their family members.

If an organization is not prepared to provide family support in countries where no government support is available, this may be one reason why women will decline these advancement opportunities and men will decline to have their family accompany them. Either of these alternatives may result in negative consequences for the organization. First, the organization may lose the talents of female or male managers it has been training for a period of time, if they decline the transfer because it means familial separation. Second, it may reduce the effectiveness of male or female managers who operate abroad without the support of their family.

As globalization becomes essential so that Singapore can continue to survive and prosper in the world, a socio-economic dilemma arises. The dilemma for women as well as men is posed when they have to choose between career advancement and being with their family. For the government it is a choice between further economic development and keeping family members together.

Individual Family and Career Choices

In most Asian countries where filial piety comes into play in most hierarchical family structures, working mothers are caught between work obligations and obligations of having to raise children and support their elderly or retired parents. This imposes a heavy burden on Singapore women since in both Western and Asian countries parental roles for men and women differ, with the mother's role requiring more time and effort (Larwood, 1983; Greenhaus, 1987).

According to the current norms and practices of mothers in Singapore, each child born means a higher maternal commitment to the family for at least the formative years of the young child, usually a two- to three-year period. This affects the shape and course of the mother's career development. From our interviews with women we found that most of them would give up work for family when necessary. The majority of women said they would make a compromise by allowing disruptions in their career development due to childbirth, or by putting less effort into their careers.

For working mothers the juggling of multiple roles poses a problem they must overcome through individual decisions and effort. This is further complicated by high levels of job involvement common among professional and managerial women. High job involvement can cause stress, anxiety and health complaints, resulting in trading off family commitments in favor of job commitments (Brown, 1996).

Singapore women have been getting married and giving birth at an increasingly older age (Department of Statistics, 1995). This is despite the government's efforts to encourage them to marry and have children early. Also, women holding managerial posts are less likely to get married as compared to their male counterparts. This decision to postpone or renounce family matters in order to begin a career is a compromise that more educated women are willing to make.

With the cost and standard of living rising rapidly in Singapore, dual-career family structures have surfaced because of economic necessity, more than out of individual career choice. As a result of conflicting interests, many women have chosen to remain single or to be married with no children. At the other extreme, those with high qualifications may choose to give up their careers altogether or take up less stressful positions so as to give more time to their families.

These common choices do not have a basis in empirical reality however. Chew and Liao (1999) have shown that being married and having children do not necessarily imply that a woman's career path will not be as good as the career paths of women who are single or are married without children. In fact marriage and parenthood were found to benefit managerial career paths. Hence there is no need for managerial women to sacrifice their family lives for career advancement. This finding supports the government's policy to encourage singles to get married, and to have at least three children early in their lives.

Those who interrupt their careers to start a family may also find themselves plagued with other worries. When married women leave the workforce to fulfill family commitments for childrearing, they may find the skills they have acquired before are obsolete; or they may have lost out to their male counterparts in terms of better promotion and job prospects, due to their lack of work experience. Employers may view gaps in work history as a signal that such events would occur again, thus being less willing to hire them (Wells, 2001; O'Connor, 2001).

Government policy can have a different impact at different ages and life stages. The government's impact through its influence on timing issues, specifically the timing of marriages and childbearing, has been limited; however the postponement of childbearing increases the potential effect of family-friendly government policies on women's careers. If a woman is young when her children are young, she may consider herself to be still young enough to decide to leave the workforce for a while. She may want to sacrifice her career to a greater extent than a woman who is relatively older who has young children. While the government's assistance in the area of childcare support is available to both women, the impact of the assistance will be greater on the career development of the older woman who feels less able to stay home with her children without jeopardizing her career.

Maids as Surrogate Mothers

One solution that Singaporean women have chosen is to rely on paid house-hold help. Singaporean professional families often employ foreign maids to assume the duties of homemakers, child-minders and sometimes care-givers. They may reduce some of a woman's home duties. However most mothers are concerned that their children may end up being closer to the maids than to themselves, or that their children may not acquire Chinese family values. Given an employee–employer relationship between a maid and a child, it may be difficult for maids to take up the role of disciplinarian. When children cease to be close to their parents and when parents may not be available to discipline children, family problems, poor discipline and other youth problems may become commonplace. For the mother and the father who are unable to have a cohesive family, morale and performance at work might be affected.

Maids may be viewed as surrogate mothers when they seem to act as a replacement or substitute when mothers go to work. The maid carries out the duties that a mother would have to do, like feeding the child, or sending and fetching the child to and from school. Some mothers fear that a young child may become confused about who the maid really is, since she seems to be carrying out duties of a maternal nature.

Foreign maids may have a very different culture, beliefs and value system. By spending a lot of time with their employer's children, a maid may incul-cate these foreign values and belief systems in Singaporean children. Thus a key women's career issue for Singapore is whether the society is ready for the introduction of a foreign culture and value system into the society, when this may not be in harmony with the values of Singapore.

One alternative to hiring foreign maids is to support childcare by other relatives such as grandparents. If this solution is desired, the government's three-tier generation flat selection scheme should be supported. This scheme allows priority when applying for flats to adults who want to stay with their parents. Grandparents could then help to take care of household responsibilities, allowing their adult children to devote more time to their careers. In this respect, the government could continue to grant more perks to encourage these three-tier generations to stay near one another (that is, within short distances).

CONCLUSIONS AND RECOMMENDATIONS

With a significant percentage of women joining the workforce, it is essential that the factors affecting the career development of women be understood and not taken lightly. As the society changes, conventional thoughts about the roles of women have to be shed and be made relevant to the world as it is today. Barriers that hinder women's career development need to be overcome and necessary changes have to be made.

A major problem we encountered was the lack of relevant Singapore statistics. Most statistics available were not in a form that was suitable for our study, since they have been generated for other study purposes. Some of the statistics available were too out of date. Hence we were unable to gain an up-to-date perspective of the Singapore situation. The interviews that we did had a sample size of 30 Singapore working women. Statistically the sample size may be too small for it to be representative of Singapore women at large. However because the objective of our interviews is largely qualitative, and our aim is to gather feedback from the women themselves, the interviews have provided us with great insight into the lives of Singapore women.

This chapter has highlighted the contributions made by the Singapore government to aid the career development of Singapore women, but there is still more to be done. From the observations and analysis of our study coupled with the feedback we obtained from the qualitative survey, we have identified various areas where the government can consider having a greater positive impact on the career development of Singapore women. Legislation should be updated, and working mothers should be given greater protection to lighten their financial and emotional burdens. The implementation of more family-friendly policies or the provision of incentives for women re-entering the workforce should be encouraged.

At this moment, family-friendly work practices are largely limited to the public sector. Most small and medium-sized enterprises and other private companies have yet to adopt practices such as flexitime, telecommuting, leave flexibility, unpaid leave and the five-day workweek. To internalize such practices would be to encourage the private sector also to adopt such practices to help women develop their careers and cope with their families. Besides implementing incentives or awards for encouragement, the government also can try to provide consultation services to the private sector to begin and maintain these practices.

Before the government can encourage more women to develop a career, they need to understand exactly what factors may be holding them back and implement initiatives targeting those concerns. Training and development is essential for career development. The most direct ways to help women develop their careers would be to encourage more of them to upgrade their skills and qualifications and to consider technical career options. For example incentives or subsidies can be given to companies who are sending a large percentage of their female employees for training or retraining. Perhaps the government can also encourage companies to arrange more of their training courses during office hours, such that it would be easier for women to attend them.

Formal or informal education can be introduced for women starting from post-secondary level to educate them on the social roles that they would have to play in the future. This would help them cope better with the dual-role conflict that is to come. Of course such education should not be limited to women, as the men would also play a pivotal role in balancing the work–family demands.

From our research, we realize that the government already has many incentives in place to help women cope with work and family demands and hence career development. However the government also needs to increase women's awareness of such incentives as well as educate them on how they can take advantage of such incentives. The government also must realize the contradictory effects of a policy that encourages increased childbearing, yet fails to provide childcare for every child on the island. At present there are more than 400 childcare centers in Singapore. What is lacking perhaps is not only the quantity of such facilities but also the quality. Better facilities as well as well-trained and well-paid professionals can increase the quality of such facilities. The government could work on training a group of childcare professionals and improve the image of this profession, as in Nordic countries, where childcare is regarded as important work. This mindset can also be instilled in the eyes of Singaporeans to increase the quality of such services. The quality of childcare facilities can also be provided through having them located more conveniently, that is, near the workplace.

An important question that we are considering is whether government initiatives will continue to yield great impact in the future. We have concluded that it would depend on the mindset of the future generations of

Singapore mothers. One possibility would be that future mothers might become so accustomed to having government support that they develop a dependency on the government. Another alternative could be that with higher education, women might no longer take to the paternalistic style of government and may decide to take control over their career development on their own. In this case the government initiatives would cease to have any significant impact.

Through our research, we have observed that the government has taken a significant role to affect female career development in Singapore. Though there may be areas they can do more to facilitate women's development, we believe that the government can only work to create an environment and infrastructure to make it conducive for women to develop their careers. Furthermore it may also be the government's intention to maintain the minimum pressure of the dual-role conflict so as to prevent a dependency syndrome in Singapore women.

The Singapore government is unique in that it adopts a paternalistic role. As such, it can influence Singaporean family lives. Its policies aim to lead the nation toward a direction it deems suitable and beneficial to the nation. However there are limits to the extent these policies can influence family decisions. If the Singapore government desires to influence these choices, it will need to provide the environment and infrastructure that would encourage citizens to move along the direction they propose for the nation as a whole. Policies implemented will have to take the form of incentives rather than punitive measures for the Singapore government to achieve its objectives effectively.

REFERENCES

Brown, D. and L. Brooks (1990), *Career Choice and Development: Applying Contemporary Theories to Practice*, San Francisco, CA: Jossey Bass.

Brown, S.P. (1996), 'A meta-analysis and review of organizational research on job involvement', *Psychological Bulletin*, **120** (2), 235–55.

Chew, I.K.H. and Z. Liao (1999), 'Family structures on income and career satisfaction of managers in Singapore', *Journal of Management Development*, **18** (5), 464–76.

Chew, I.K.H. and W.C. Zhu (2002), 'Factors influencing Singapore managers' career aspiration in international assignments', *Career Development International*, **7** (2), 96–108.

Chew, I.K.H., H. Halim and T. Matsui (2002), 'Gender differences in career self-efficacy in Singapore', *Australian Journal of Career Development*, **11** (2), 30–37.

Department of Statistics (1995), *Statistics on Marriages and Divorces*, Singapore: Government of Singapore.

Department of Statistics (1999), *Yearbook of Manpower Statistics*, Singapore: Government of Singapore.

Department of Statistics (2001), *Yearbook of Statistics*, Singapore: Government of Singapore.

Department of Statistics (2002a), Singapore: Government of Singapore, http://www.singstat.gov.sg/keystats/economy.html#labour.

Department of Statistics (2002b), Singapore: Government of Singapore, http://www.singstat.gov.sg/keystats/mqstats/ess/aesa24.pdf.

Greenhaus, J.H. (1987), *Career Management*, Fort Worth, TX: Dryden Press.

Larwood, L. (1983), 'Career strategies and success in fourteen corporations', Academy of Management Annual Meeting, Dallas, TX.

Ministry of Education (2003), Singapore website, http://www1.moe.edu.sg/esd/index.htm.

Ministry of Manpower (1995), *Women Returning to Work*, Singapore: Manpower Research and Statistics Department, Government of Singapore.

Ministry of Manpower (1999), *The Labor Force Survey of Singapore*, Singapore: Manpower Research and Statistics Department, Government of Singapore.

Ministry of Manpower (2000), 'Flexible work arrangements', occasional paper 1/99, November, Singapore: Singapore Manpower Research and Statistics Department.

Ministry of Manpower (2002), 'Conditions of employment', occasional paper 3/200, Singapore: Manpower Research and Statistics Department.

Ministry of Manpower (2003) *Yearbook of Statistics*, Singapore: Manpower Research and Statistics Department.

O'Connor, V.J. (2001), 'Women and men in senior management: a different needs hypothesis', *Women in Management*, **16** (8), 400–404.

Singapore Ministry of Community Development and Sports (2002), *Handbook on Making Your Workplace Family Friendly*, 2nd edn, Singapore: Family Development Division, Government of Singapore.

Wells, S.J. (2001), 'A female executive is hard to find', *HR Magazine*, **46** (6), 40–46.

APPENDIX 6.1   QUESTIONS AND RESULTS OF FACE-TO-FACE SURVEY

Self-concept

1. Do you see yourself more as (a) a wife and/or mother (homemaker), or (b) a career woman?

Career woman	2	(6.67%)
Wife	3	(10.00%)
Mother (homemaker)	2	(6.67%)
Wife, mother (homemaker), career woman	14	(46.67%)
Wife and mother	9	(30.00%)

2. Would you be willing to give up your work for your family, or your family for your work?

Give up work for family	30	(100%)
Give up family for work	–	

3. Do you want to develop your career or are you satisfied with where you are right now?

Satisfied with where I am now, I'll just stay put	11	(36.67%)
There is room for development	2	(6.67%)
Would like to gain more learning experience	1	(3.33%)
I wish to develop my career further	16	(53.33%)

Career Preparedness

1. Has your academic qualification affected your desire to move up the corporate ladder?

Yes. Kind-of	2	(6.67%)
Yes	8	(26.67%)
Yes. Very much affected	1	(3.33%)
Not really	3	(10.00%)
Maybe, somewhat	3	(10.00%)
No	13	(43.33%)

2. Do you want to improve your current skills or qualifications? Why?

Yes.	20	(66.67%)

    – To open up more career opportunities.

– To adjust to the changes. Stay relevant.
– Improve my skills to upgrade myself to be
  a better person.
– For personal development and satisfaction.
– Improve my skills to upgrade myself to meet
  the demand of the competition with
  younger generation.

No.   10   (33.33)%

– Not at this moment due to family commitment.
– It's too late.
– No unless necessary.

Opportunities Available in Society

1. Do you think society is supportive of women having careers?

Generally ok, not discouraging, but does not offer much help/support.	1	(3.33%)
Yes	13	(43.33%)
No	8	(26.67%)
Yes, to a certain extent, not full support	5	(16.67%)

2. Do you think gender has a part to play in determining one's chances of promotion in your company/ organization?

Yes	10	(33.33%)
Not Sure	2	(6.67%)
No	15	(50.00%)

3. If you leave your current position, do you think it would be possible to rejoin the workforce in the same position (i.e. similar remuneration and job scope) later on?
    Why?

    Yes.   15   (50.00%)

    – It's easy to find a job in Singapore.
    – Yes, but not the same pay because of age factor.
    – Job-scope is standard and not age sensitive.
    – Yes, because of her experience which is an
      important factor.
    – Yes if we upgrade our skills and knowledge
      because we are going into a phase called
      knowledge based economy.

Maybe	5	(16.67%)

Because of my specialized skills and
good performance.
It depends on the economy and how well
the industry is doing.

No.	10	(33.33%)

– Cannot catch up.
– Because of competition

Influence of Marriage, Pregnancy and Childbirth

1. Would you delay your marriage and childbirth in order to develop your career?

Maybe	2	(6.67%)
No	22	(73.33%)
Depends on my age	2	(6.67%)
Yes	4	(13.33%)

2. Did getting married/ having children affect your work life in any way?

Yes – half the time is devoted to the children (1 person said)	19	(63.33%)
Not applicable	5	(16.67%)
No	6	(20.00%)

3. If given a choice, would you stop work to take care of your children/ family? Why?

Yes	21	(70.00%)

– Family is my top priority. We can come out
  to work when children have grown up.
  I want more time with my family.
– If it is necessary. If not, I would avoid doing this.
– I will work part-time.

No	9	(30.00%)

– Not for me because my children have grown up.
– Parents taking care of children.

4. Is your family supportive of you having a career?

Yes	26	(86.67%)

– Because we needed the money. But my
  children were not when they were younger.

– But not now because my children are young.

No   4   (13.33%)

Impact of the Government

1. Do you think the government has played any role in your career development thus far?

No	8	(26.67%)
Not sure	2	(6.67%)
Don't think so	2	(6.67%)
Yes	18	(60.00%)

2. It is reported in a survey that very few women hold senior management positions in companies in Singapore. Why do you think this is so?

    - There are many to choose from and because they tend to think that women are more interested in caring for the family than in their careers. Only women who are very smart and able to devote all their time (whether married or single) to the companies are considered. These are few in number.
    - Not given a chance at all!
    - They focus more on family than progressing in corporate ladder.
    - Because it is difficult for women to juggle work and family.
    - They have to think about work and family.
    - There aren't that many professional working women maybe 30 years ago, for enough women to achieve senior management positions vs. men. Also, women have additional roles and responsibilities of being homemaker, and most do not have the support rendered by family or society to be able to build a successful career, and simultaneously maintaining a family.
    - Because of their family commitment.
    - No, it is based on meritocracy.
    - Have to sacrifice to make time for family (two responses).
    - Traditional mindsets that men should be leaders in the organizations.
    - Women's innate nature to put family first.
    - Less energy as they grow older.
    - Glass ceiling exists.
    - Husbands prefer them to not have a job.
    - Difficult to juggle both.

3. How do you think the government can encourage more women to move up the corporate ladder?

- Provide more childcare centers, income tax rebate, flexible working hours, telecommuting.
- Training and upgrade courses should be arranged to be held during office hours so they will be options open to them.
- Let them work at home.
- Shorten working hours or days for women or let them apply half day work until the child reaches secondary four age (at present, only can apply if your child is below six).
- Sponsor more companies to open up child-care centers at the workplace.
- Flexi work arrangement. Be more sympathetic to their need to care for the family.
- By providing more benefits for working women with families, in terms of health benefits, childcare facilities, paid leave etc.
- Sponsorship for higher learning for professionals.
- Less stressful education system.
- 24 hour childcare service when parents are out-stationed.
- Extend flexi-work to private sector.
- No pay leave.
- Five-day work week.
- After-school care (retired teachers).
- See contradiction in objectives.
- Increase maternity leave to three months paid and another three months unpaid.
- Housing application for parents to stay near them.
- Compulsory pensions to encourage to work longer.
- Provide career planning.
- Decrease maid levy.
- Find out the reasons for hesitation first.

Demographics

1. Age

20–24	3	40–44	4
25–29	5	45–49	8
30–34	6	50–54	2
35–39	2	55–59	

2. Marital status

    Married   25
    Single   5

3. Number of   Respondents
    Children

    1   7
    2   10
    3   4
    0   9

4. Educational attainment

     0   Primary and below
     0   Lower secondary
     4   Secondary
     7   Post secondary/diploma
    18   College or university degree
     1   Postgraduate degree

5. Occupation

    18   Managers and professionals
     1   Technicians and associate professionals
     6   Clerical workers
     2   Service and sales workers
     0   Production craftsmen, plant and machine operators
     0   Cleaners and laborers
     3   Others

6. Number   Respondents
    of years
    employed

    1–5 years   5
    6–10 years   5
    11–15   5
    16–20   2
    21 or more   8

APPENDIX 6.2   TWO INTERVIEW RESPONSES

Interview Agenda:

1. Introduction of research topic.
2. Objective of interview – to answer the question: 'does the Singapore government have an impact on the career development of working mothers?'
3. Explanation of concerns with respect to women's career development: career preparedness, opportunities available in society, pregnancy and childbirth, childcare.

Executive Director, Singapore National Employers' Federation (SNEF)

1. With respect to career preparedness, that is the kind and quality of education women receive, the kind of information they gather for their careers, their mental and physical preparation, do you think the Singapore education system has done well to prepare women for their careers?

   Yes, too well in fact. Women seem to be quite good at their studies, especially in their languages. The new economy is very suitable for women to establish a career. They are especially good at certain fields, for instance, Human Resource practitioners are mostly women. Employers are satisfied with the Singapore education system. For instance, a survey showed that employers prefer Singapore graduates, followed by British university graduates, Australian university graduates, and finally graduates from the States.

2. Is there anything lacking, which you think the government can do to maybe improve the education system to help women be better prepared for a career?

   Well, I think the education system is already very good in terms of providing technical knowledge. In that aspect, they are rather well prepared already. With regards to mental preparation towards the dual roles women play, it really depends on their individual appreciation of their roles in the society. However, what the government can do is to provide, like a national service that requires female graduates, upon graduation to attend a course to prepare them with their upcoming challenge in life. That is, to pursue a career and maybe to not neglect their other role to find their partner and have children.

3. Are female employees given equal opportunities, taking into consideration the prevalence of globalization, overseas postings, and inter-company exchange programs?

As far as employers are concerned, there are always opportunities given to women as they are very competent. However, it is always the case whereby female employees turn down these opportunities as they put their families first-place. It comes down again to the personal choices they make within their families. It is a family decision. Being an Asian country, the tradition is for men to be the sole breadwinner.

The government may give grants, enact laws to stipulate that employers should send their families overseas with the mother but there are various other considerations like the children's education. There is a limit to what the government can do here.

In fact, the government has done a lot for them already in terms of tax reliefs, paid maternity leave, two months off to give birth.

4. Do employers feel that pregnancy and childbirth will disrupt a woman's career?

Actually, from the employer's standpoint, pregnancy is not a major disruption to a woman's career development. In Singapore, men take leave too for their annual reservist. All men are eligible for National Service every year until they turn 40 for up to 40 days per year. Women only take eight weeks off during the year they are giving birth and they are not pregnant every year! In totality, men take time off their employment more often, and possibly for a longer time than women. Hence, disruption from their career is not a big issue in Singapore.

5. What has the government done for women to address their concern about childcare issues? In what area is the government not doing enough?

I feel the government has done its part to subsidize childcare centers, allow for maids to work in Singapore, give baby bonuses. However, what may be lacking is that there are not enough childcare centers. Also, they should be located at better locations.

6. Where do you think will be a better location then? How about childcare centers at the office building itself?

There are different views to that question of a better location. For instance, some of the feedback we received is that mothers are afraid they may be distracted from their work if the children are too near them. Also, another issue is that hospitals and government institutions like the Ministry of Defense have a large space to build a childcare center. Smaller companies may not have that kind of infrastructure or resources. It may not be feasible. Hence, what the government can do is probably make it cheaper for companies to have a childcare center at locations like town areas where rental is high.

7. From the private sector's point of view, do the government initiatives adequately address the concerns working mothers have with regards to their career development? Has it done enough compared to other countries?

Definitely, it is more than sufficient. However, it is not excessive to other countries. For instance in the States, women may receive longer paid maternity leave, but the society can accept it as they are more developed. Compared to them, we are not there yet in terms of our economic development. Hence, how much the government should do should be parallel to our economic performance too. To spend more on women's welfare, we need to have the money too!

8. Is it fair and appropriate for the government to require organizations to be more family-oriented and family-friendly?

Yes, definitely! It should not be skewed towards feminism but the overall welfare of the family. It affects not just women but men as well. The government would want Singaporeans to have a balanced life and be happy.

Assistant Divisional Director, Labor Relations and Welfare Division, Ministry of Manpower

1. Are there any policies or initiatives by the Ministry of Manpower to help women remain in the workforce during and after childbearing?

Basically we have a provision for the women folk in terms of maternity leave, which is actually four weeks before and after delivery to allow them to recuperate and perhaps take care of their child during this period. At the same time, we have a provision for pregnant women in the workforce preventing them from being sacked during pregnancy. They can actually make an appeal with the Minister if such a situation arises and we will take action to investigate and remedy the situation.

2. Most women actually work part-time so that they can take care of their families at the same time. Does the government have any measures to ensure that part-time working would be rewarding?

Perhaps the issue here is not about making the part-time working experience rewarding but to make sure that part-timers also receive similar benefits, part thereof if not in full. To do this, we actually have in place a set of part-time regulations as part of the Employment Act, which stipulates that a part-time worker working a minimum number of hours will be entitled to the full benefits of a full-time employee. For workers who do not contribute that certain number of man-hours, he or she will be entitled to the benefits on a pro rata basis.

Although these regulations will seem beneficial to largely women, these regulations are essentially gender-blind as they aim to protect the welfare of part-time workers in general.

3. Are there any new policies or initiatives in place to provide for equal opportunities at work?

It has always been the Ministry's aim to provide equal opportunities for all at work and it is not only gender-based. Recently, we had a series of regulations for anti-discrimination job advertisements. For the purpose of recruitment, employers can no longer specify the gender or race preference as long as both man and woman regardless of race can do the job. With respect to age also, these regulations will prevent discrimination as long as we deem the job suitable for workers of all ages.

4. How do you see the government's involvement in career development of Singapore women?

First of all, I need to highlight the point that career development refers largely to issues such as training and development, which are company specific. However, the government actually works on a tripartite basis whereby there is constant feedback between the three parties, employees, employers and the government. This close cooperation will help the government understand the employees as well as the employers to create the suitable policies to cater to the needs of the people.

5. Do you feel that it is necessary for the government to stipulate ratios for the percentage of females and males in the upper levels of management of corporations?

Basically, we always believe in meritocracy and it is always an issue of the best man or woman for the job and not an issue of 'you should be entitled to the job simply because you belong to a particular gender group'. In fact, many others have tried to implement something like [this] but results have not been that favorable. We definitely do not want a case of people occupying certain positions just to make up the numbers.

APPENDIX 6.3   ANTI-DISCRIMINATION PROVISION IN THE PENAL CODE OF SINGAPORE

Article 12:

1. 'All persons are equal before the law and entitled to the equal protection of the law.'
2. '(no) . . . discrimination against citizens of Singapore on the ground only of religion, race, descent or place of birth . . . in the administration of any law relating to . . . the establishment or carrying on of any . . . employment.'

We note that Article 12 does not mention gender as a factor that is used to discriminate against persons seeking employment. However this Article has served to minimize discrimination in the employment market in general.

7. Women's development in Hebei Province, PRC

Yong-Qing Fang

The women's movement has progressed with the world's economic development. The first International Women's Assembly was held in 1975 in Mexico City. The main agenda of the meeting was the shaping of a declaration of equal status for women and a declaration of women's contribution towards peace and development.

This chapter will trace the path from the international declarations of women's rights through the formulation of the national policy of the People's Republic of China, to the adoption of Hebei provincial goals for policy implementation. The chapter will end with a summary of the impact of these policies on the lives of women who live in Hebei Province (see Figure 7.1). It will describe the broad perspective of all rights for women, narrowing to an analysis at the provincial level of the specific impact on women's ability to train for and participate in careers of paid employment.

INTERNATIONAL WOMEN'S RIGHTS

The meeting in Mexico City was the first meeting on the study and discussion of women's development held in the international arena, organized under the auspices of various governments. The major outcome of the 1975 International Women's Assembly was a declaration known as the Mexican Declaration or the World Action Plan for Women's Development. Representatives of the PRC government attended this meeting. The pact was approved during the United Nations meeting on 18 December 1979. On 3 September 1981, after the approval of 20 nations, it became an international pact. As of 1989, ten years after the birth of the pact, nearly 100 nations had agreed to be bound by the pact, the result of over 30 years of hard work by the United Nation Committee on the Status of Women.

The author wishes to thank Zhao Lijuan for her valuable contributions to the collection of data and other materials as well as to the early version of this chapter.

The pact required participating nations to take necessary actions to eliminate all discrimination against women and to guarantee that women receive adequate development and progress in all domains, especially in politics, social affairs, economics and culture. It allowed women to enjoy human rights and basic freedom under the condition of gender equality including: (1) equal rights to education; (2) equal employment opportunities such as equivalent selection of career choices, promotions, job training and retraining, remuneration and incentives for performing the same job; (3) assurance of healthcare and safety, including the right to reproduce through paid maternity leave or leave with equivalent social benefits, assurance of retention of job, tenure and social benefits; (4) political rights including the right to vote and to be candidates in all elections including planning and administrating government policy, eligibility for any position in government and civil service, and participation in grassroots and political activity in non-government organizations. As a participating nation, PRC has affirmed its commitment towards the pact.

The second United Nations Women's Decade pre-meeting was organized in 1980 in Copenhagen, Denmark. The second meeting accelerated realization of the goal of equal development and peace raised during the United Nations Women's Decade. It also summarized the achievements and obstacles faced during the previous five years, and developed action plans for the next five years. The meeting listed women's employment, healthcare and education as important components for women's development. Leading a 23-member delegation to the convention, the vice-chairperson of the National People's Congress and the chairperson of All China Women's Federation (ACWF), Madam Kang Ke Qing signed the pact 'towards elimination of all discriminations against women' at the meeting on behalf of the People's Republic of China.

IMPACT OF THE INTERNATIONAL WOMEN'S MOVEMENT ON PRC

The fourth International Women's Assembly was held in Beijing in 1995. The main agenda was an action approach towards development and peace. Secondary agendas included healthcare, education and employment. The assembly approved the Beijing Declaration, and clearly mapped out a program for women's development.

In 1992 the PRC promoted the Law on the Protection of Women's Rights and Interests. This was followed in 1995 by the Program for the Development of Chinese Women (1995–2000). These legal and policy efforts have been described in Chapter 3 of this volume and they clearly

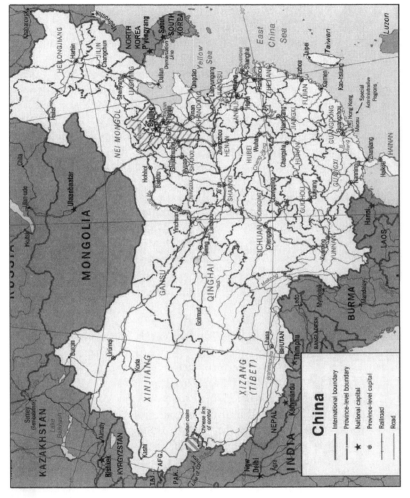

Figure 7.1   People's Republic of China, Hebei Province.

reflected a desire on the part of the PRC to align itself with international standards in this domain.

Although according to the Chinese Constitution, women enjoy equal rights in politics, economics, culture, society and family, the belief that 'men are superior, women are inferior' is still deeply rooted in Chinese society, which is traditionally a male-dominated culture. Attempts to expedite women's development through state laws and government policies have yielded significant results from legislative and policy perspectives; however many problems persist.

When China was transformed from a planned economy to a market economy, the governmental functions were reduced. Enterprises began to possess the power of hiring and firing workers. Profit, cost saving and high efficiency became the first things enterprises pursued. On the other hand, the reduced efficiency and increased medical fees associated with women's reproduction became a burden on the individual enterprises, and many firms hired men instead of women. All of these factors restricted the realization and development of women's rights.

Although not all discrimination could be eliminated instantaneously, analyses and research about women's development will assist in making the policies more complete and more effective. This chapter uses the example of one province to clarify and exemplify how local efforts influence the practical and specific circumstances of women in many parts of the PRC.

HEBEI PROVINCE PRC

Hebei Province covers an area of 187 700 sq km. It has 64 million people, comprising about 5.3 percent of China's population. The people in the province include 54 of the 56 ethnic groups that exist nationwide, including the Han, Hui (Muslims), Man (Manchurians), Menggu (Mongolians), Chaoxian (Koreans) and Zhuang. Hebei Province is made up of mountains, sea coast, rivers, highlands and basins. Surrounding but not including the national capital of Beijing, and extending to Bohai Bay, the province has 11 cities and 138 counties. Hebei provides China with grain, cotton and edible oil. Land suitable for farming spans 6.52 million hectares, making this province the fourth-largest in arable land in China (Bohai Strategic Development Committee, 1996).

In 1995, the same year the International Women Assembly was held in China, the Hebei provincial government drafted the Hebei Women's Development Program, providing a series of quantitative objectives for achieving equality and creating developmental opportunities for women. In 2001, the Hebei government further set 2010 as the target year for accomplishment of the Hebei Women's Development Program. The Hebei govenment extensively studied and analysed the status of women and implemented policies to solve significant problems.

This chapter will analyse the Hebei Women's Development Program and other regulatory documents and local policies in order to study the effect of their implementation on women's development, particularly with respect to women's employment. The areas of study include:

1. Women's education and training (educational rights).
2. Women's career advancement (employment rights).
3. Women's employment situations (employment rights).
4. Working women labor protection (labor protection rights).

The legal basis for these rights is the People's Republic of China's Law on the Protection of Women's Rights and Interests (1992) which advocates gender equality. These rights are seen as interconnected and forming a logical progression that leads to women's equality in the PRC. The right to live promised by law is the most basic and fundamental right women can be offered. Good education is the foundation to economic and political rights for women. Economic rights, in turn, are the assurance for women's independence. Women's development and promotion are dependent on women's political rights, which give women the means to protect their other rights, and are thus rights of a higher level. The various rights are inter-connected, affecting women's status from different angles. All are essential to the development of women in the PRC, and implementation at the provincial level creates the realization of these rights in women's lives.

The Role of Local Law and Government Regulations

Between the establishment of the PRC in 1949 and 1992, the PRC People's Assembly, the state office, the PRC National Women's Committee, the Hebei People's Assembly, the Hebei provincial government and the Hebei Women's Rights Committee implemented over 110 laws, regulations and papers to address the issues of women's rights and development. In 1988, the central government state office announced a Women's Labor Protection Regulation and the Hebei provincial government issued the Hebei Province Women Labor Protection Regulation, giving a set of precise regulations about women labor's safety and protection. In 1994, the Hebei People's Assembly issued the Hebei Province Women's Law. In 1995, the central government state office enacted the Chinese Women's Development Program, an action-based approach to achieve equal development for women, which was a program suitable for China's situation. In 1995 and 1996, the Hebei provincial government implemented the Hebei Women's Development Program. The program focused on legal rights of women, improving the quality of life of women, encouraging women's participation in social and economic development and new problems faced by the women in development process. It institutionalized the rights of women in areas such as politics, careers, education, labor protection, healthcare and human rights (Department of Women's Rights of Women's Association of Hebei, 1995a and 1995b).

To establish a realistic and feasible target system for achieving women's development, the province conducted a survey throughout the government in 1994. The results showed that in the areas possible for promotions for women, the proportion of females was relatively lower than men in all levels of positions in governmental agencies, institutions and enterprises. It was especially lower in the top management levels of enterprises and institutes. Females occupied only 0.2 percent of the total high-level management positions in enterprises, 0.01 percent and 0.04 percent in governmental agencies and institutions respectively (Department of Statistics of Hebei, 2000). Gender discrimination existed in nearly every high-level occupation in females' career development.

In female education and training, there were fewer women at every level of the educational ladder. The same case applied for technical degrees. In Hebei Province there were 160 000 university students in 1994, 43 percent of whom were women. There were 830 000 people with bachelor's degrees, 316 000 (38 percent) of whom were women. There were 614 000 illiterate persons, 444 000 (72 percent) of whom were female. The opportunity to receive vocational training was greater for males than for females. Women were also treated discriminately in *xiagang* and re-employment exercises. *Xiagang* is a unique phenomenon found in China. It refers to workers who, for operational or other organizational reasons, cease to work for a company but still officially remain on its payroll at only a fraction of the original wages (Fang, 1999). Women were not protected fully regarding employment security and there were still problems with the proper execution of the relevant laws and policies to protect women's rights.

One important reason for the inadequate protection of women's rights was that leaders in different levels of administration were not aware of the law and policies. In addition, a large number of women were not aware of the existence of the protective law and policies. They did not know how to protect their rights, nor did they know how to turn to the law when their rights were violated.

Even though some men and women knew gender equality was the law, they would disregard the laws due to their traditional mindset. The conventional opinions that 'an incapable man is better than a capable woman' and beliefs in women's traditional role as 'husband's assistant and son's teacher', as well as the belief that 'a man's success is a woman's honor' were all barriers to the implementation of law and policies.

The third reason for the discrepancy between law and practice was that the existing laws and policies focused on authorizing and forbidding, which caused the Women's Law to be more a source of slogans and less a force for practical actions. The punishment for poor implementation and breaking the law was not harsh. The lack of operational reference and powerful monitoring mechanisms made the relevant laws and policies a toothless tiger.

Target Systems for Women's Development

The Hebei provincial government responded to the findings of the evaluation study of 1992 and to the implementation of the 'women's laws' of 1992 and 1994 and the Women's Program of 1994 with a specific program to provide opportunities for women's development in Hebei Province. In 1995, the government of Hebei Province launched the compelling Hebei Women's Development Program (1995–2000). In this program, 11 objective areas were designed to support the existence and development of women and thorough protection of women's rights. The objectives were to:

1. Strengthen the cultivation and promotion of women leaders and enhance women's involvement in decision making regarding national and social issues.
2. Expand the career fields for women and increase the number of working women.
3. Implement the People's Republic of China Labor Act and the Hebei Women's Labor Protection Regulation with the aim of improving the safety and health levels of female workers.
4. Acknowledge women's valuable contribution to human reproduction, and gradually establish special funds for social assurance for bearing and rearing children and improving the health of mothers and children.
5. Enhance the educational level and quality of education provided to women.
6. Improve the capacity and quality of women's healthcare services so as to enhance women's health level.
7. Protect women's right to reproduce, and provide quality service for their reproductive health to improve the gender-balanced structure of the population and to improve the health quality of the population.
8. Effectively stop criminal acts of violence against and deception of women, including stopping the illegal trade of women, prostitution and trading of brides.

9. Stress and assist the development of women in poor and remote as well as minority areas. Especially, protect underage females and elderly females as well as handicapped females.
10. Improve the social environment for women's survival and development. Enhance the living quality of women.
11. Build a system for monitoring the status of women. Propose timely policies for enhancing women's position; build a women's database in the relevant statistical department, set up a statistical index of gender balance, and provide timely analysis reports addressing gender issues.

This comprehensive system included various fields related to women's development. It created both macro and micro environments for the realization and development of women's rights. Under this framework, there were nearly 30 detailed targets scheduled to be implemented gradually over the years. Every target was delegated to specific persons. In total over 20 governmental departments with 60 offices were involved and a Hebei Women's Rights Committee headed by the provincial governor with the participation of leaders on different levels was set up to direct, check and monitor the implementation and give timely evaluation.

The following analysis will summarize the progress of this committee. It will emphasize targets related to women's training and employment but will also include education and political development.

Not only is political activity an important mechanism for women to influence their rights in other areas, one must remember that in the PRC, political cadre jobs occur in every department of every enterprise, in addition to the huge number of positions in government bureaus and offices. Thus progress toward equality in political positions means progress not only in government but also in employment.

Measures, Action Items and Results

To ensure the successful implementation of the program, the Hebei Provincial Government further issued 'Suggestions regarding the implementation of the plan for women's development in Hebei' which were action items leading to the targets. To ensure the realization of the Hebei Province Women's Development Program, Hebei Province required every department to commit funds and to cooperate and to do their part. There was also a plan for annual assessment of their performance. The Hebei Provincial Statistical Department focused on data collection and ensuring correctness of the data. The target systems and progress of a few selected target areas relevant to women's training and employment are presented below.

Target 1: The Involvement of Women Leaders in Policy Consulting and Making

The proportion of women candidates in all levels of representatives should be no less than 25 percent. The proportion of women members in the Political Conference Committee should be no less than 13.3 percent. The leader teams in all levels, from province, city and county to village, should have at least one women member. At least 50 percent of governmental agencies at the province, city and county levels should have women leaders. The provincial labor office was designated as the responsible unit overseeing implementation.

Specific action items included: to select 1000 women officers to receive training in grassroots organizing every year; to assign 1000 women leaders from grassroots organizations to higher-level positions to receive training; to select 1000 women leaders to receive higher education in cadre training schools or universities; to emphasize cultivating promising women leaders with the aim to give systematic training to 15 000 women leaders within a five-year period.

Progress Toward Target 1

Increase women's participation in politics
In 1999 there were 627 300 women leaders in the province, about 39.5 percent of the total leaders. That was a 33.4 percent increase from 1994 figures. Leadership at specific levels however had not yet reached the 25 percent target. The ninth people's assembly meeting consisted of 120 people, of which 26 (21.6 percent) were women. The ninth provincial political consultancy assembly consisted of 762 people, of which 159 were women (20.87 percent). Women representatives of people's assemblies at the city, county and town level were 21 percent, 22.3 percent and 25.71 percent respectively. There were seven women committee members (22.6 percent) at the ninth national government association meeting, an increase of 12.58 percent from the previous meeting. There were 116 women committee members (15 percent) at the eighth provincial political consultancy assembly, an increase of 1.5 percent from the previous meeting. These women came from difference areas and participated actively at the meeting, and provided many constructive recommendations.

Groom and select women leaders
Under the Hebei Province Five-year Program for Grooming and Selecting Women Leaders, a number of highly qualified women were assigned to various leadership positions to participate in decision making. In 1999

there were 627 300 women leaders in the province (39.5 percent of the total), an increase of 1.4 percent from the previous year. Chinese Communist Party leadership exceeded that of departmental leadership: 100 percent of the city party and county party, 98.6 percent of the town party, 50 percent of province departments, 54.9 percent of city departments and 53 percent of county departments had at least one women leader.

The ability of women workers to manage social issues had increased tremendously. As of the end of 1999, women representatives made up 209 700 (34.4 percent of the total), an increase of 0.6 percent from 1995. There were 187 780 women labor committee members, an increase of 1100 from the previous year. As of 2003 there were 339 950 women leaders in the entire province, most of whom were working at the grassroots level providing timely assistance to other women.

Target 2: Expand Occupational Choices and Employment of Women

The number of women employed in state-owned enterprises (SOEs), collectively owned and foreign direct investment (FDI) enterprises is to increase from 2 005 600 to 2 659 400. The number of women employed in township and village enterprises (TVE) is to increase from 2 117 400 to 3 306 200. Designated departments were provincial labor office and provincial township enterprise offices.

The action items covered the following areas: (1) enforce labor law and increase labor supervision to boost women's re-employment; (2) set up organizations providing complete job introduction, training, employment and information services in all cities and towns in the province; (3) increase job training to increase the technical skills and the overall qualifications of women; (4) develop township enterprises in order to provide women with more employment opportunities; and (5) all cities and counties will implement a reproduction foundation to prevent additional burdens due to women's labor, so as to make the environment more conducive for women's employment.

Progress Toward Target 2

Agriculture sector
In Cangxian County, 360 000 village women who maintained and expanded the country's largest production base for jujubes, a type of date, have also contributed to the local production of poultry and meat products. This is the result of the men going to work away from home at construction sites and industrial firms in towns and cities (*China Daily*, 2002). However some women in the rural areas are not content with their current status in

managing agricultural activities. Some 120 million rural women have taken part in the program of 'Earn more Income through Science and Technology' since 1989 (*China Daily*, 2001).

Non-agricultural industrial sectors

At the end of 1999 there were 32 572 300 women in Hebei Province, about 49.25 percent of the total population. There were 2 143 200 women workers, about 38.02 percent of the total labor force. Of these, 1 638 100 were employed in state-owned enterprises and 266 600 were employed in municipality-run enterprises. In FDI-linked enterprises, the employment figure for women reached 238 500.

Labor departments of every administrative level increased their commitment towards women's employment. This included providing services for job introductions, job training and job information, actively guiding and promoting women's employment, actively developing jobs that meet the characteristics of women, and developing social service and labor service enterprises. In 1999, various departments had trained 80 600 women and successfully created employment for 121 800 women. The labor and employment service industry is gradually moving towards social services, using multiple channels and multiple methods to create employment opportunities for women. By the end of 1999, there were 91 000 registered unemployed women – about 56.2 percent of those unemployed, and about 4.1 percent lower than the previous year.

Actively promote re-employment and welfare of *xiagang* (unemployed)

In 1999, there were 162 260 *xiagang* woman workers in SOEs in Hebei Province. Through re-employment projects, 61 600 women were re-employed, achieving a re-employment rate of 37.9 percent. At the end of 1999 there were 101 000 *xiagang* women, about 48.8 percent of total *xiagang* workers. *Xiagang* women in the province have received some forms of assurance of basic living subsistence. Between 1994 and 1999, unions at all levels have provided services free of charge, 2400 women's training programs have trained over 80 000 people and assisted 8700 *xiagang* women workers.

Professionals

Women professionals have became a prominent force in the Chinese economy. There were 499 200 women professionals in 1999, making up 46.29 percent of the total number of professionals in Hebei Province. Among these women professionals, 28.13 percent were highly skilled professionals. The number of professionals in 1994 is not available so the exact increase or decrease cannot be calculated.

Target 3: Implement the People's Republic of China Labor Act and Hebei Women's Labor Protection Regulation to Improve Job Safety and Healthcare of Women Workers

Improve labor conditions

Protect and ensure safety and health of women workers according to the law. Women's labor protection measure should be implemented in 87.2 percent of the enterprises, and a system of health checks should be implemented in 93 percent of the enterprises. The responsibility was assigned to the Provincial Labor Office, Provincial Health Office and Provincial Main Labor Union.

Action items included: (1) Classify women's labor protection into safety production regulations, perfect enterprise safety and hygiene regulations, and implement regular health checks and treatment for women workers. (2) Enterprises are to set up a washroom, shower room and pregnancy rest room for women employees, are not to put women employees into jobs which may be a hazard to their health, such as underground mining and poisonous environments, and are to provide necessary care and protection for women employees during their menstruation, pregnancy, maternity and breastfeeding periods. (3) Labor departments are to be responsible for supervising the distribution to women of protection gear and equipment. Encourage relevant institutions to conduct research and development.

Progress Toward Target 3

According to information provided by the Provincial Labor Office, many Hebei women's protection activities were systematized and put in place. Of the 1710 enterprises inspected under the women's labor protection regulations, 1314 (76.8 percent) had fully implemented the regulations. The setting up of the 'four rooms' (women's washroom, shower room, changing room and nursing room) required by the regulations was also well under way. The 'four check-ups' (regular physical examinations plus obstetrical examinations) were also widely executed.

Labor agreements are a primary mechanism for protecting women's health and safety rights on the job, as well as providing a major source of general medical care, that lingers in some (but not all) organizations from the previous state system where work units provided for the health of workers. In 1999, 209 700 women attended labor representative meetings – about 34.44 percent of the total attendees, a 0.6 percent increase from 1995. Of the units which signed a collective labor agreement, 92 percent had established women workers' units, 91 percent had included special benefits in the agreement, 75 percent were able to monitor the implementation and 67 percent were able to solve problems that arose. Of those that signed agreements, 89 percent met the standards of the women labor protection and benefits regulations.

Women played an active role in managing labor disputes. There were 13 887 women in labor dispute mediation committees. They handled 2 580 cases and successfully settled 2060 cases at the lower levels, maintaining the benefits of women in labor.

Problems still exist however. For example in Baigou Zhen, Hebei province, famous for baggage manufacturing, the rights of many women workers were seriously violated. The town was the largest baggage processing and sales area in China. It produced 120 million pieces of baggage annually for sale to every part of China and to over 20 countries. Even in a sluggish market in 1998, the economic value of the production of the township enterprises, independent enterprises and privately owned enterprises stood at RMB$1.88 billion. The value of market trade was RMB$5.1 billion, tax revenue was RMB$ 17.59 million and the average income for farmers was RMB$4650.

In September 1998, relatives of nine women workers (aged 18 to 19 years) complained to the provincial women's union that the young workers were made to work with a glue compound in a baggage production factory with no protection. The boss of the factory falsely assured them that it was safe and they just had to get used to it. After about six months a few women were totally paralysed and they were diagnosed to have suffered from prolonged exposure to a toxic substance. In another factory, such abuse had resulted in the death of a worker and left two workers critically ill. Many slightly more fortunate women escaped this terrible fate when they left the jobs due to their ailing health. These cases prove that even with legal protections in place, some women are still not able to benefit from legal equality.

Setting up a women's legal service center
In December 1995, a Women's Legal Service Center was set up in Qianxi County, Hebei. The center provides legal consultations to women whose rights are infringed upon and provides litigation and non-litigation services free of charge (Chen, 1999). Of 400 cases seen in this center between 1995 and 1998, one-third concerned violence against women.

To raise rural women's awareness of their individual rights as citizens, staff at the center looked for ways to take their services to places where rural people go regularly. They decided to open a legal desk (actually a stall) at the main local markets, a public place where people meet once a week to buy and sell goods. At the stall, staff members distribute printed materials on the Law on the Protection of Women's Rights and Interests, and answer queries from rural women regarding the legal implications of divorce, property rights and domestic violence.

Since early 1998, the center has organized a series of activities on violence against women, and also legal training workshops, which are held in the markets every second week. These activities have become extremely popular among rural women, as they can buy and sell goods and learn about their legal rights in areas such as marriage and property at the same time (UNIFEM East and South East Asia, 2001).

Most of these measures target educating women about their legal rights; however such education is still insufficient to encourage these women to exercise their rights. Future additional steps are needed. Publicity of the successful cases of these centers might boost women's confidence and encourage them to seek these centers' help. In addition to educating the female workers about their rights, it is important to educate employers and male co-workers. Such education would be most effective if it aims at changing the traditional mindset that women should remain at home doing domestic chores and not speak up for themselves in the external social arena.

Target 4: Recognizing the Value of Women in Human Reproduction, Implementing a City Worker Reproduction Foundation

The province is keeping pace with the nationwide social assurance reform. The goal of the reform is to convert the old enterprise-based welfare system into a new societal-based social assurance system, and to extend social assurance from SOEs to cover the entire workforce in all industrial sectors. All enterprises need to pay premiums for their employees into the Social Overall Arrangement Funds (SOAF). The provision of the funds also covers women's special needs through the Social Overall Arrangement for the Funds for Women's Parenthood.

Progress Toward Target 4

Since 1995, organizations that participated in the foundation included state-owned, collective, foreign investment, publicly-owned, jointly-owned and privately owned organizations. At the end of 1998, 13 413 reproduction insurance units covered 1.54 million people province-wide and 12 607 women benefited from the insurance scheme. The scheme created the conditions for equal employment opportunities for women by making provisions for assistance for them while pregnant, immediately *post partum* and when nursing.

In October 1994, the system of Social Overall Arrangement Fund for Women's Parenthood was instituted within Qianxi County, under Tangshan City, Hebei Province. A study monitoring its implementation over three years found that the program provided good conditions for assisting women in obtaining employment. Such activities and measures made people in the county pay attention to the implementation of laws and regulations about protecting women's rights and interests, and heightened their consciousness about gender equality (Chen, 1999).

Target 5: Women's Education and Training

Develop women's education, and eliminate illiteracy among young women. Departments responsible for this area were the Provincial Education Commission, Provincial Labor Office, Provincial Personnel Office, Provincial Women Union, and the Provincial Youth League.

Actions to be taken included: (1) Further enforce nine years of compulsory education. (2) Gradually reduce the ratio of educational difference between boys and girls and increase the admission of girls to school. Include this as part of annual performance appraisals of officials. (3) Run the schools in a locally appropriate manner, and reduce or waive the fees for students with special financial difficulties. (4) Broadly mobilize social forces to implement the Hope Project and Spring Bud Plan to bring female school drop-outs back to the school and to control the drop-out rate to about 1 percent. (Project Hope is a nationwide project launched by the China Youth Development Foundation aimed at providing financial assistance for school drop-outs in poverty-stricken areas in China. The Spring Bud Plan is a public service sponsored and organized by the Children's Foundation of China under the leadership of ACWF. Its long-term strategic task is to assist the state to promote nine years of compulsory education and to help girl drop-outs return to school. The program raises funds from China and abroad to set up Spring Bud Classes in China's poor areas). (5) Achieve gender equality and fair competition in the admission exercises of institutes of higher education. Except for the selected areas under state directives that forbid women (for example ocean freighter operation), all professions are not allowed to cite any reasons to reject women's admission or to raise the entry requirements for women. In recruitment no companies or government units shall use any unfair excuse to reject women graduates. (6) Strengthen and improve women's vocational education and job training, and organize and develop professions that are advantageous for women. Open up professional training courses which suit women's characteristics in vocational schools, vocational institutes and labor departments in every city.

Progress Toward Target 5

'Saving a girl who missed the chance to be educated is equivalent to saving a future mother, which in turn is equivalent to saving a family, which in turn is equivalent to saving the entire society.' This common understanding of the importance of women's education has led to the raising of over RMB$ 12 million to aid 23 754 girls who were not in schools, improving the education infrastructure for girls in the province.

In 1995, the school admission rate for girls seven to 12 years old in the province was 99.1 percent, 0.3 percent lower than that of boys. There were about 34 800 girls who were not enrolled in schools, 57.3 percent of the total number of children who were not enrolled. In 1999, the admission rate for girls increased to 99.9 percent and the rate was not different from that of boys. The number of girls who were not enrolled in schools decreased to 4000, a reduction of about 30 800 (9.6 percent) from 1995. Girls made up 47.7 percent of the total number of children who were not enrolled. The drop-out rate for girls has also been diminishing. In 1999 the drop-out rate for girls in the province primary schools decreased to 0.3 percent (14 000 girls), about a 0.27 percent decrease from 1995. The drop-out rate for girls in secondary schools also decreased from 1.9 percent in 1995 to 1.4 percent by 1999.

The campaign against illiteracy also showed results. The campaign focused on primary and secondary schools, as well as schools for adults. In densely populated areas the emphasis was on conducting lessons, while in sparsely populated areas the emphasis was on offering education on the doorstep. Besides education on culture, the campaign also focused on education about law and technology. In 1999, 43 600 cases of illiteracy among young people were eliminated, of which women comprised 70 percent.

Surrounding the strategic implementation of the technological boom, women associations in Hebei organized various learn and compete activities, providing technical training and organizing competitions. In rural areas the government organized a campaign of 'Ten Thousand Technicians, plus One Million Female Farmers, to Apply One Hundred New Technologies'. Nearly 1000 women participants picked up two or three practical skills. In 1999, 37 923 people received some forms of technical training, 27 059 received the green certificate and 9500 women received agriculture technician certificates. That brought the total number of women agriculture technicians to 67 798, an average of one per village, thus reaching the program goals. In cities and townships similar campaigns were also organized, such as 'Ten Industries, One Hundred Positions, One Thousand Star Performers' showcases and skill competition. In 1999, the province organized 6600 job skill competitions. Women won recognition and admiration for their own ability and achievement. The downsizing of state-owned enterprises resulted in more *xiagang* women workers, but many of them are displaying their capabilities in privately owned and publicly listed companies.

Target10: Improve the Social Environment for Women's Development and Improve the Standard of Living of Women

Action items: Achieve 48 percent of all children province-wide attending three-year pre-school (95 percent for city children attending three-year preschool), 97 percent of rural children attending a one-year pre-school. Achieve 85 percent of enterprises that set up a resting and socialization area for women. These measures would help women reduce their housework and childrearing burden and set up women's social support networks.

Progress Toward Target 10

In order to create a more conducive environment for women's development, women need to be liberated from the burdens of household chores. At the end of 1999, there were 5691 childcare centers, higher than the 3372 centers existing in 1995, taking care of a total of 1 175 800 children. In addition, 10 400 social activity facilities and 22 000 residents' service points were set up in the province.

CONCLUSIONS

Facts and figures revealed that the Hebei Women's Development Program had made great progress, even though more work remains to be done before the women of Hebei achieve the goals set forth in the UN proclamations as well as PRC and Hebei Provincial goals. Within the scope of this study, three areas had met their targets while another area stands a good chance of meeting its target. However there were many difficulties and problems.

Difficulties and Obstacles in Realizing the Goals

One consequence of the agricultural program instituted to implement Target 1, of providing employment for women, has been a feminization of agriculture, in which women have been left to do an increasing share of the farm work. Where opportunities for non-agricultural employment have become available, men have been the first to leave agriculture to take up such employment. Thus agriculture has increasingly become the responsibility of women, especially married women. Often these jobs are more suitable to men, such as those in construction, transportation and so on. Leaving home to work in a distant place and unfamiliar environment may also be perceived as safer for men than for women. As a tradition in rural China, men have always been the majority among those who leave their hometown in search of better livelihood for their families and themselves. If this trend continues, it would indicate a relative worsening of rural women's economic capabilities since the agricultural sector typically provides lower incomes than other industry (Summerfield, 1994).

This trend began before the programs described for Hebei Province. Between 1982 and 1987 the concentration of women in agricultural activities increased from 43.69 percent to 44.52 percent (National Bureau of Statistics of China, 1990). The 1990 national census found that women comprised 48 percent of farm workers (Khan and Riskin, 2001). Some variation may be because of reporting differences, but there is a disturbing trend that parallels agricultural projects supporting women's employment. A 1992 study (Xianfang, 1992) showed that women account for 60 to 70 percent of all farm labor; by the mid-1990s, another report claimed that 60 percent of all agricultural labor was performed by women (Jacka, 1997).

In official explanations of the feminization of agriculture, women's responsibility for domestic work is commonly cited as an important factor. One reason why women themselves say they choose to work in agriculture is that it gives them a degree of flexibility in combining their various responsibilities. As one woman explained, 'During harvest or planting, you might have to put in long hours, but you can catch up with the household work in the slack season. It would be hard to keep factory hours and do the rest of the work after' (Jacka, 1997). The seasonality of agricultural work contributes in another way as well. During the slow months in agriculture (October to mid-March) many men emigrated in search of wage labor. Therefore it was the women who became heavily involved in the project's slack season activities such as planting trees, building earth works, digging wells and leveling land, in spite of the obvious physical demands of these activities (*China Daily*, 2002).

A second problem is that the re-employment rate of *xiagang* women workers has decreased. The re-employment rate in 1999 decreased 9.8 percent from 1995, to 37.9 percent. This was due to an increase in the number of *xiagang* women workers, an increase in gender competition, and old beliefs of employing units, all working to limit the area of job search and increasing the difficulty of re-employment for women.

This trend parallels the experience of Chinese workers as a whole, and has not occurred just in Hebei Province. However it provides a pessimistic view of the future if programs such as that in Hebei Province have been unable to keep up with the increasing numbers of workers laid off from closing or streamlining state owned enterprises.

A third problem that came to light in this evaluation is the weak effect of women's labor protection policies in non-state-owned enterprises (Women's Association, Chao Yang District, 2002). In some foreign directly invested (FDI), privately owned or township enterprises, many women do not enjoy the protection offered by law due to employers' poor understanding of the law and their profit-centered goals.

In 1999 there were 1 638 100 women workers in state-owned enterprises, down from 1 854 200 in 1995. In collectively owned enterprises the number decreased from 544 300 to 266 600 in 1995. In privately owned enterprises the number increased from 129 900 to 238 500. The high employment rate in privately owned enterprises accelerated women's development, but also caused some serious problems.

In recent years accidents in independent and township enterprises occurred repeatedly. It appears that the economic revenue of these areas was gained at the price of the lives and health of the women workers (Wu, 1999).

A fourth problem is that the drop-out rate for girls in primary schools and secondary schools has rebounded. In 1999 the drop-out rate in primary schools edged up 0.14 percent. The drop-out rate in secondary schools increased 0.34 percent, higher than that of primary schools. This increase occurred because of economic reasons and traditional beliefs. In rural areas the cost of education has been continually rising, increasing the financial burden of poorer families. Hence many parents have stopped the education of their children. Also many parents believe that education is useless, and this thinking was reinforced by the fact that students found it harder to find a job. In addition many parents believe their child lacks the talent to study, and she should stop education once she has gained some skills. This focus on short-term benefits may be very shortsighted, but persists.

Suggestions and Solutions

Much work still needs to be done to strengthen the work of women's employment and protection of women's rights and safety. At the end of 1999, the number of *xiagang* women workers stood at 101 000, 48.8 percent of the total. To solve this problem, every labor unit will have to take a serious and systematic approach toward the re-employment of *xiagang* workers. All organizations and the media could play a role to educate *xiagang* workers, to change their old beliefs, and to encourage them to seek re-employment actively. At the same time, if women are not to suffer disproportionately from these efforts, there needs to be continued promotion of labor law and women's labor protection and regulations. This will increase the power of the law, especially among joint ventures, township enterprises, independent enterprises and privately owned enterprises that have a different relationship to the PRC central government and which may take these laws less seriously.

To control the loss of primary school and secondary school students, serious educational reform must accompany parental education for the need for education. This reform needs to require schools to better manage their students, improve teaching ideas and methods, and promote the willingness of students to study. There is also a need to adjust the curriculum so that school knowledge is relevant to the local conditions.

There is also is a need to improve awareness of the law requiring compulsory education of girls through grade nine and to inculcate a new belief in the society and the parents. 'Education strengthens the clan, strengthens the country, increases quality, and changes fate' has become quite a well-known slogan in the province. This belief might fall on more fertile ground if efforts were made through various programs and activities to solve the admission difficulties faced by children from poor families. If all of these efforts do not encourage girls to catch up and participate in the educational system, the province needs to offer remedial education to teenagers below 17 years of age who have not completed secondary education.

For all of these difficulties, the PRC and the provincial government clearly needs to protect women's rights actively and to promote women's development. Under the women's development plan for 2000 to 2010, programs are aimed at eliminating specific problems faced by the program through law, government policies and shaping public opinion. In particular it may be possible to work with non-governmental organizations to improve the awareness of women's protection laws. When women are aware of their rights, they may defend them more actively, hence laying the work for future implementation of law and policies.

The evidence from 1978 to the present shows the positive effect on women's development and gender equality of governmental intervention, including implementation and execution of law and policies. This evidence shows that even under market conditions governmental intervention has a positive effect on women's development because of the immaturity of the market mechanism and the presence of market imperfections. After thousands of years of feudal influence, old distorted beliefs persist that men are superior to women, and that men should work and women should care for the household. These beliefs have resulted in distorted expectation in men's minds, bonding women to the kitchens. Under limited resources conditions where benefits are reallocated, women's welfare is often placed behind overall welfare or men's welfare by the invisible hand of the market. China needs to adopt an aggressive approach to stop these gender inequalities in all domains.

The law and government policies, coupled with execution of the right intensity to stop the gender inequality that results from these beliefs, will promote the welfare and development of women. Today's productivity depends on intelligence and knowledge, and this is an advantage to women. The progress of science has weakened the importance of physical strength needed to do many jobs, and thus weakened the average man's advantage. In this respect, women are able to compete on an even ground with men. Facing these opportunities, women must abandon all thoughts that restrict their development, institute 'self-respect, self-emphasis, self-dependence, and self-strengthening', and gain greater development and higher status through knowledge. When women can continue their wide participation in society even without special incentives, then the society will really be equal.

REFERENCES

Bohai Strategic Development Committee (1996), *Perspectives on the Development of the Bohai Bay Area*, Beijing: China Reform Publishing House.

Chen, M.X. (1999), 'From legal to substantive equality: realizing women's rights by action', *Violence Against Women*, 5 (12), 1394–410.

China Daily (2001), 'Chinese women hold up half the sky', 24 August, http://www.china.org.cn/english/2001/Aug/18032.htm.

China Daily (2002), 'Rural women still face inequalities', 1 February, http://www.china.org.cn/english/2002/Feb/26285.htm.

Department of Statistics of Hebei (2000), *Reports on Women's Development*, Shijiazhuang, Hebei: Department of Statistics of Hebei.

Department of Women's Rights of Women's Association of Hebei (1995a), *Blueprint for Chinese Women's Development: A Handbook (1995–2000)*, Shijiazhuang, Hebei: Women's Association of Hebei.

Department of Women's Rights of Women's Association of Hebei (1995b), *Guidelines for Women's Development in Hebei Province: A Handbook (1995–2000)*, Shijiazhuang, Hebei: Women's Association of Hebei.

Fang, Y.Q. (1999), 'Two challenges facing the Bohai Bay region', in J.J. Williams, S.B. Chew, Y. Cao and A.M. Low (eds), *Business Opportunities in Northeastern China*, Singapore: Prentice Hall, pp. 125–32.

Jacka, T. (1997), *Women's Work in Rural China: Change and Continuity in an Era of Reform*, Cambridge: Cambridge University Press.

Khan, A.R. and C. Riskin, (2001), *Inequality and Poverty in China in the Age of Globalization*, New York and Oxford: Oxford University Press.

National Bureau of Statistics of China (1990), *China Statistical Yearbook*, Beijing: China Statistics Press.

Summerfield, G. (1994), 'Economic reform and the employment of Chinese women', *Journal of Economic Issues*, 28 (3), 715.

UNIFEM East and South East Asia (2001), 'Providing legal information to rural markets', 2 November, http://www.unifem-eseasia.org/Resources/EVAWmaterial/VAW-NGO/china.htm#one.

Women's Association, Chao Yang District (2002), 'Women's right in privately owned enterprises cannot be neglected', http://www.cyw.com.cn/rightsview.php?nmid=19.

Wu, M.R. (1999), 'Warning bell from the worker poisoning incident', *Democracy and Law*, **17**, 31–3.

Xianfang, M. (1992), 'Rural females in the labor force transition in China's countryside', in Women's Association of Hebei Province, *Insurance and Benefits for Female Employees*, Shijiazhuang, Hebei: Women's Association of Hebei Province.

PART III

Conclusions

8. Chinese women, half the sky, little ground: comparative comments on Chinese women's lives under various government systems

Cherlyn Skromme Granrose

If we look at the reports from the previous chapters, what can we say about Chinese women at the turn of the twenty-first century? Certainly they are employed in great numbers and work to hold up half the sky, but they do not receive equal wages for their work and they do not hold positions of equal status to men in any of the societies we have examined in this volume. Despite a variety of government efforts and a variety of government systems, there is no system that has been able to overcome the Chinese ancient traditions to value sons over daughters.

In this conclusion I will use the theoretical framework described in the early chapter that highlights national career identity, national career beliefs, national career behavior and national career processes, to give an initial structure to the discussion of how each government system has or has not influenced women's work lives. In order to explain the overall findings in each location, I use both Western theoretical explanations of why gender differences might arise as well as Chinese cultural foundations of Taoism, Confucianism, Buddhism and Legalism.

In the brief review of the Western theories described in Chapter 1, gender role socialization theory posits that gender differences in employment arise because boys and girls are taught early in their lives to prefer different things, and this leads them to select different careers that lead to differences in pay and opportunity. In addition, different gender roles may lead to gender role conflict that may also interfere with employment in a variety of ways (Sullerot, 1971; O'Leary, 1977; Pleck, 1985; Eagly, 1987; Moen, 1992; Geib and Leuptow, 1996). Human capital theory posits that women tend to obtain less education and also tend to leave the labor force for childrearing, thus bringing less human capital to the labor force, and therefore women receive lower lifetime wages and opportunities (Mincer, 1962). The dual labor market theory claims that women select a different range of jobs and occupations that are more compatible with childrearing, but because they tend to be in jobs with lower hours worked or more flexible hours they receive less pay and are offered fewer opportunities (Bosanquet and Doeringer, 1973). Discrimination theories propose that even when all of the differences due to the previous gender-related employment explanations are taken into account, a significant amount of the lower wage and status attainment of women in most occupations and nations remains, and is due to resentment by males and attempts by males to retain a power advantage. By applying each of these explanations to each of the locations described in this volume, we may be able to gain some insight into the processes by which the Chinese culture and the government structures affect the employment of Chinese women.

The chapter includes a discussion of how the different government systems have responded to the Chinese cultural traditions outlined in Chapter 2. The Taoist tradition favored small government and thought the important issues were the relationship between humans and the natural world, and acceptance of the natural force of the universe. This force might sometimes be personified as female, maternal, dark, universal and sometimes to be feared. Confucianism was more specific in its elevation of loyal, obedient, studious sons, and benevolent, just, wise, paternalistic, proper rulers. Women occupied a status somewhere far below sons. Buddhism was imported from India but has had an influence on all Chinese nations. The idea of escape from a painful real world through meditation, piety and good deeds and tolerance rather than protest of a painful reality persists today. Women are seen as temptation to be avoided in most Chinese Buddhist practices. Legalism has provided one of the most persistent government practices, that of education and examination as the route to government office. This route was open only to men traditionally, but in some modern societies has also provided the way for women to excel if they have been able to gain access to the education system. This chapter concludes with some recommendations gathered from preceding chapters of what governments might do to aid employment of Chinese women.

Each society will be examined in light of both Western and Chinese principles to clarify what persists and to determine what remains to be done to open the doors to equal opportunity to all. The comparisons are not statistical and must be taken with serious reservations because there are quite different capacities to obtain accurate information from official or academic sources in each location. In spite of this qualification we can still find some interesting comments to make about the influence of government on the employment lives of Chinese women in different locations.

As seen in Table 8.1, and reported in Chapter 3, the People's Republic of China (PRC) has by far the largest number of people and the largest number of women, over 0.5 billion, spread over the largest physical territory, almost 10 million sq km, of all of the locations. This size differential is so much greater that it dwarfs all of the other nation-states combined.

Table 8.1   Factors contributing to gender differences in employment of Chinese women

	People's Republic of China	Taiwan	Hong Kong	Singapore
National career identity	9 600 000 sq km, 1.26 billion people, 48.4% female, 93% Han Chinese; secular.	36 000 sq km, 23 million people, 49.0% female, 98% recent and old Chinese immigrants; Buddhist, Taoist, Confucian.	1070 sq km, 6.7 million people, 51.0% female, 95% ethnic Chinese; Buddhist, Taoist, Christian.	616 sq km, 3.4 million people, 49% female, 76% Chinese, 16% Malay, 6% Indian; Buddhist, Taoist, Muslim.
National career beliefs	Education is not necessary for women; women are responsible for home, men for outside; disputes should be resolved outside of courts; party ideology is equality for all, including women.	Work centrality is high; collectivisim and power distance societal values are high; norms are that women should retire when they marry or get pregnant.	Materialism, individualism, gender egalitarianism are high; work ethic is high; patriarchal family structure with sons valued.	Patriarchy and paternalism are beneficial to the society; delay in marriage and childbearing are desired, education is highly valued; use three-generation families for childcare.
National career behavior of women	41% of college students are women; 39.18% women LFP, majority of women work in agriculture; women are 52–61% of unemployed, lowest % re-employed; do the majority of housework, childcare and eldercare.	47.8% of college student are women; 80% LFP of women before marriage; 30% after marriage; 49.5% total LFP of women; most do not return after childbearing; occupations stereotypical female teacher, nurse etc.	54.6 % of college students are women; 49.2% LFP of women; unemployment lower for women- become homemakers when jobs move to PRC; moderate occupational stereotyping.	51% of college students are women; 53.4% LFP of women, most in stereotypical occupations; many delay marriage and childbirth; professional women remain in LF, others leave after childbirth; international travel of wage earners.

Table 8.1   (continued)

	People's Republic of China	Taiwan	Hong Kong	Singapore
National career processes	Communist, large CCC party civil service; socialist with market characteristic; moderate centralized civil service; constitution and 1992,1994 law for equal rights and safety, rarely enforced; discrimination in private sector higher.	Democracy with history of martial law; market economy; moderate civil service; safety, maternity leave, pay protection; right to work 1949, gender equality constitutional amendment 1994; Equal Employment Opportunity Act 2001.	British colony till 1997 then PRC with autonomy; laissez-faire market; large civil service; 1981 equal pay for civil service; EEO Bill of Rights order 1991 prohibits gender discrimination, no other gender policy; family gives welfare.	British colony to WWII then democracy; centralized market economy; moderate civil service; no gender law; policies support women's careers but 2001 bonus for childbearing; government support childcare; three-generation housing.

The career-related beliefs that shape the lives of PRC women begin with beliefs that access to education is more important for men than for women. The Legalist tradition of using education and examinations as access to important government positions for men persists in some form in both the Chinese Communist Party (CCP) access to government positions and in access to higher education. The Confucian tradition that women should be absent from the public sphere and men dominant in the public sphere seems to persist in some areas in spite of vigorous government efforts to remove remnants of Confucianism from the society. These beliefs are counteracted by other strongly advocated official positions of the CCP that women should be given equal access to social opportunities and positions.

If there is anything one can say about PRC it is that any generalization is bound to be false when discussing such a large and complex nation. The employment behavior and experiences of a professional woman, or an unemployed displaced migrant woman in a coastal city where movement toward market economic processes is common, are vastly different from the employment experiences of women in the agricultural interior. That said, first, the employment experiences of the majority of Chinese women on average are experiences of rural agricultural workers with a grade school education who combine homemaking, childcare, eldercare and farming to produce goods for state requirements as well as family needs. There is a high probability that some male family members as well as some young adult unmarried female family members have migrated to cities or coastal areas to find other employment.

Women in PRC who are not employed in agriculture are more likely to be employed in health, social welfare, education or arts in a state-owned enterprise or other collective enterprise, and are less likely to be found in the upper levels of the organizations in which they work. The next most common experience of Chinese women is to be unemployed, not receiving retraining or educational services from the government in spite of its major efforts aimed at re-employment, or making a living by small vendor operations in urban areas, or living with family members who are employed. A smaller number of women are employed in market-oriented enterprises. In aggregate, PRC women are more likely to be unemployed, less likely to be educated, less likely to be hired or rehired and less likely to be promoted than men. The pay gap is approximately 60 percent. A small, fortunate and growing minority has obtained a university education. Some of these highly educated women have only been able to obtain secretarial jobs because of gender discrimination in the Chinese market sector. Others work in Western joint venture market-oriented businesses or in the upper levels of government along the seacoast or in the major metropolitan areas. These women have the opportunity to live a very different urban life from the average agricultural majority.

As citizens of PRC, women are influenced by a government with an official 1949 Constitution that offers gender equality. They could also theoretically benefit from Women's Laws passed in 1992 and 1994 which focus on gender equality, as well as female health, safety and protection. The ideology of the Chinese Communist Party is that men and women are equal, and this policy does have an influence to the extent that the cadre of party members that occupy every employment organization contain both men and women, and they promote this official policy.

The implementation of the gender equality laws as explored and evaluated in Chapter 7 revealed that the common perception of the role of law in the PRC is to authorize and forbid rather than to protect women. Since there are few enforcement mechanisms, and since punishment for breaking these laws is not harsh in a society in which harsh punishment is often seen as the measure to which a law should be taken seriously, the law is seen as a 'toothless tiger'. In conjunction with international efforts to support women's rights, especially during the 1997 International Women's Year celebration, PRC has made greater efforts to enforce these laws at the provincial level. The report of Chapter 7 reveals that government efforts were somewhat successful in increasing access of girls to elementary education, and increasing access of women to lower levels of government and party positions of power, but less successful in aiding unemployed women and in aiding women being discriminated against in market-oriented firms. The laws meant to help or protect women are often used as excuses not to hire women into market-oriented firms not tightly controlled by the government. Recent government efforts do provide women with information about their rights under these laws, but as their Buddhist heritage would predict, there are only a few instances where women act on this knowledge.

There is no doubt that PRC women are not equal to men in most dimensions of positive employment experience, even if we take into account protective laws that give them time off or extra benefits for menstruation, childbearing, nursing and early retirement. While in some cases the laws may provide advantages that some men may covet or feel are too advantageous to women, in many other cases these protections have not been enforced or have been used to deny women employment or advancement.

If we compare the description of the PRC to the various Western explanations of why these gender disparities might occur, we see that every one of the theories gains some support, although gender socialization probably receives only mixed support (see Table 8.2). There are also some clear Chinese cultural influences that appear. Within the CCP and the state-owned enterprises there is less gender role segregation than in other areas of society. There are more women employed in female stereotypical jobs than in non-stereotypical jobs outside of agriculture, especially in the more privatized sectors less influenced by the Communist Party and the government, and more influenced by traditional Chinese Confucian principles favoring sons above daughters. This suggests that the government does play a moderating role in socializing citizens about equality of men and women. This moderation in the remaining state-controlled sectors of the economy is probably the largest role for the government in the PRC, since the legal role is becoming less prominent as more and more organizations join the market economy and are less and less under central government control.

A mixture of socialization appears to be occurring, some from Chinese cultural traditions that support the subservient roles of women and others from the Communist tradition that support women's equality. The move to a market economy threatens the employment opportunities for women to the extent that it supports traditional gender socialization beliefs.

The support for human capital explanations come from the lower access to education that women have compared to men, a Confucian tradition and a Legalist tradition, and the enforced time off from work for female reproductive activities and the tradition of giving less education to daughters than to sons that results in lower human capital accumulation for women.

A dual labor market explanation also describes what is occurring in PRC since women are more likely to remain in rural areas in agricultural occupations, are more likely to be laid off from factory jobs first and less likely

Table 8.2   Theories to explain gender differences in employment of Chinese women

Theory	People's Republic of China	Taiwan	Hong Kong	Singapore
Gender role socialization	Both men and women do physical labor; women are childcare workers and housekeepers.	Women have primary childcare; are expected to retire at marriage or childbirth; occupational stereotyping.	High gender based division of labor in and out of family; women have high childcare and homemaking work.	High gender stereotyping; social support for women to bear children.
Human capital theory	Men have more access to higher education.	Men have more higher education.	Men have more higher education.	Women have access to higher education.
Dual labor market theory	More men in manufacturing and government; more women in agriculture, not always childcare.	More women in low-paying, low-prestige jobs, childcare related.	More women in textiles and fluid unstable jobs not necessarily due to childcare choice.	Not sufficient data; not always related to childcare choice.
Discrimination	Government and SOEs- moderate job discrimination; high lay-off, rehire discrimination; high discrimination in private sector little government enforcement; wage gap 60%.	High social, job, wage, promotion discrimination; law too new to determine enforcement; wage gap 35%.	Moderate social discrimination and job discrimination; a few women in high positions in government and firms; wage gap 73%.	Moderate social discrimination; Low discrimination in women job entry; higher discrimination in promotion, wage gap unknown.

to be rehired, and therefore are more likely to be surviving in marginal, part-time and transitory jobs that pay less and offer few future opportunities. This description of how women end up in a separate labor market with lower human capital to contribute also provides support for a discrimination theory of gender differences in PRC. The failure to object to this discrimination and to accept their fate is reflective of a Buddhist approach to the Universe. The large number of women still engaged in agriculture also reflects occasions when older Taoist beliefs may emerge if the hold of the central government relaxes.

The second location, Taiwan, is 20 percent of the geographical size and has 33 percent of the population of the single PRC province of Hebei. It is located across a narrow strait from the Chinese mainland but offers a very different employment experience to the Chinese women who live there. Here the ancient Chinese traditions of Confucianism, Taoism, Legalism and Buddhism have not been countermanded by Communist Party dogma; rather they have been joined by a small Christian minority. The career-related beliefs that value work and study and family loyalty are still central to many people's thoughts. Taiwanese also retain Confucian values of high power distance or deference to authority that give government as well as family patriarchal elders great moral authority; however younger women are showing some signs of independence that belie traditional Confucian values.

Rather than finding the average woman employed as an agricultural worker, because the educational level of the population is higher and a higher proportion of women has access to more education, the average Taiwanese woman is more likely to be employed as a clerk, factory worker, technician, service worker or government worker, but the work place is gender-segregated with women occupying gender-stereotypical occupations. The labor force participation experience of Taiwanese women differs by age and education. About 80 percent of women are employed before childbirth, but less than 30 percent remain in the labor force after they have children. The proportion that remains employed after marriage but before childbirth is increasing and the proportion that remains in the labor force after childbirth is higher for those with more education. The wage gap is about 35 percent but the unemployment gap favors women slightly over men, unlike that of the PRC. This may occur because women who become unemployed become homemakers.

The active role of government influence in employment of women in Taiwan has been a recent phenomenon in every area except education, where the government has long been active in promoting educational opportunities for all children. A constitutional amendment promising gender equality was passed in 1994, and an equal employment opportunity Act was passed in 2001. Thus Taiwan serves as a fair example of the effects of government with a market economy and a traditional Chinese culture heritage. The results have been government policies and legislation that emphasized the protection of women more often than the promotion of opportunities for employment of women, and a society that emphasizes the importance of family roles more than employment roles for women, certainly reflective of Confucian ideas of women with internal family roles and men with external public roles. Neither a large government program nor legislation in support of childcare exists that would facilitate employment of women, who now remain home after childbirth because they are the primary child caregiver. The wage gap is noticeably smaller in the category of government workers and business managers however, which provides some evidence that the government may be setting an example that sets a positive precedent for the future.

Occupational segregation by gender strongly supports the gender socialization explanations of employment differences in Taiwan. Support for dual labor market explanations and discrimination theories of gender differences in Taiwan are also apparent since so many women leave or are forced out of the labor force at the time of their first childbirth. Fewer women return to the labor force after childbirth, so the lack of large numbers of women in part-time work while children are in school does not fit that part of the dual labor market theory. The human capital theory is only partly supported. Women do obtain education in Taiwan and their early job experience is rapidly approaching that of men, but they are more likely to go to junior college than to university than are men. They obtain jobs at similar times early in their careers, but upon marriage or childbirth many are likely to leave the labor force, thus obtaining less total job experience. If they never return, this behavior may explain in part the smaller numbers of women in high positions of power in business and government. This explanation must be complemented by gender socialization and discrimination explanations as the few women who have attained higher positions are more likely to be single or to have no children, or to be wealthy enough to obtain alternative private childcare.

Hong Kong is an even smaller island, and a territory even more tightly connected to the PRC than Taiwan. In 1997 Hong Kong returned as a Special Administrative Region of the PRC from its previous status as a British protectorate. The combination of 99 years of British colonial rule and thousands of years of Chinese cultural influence have left a mixture of Hong Kong values and beliefs that differs from the largely Chinese heritage of Taiwan and the 50 years of Communist Party influence of the PRC. The career beliefs are more individualistic, more materialistic and more gender-egalitarian than the PRC and Taiwan, but the high work ethic, patriarchal family structure and high value placed on sons that sound like strains of Confucianism remain in place as well. Legalist traditions of valuing education and using education to gain government jobs have been modified by a British civil service tradition that bears some striking similarities to the older Chinese examination system. Social norms support women remaining in the labor force after childbirth, but they also support women providing the majority of homemaking, childcare and eldercare.

The average Hong Kong woman has lost her factory job to a worker across the border in PRC and now works in a wholesale or retail shop, hotel, bank, restaurant or other service job for pay that is about 75 percent of that of her male colleagues. Increased opportunities to finish high school and get more education have kept many younger women from working until they are out of their teens, and high pressures to retire and to provide childcare for an employed daughter's children urge women to leave the labor force in their fifties, but most women work from age 20 until their late forties or fifties.

Hong Kong women are delaying childbirth and having fewer children in order to pursue their careers. They do not leave the labor force to stay home with their children in the same numbers that occur in Taiwan, unless they have lost their jobs and have not been able to find another one during the process of shifting jobs between HK and PRC that has been occurring during the 1990s, or unless they could not find adequate childcare.

The role of the government has been even less proactive in Hong Kong than it is in Taiwan, although equal employment legislation was passed earlier, in 1991, and the British civil service implemented various equal employment policies for government workers in the 1980s. Laissez-faire market economy philosophy was also extended to other aspects of social policy, and the role of government has been largely absent in women's lives both before and after the shift to PRC control. The women's Bill of Rights, while on the books since 1991, was sporadically enforced before 1997 and, given the tradition of low levels of law enforcement in the PRC, there is no evidence to suppose that law enforcement will improve in the future. Most social services are provided in the family unit without government help, but this is increasingly difficult as families live in different parts of the city. This geographical distance is having an increasingly strong impact on working mothers as fewer aunts and grandmothers are available for childcare.

The horizontal gender segregation of the labor market suggests that gender role socialization processes in accordance with Chinese and British traditions are still strongly evident in Hong Kong today. Women appear in occupations caring for others and are less likely to do stereotypically masculine work. Although educational opportunities for women are increasing, men still have educational advantages, supporting human capital theory explanations for gender differences in employment. The marginalization of some women in the labor market might be interpreted as supporting the dual labor market theory if more women left the labor market to raise children, but in this case the evidence seems to support a discrimination theory or a human capital theory more than a dual labor market theory as an explanation for gender differences. In Hong Kong society, the expectation is not universal that young women will leave to care for children, but many young women have lost their jobs, and do not have enough education to obtain the type of jobs that have not migrated to the PRC.

They have stayed home with children out of lack of job opportunities rather than choosing part-time work as a flexible childcare option. In this case the government policy that fails to support sound childcare provisions acts as an employment discrimination factor when it is combined with a socio-cultural assumption that mothers rather than fathers are primarily responsible for childcare. In this volume we have been attributing this to a Confucian heritage; however in the Hong Kong case it would be equally fair to attribute it to a European or British heritage as well.

Singapore, the final location, is the smallest island of all, only 616 sq. km with half as many people as Hong Kong, only three-quarters of them Chinese. The influence of 16 percent Malay Muslim, 6 percent Indian Hindu, and 2 percent Western European minorities compressed into such a small geographic area, even in the face of a large Chinese majority, makes this one of the most complex ethnic social systems addressed in this volume, although the PRC contains a larger number of minority citizens. Singapore also experienced British colonial influence but has had self-rule since the mid-1940s. Singapore has chosen a very different, strong, paternalistic, Chinese-influenced form of government with free market capitalism rather than the live-and-let-live atmosphere of the British government in Hong Kong.

The career beliefs of the Singaporean society include strongly Confucian patriarchal family and educational values and a strong work ethic, combined with a Western attitude among young women that they can have the careers they want if they have small families and delay childbearing in order to pursue economic opportunities.

The average Singaporean woman is employed in personal service work, manufacturing or retail sectors. She has had fairly equal access to education. The educational opportunities in Singapore are tied to examination as in the old Chinese legalist tradition; however both men and women are eligible to sit for the examinations and at the current time more women than men obtain university degrees. The educational opportunities are not completely open to all however, since some families, especially poor and minority families, still use limited financial resources to favor sending boys rather than girls to Chinese and English language schools that prepare students more fully for the path toward university entrance examinations.

Occupational segregation exists as a perpetuation of gender differentiation in educational major. Girls still are more likely to prepare for careers in caring professions than in building, but they are also more likely to major in business. Those women who have obtained a college or university degree are likely to remain in the labor force following childbirth, whereas those with less education are more likely to leave the labor force after childbirth and are unlikely to return to part-time jobs later in their lives.

In spite of a strong, controlling central government with many social welfare policies, Singapore has no equal employment opportunity legislation or constitutional provisions. There are individual policies that support careers for women, especially those supporting educational preparation; however these policies are sometimes in conflict. The government, concerned about a low and falling birth rate among the more educated Chinese population compared to a higher birthrate among the Malaysian population, has proposed a financial bonus for women who bear children, and the government is also actively supporting childcare facilities sponsored by businesses; however there are too few facilities to meet the need and the government has not been able to fill the gap. Women are coping using Filipina maids and resident grandmothers.

Gender socialization theory explains much of the difference in Singaporean women's employment experience, since they have fairly equal access to education yet choose gender-related majors and occupations. There is a clear expectation that Singaporean women will be the primary caretakers of their children, or at least be responsible for their care if not delivering it themselves. The delay and decline in childbirth speaks eloquently that the women themselves may not be adopting this ideal as completely as others around them may be insisting on their fulfilling this role.

Little support exists for human capital theory in Singapore, since most women get equal amounts of education and stay in the labor market; only a few leave after childbirth. We do not have enough evidence about a secondary labor market to identify any support for a dual labor market theory, but the very small number of women engaged in part-time work suggest that this theory is not a large explanation of women's experience in this location.

We are left with a very large gap in the number of men compared to the number of women in top government and management positions in Singapore, and the remaining explanation seems to be that a significant amount of gender discrimination exists with little help from the government and little legal recourse for those women who are victims. It is more difficult to tease out the Chinese cultural influences in Singapore because of the multicultural context; however the Confucian paternalistic, masculine government, and legalistic educational system do seem obvious remnants of Chinese culture in spite of British and Malay as well as other entrepôt trade influences.

SUMMARY

If we look at Table 8.2 we can see a summary of the evidence for each Western explanation for different employment experiences of men and women in each nation-state. In making these comparisons we must acknowledge first that the theories were developed to apply to Western, not Asian contexts; and second, that we have reduced each theory to its few key principles in order to make these comparisons, and many details have been lost by these simplifications. However the comparisons would be impossibly confusing without the simplifications, and the reliability of these data do not warrant more detailed comparisons. Because these are the theories that have been used most often in the existing literature on women's employment, it seems important to make this link to give some indication as to what seems to apply and what does not seem to apply to Chinese women.

First, we see that that in every instance there is a great deal of evidence that gender role socialization is occurring to encourage women to select careers that differ substantially from those of men, and there is only one instance where a government policy or political process has had even a small influence on gender role socialization. The only instance where one might say that the government has had an effect in this domain is in the PRC where the CCP has insisted to some extent that both men and women play a role in the party and that childcare should be provided at all levels so that both men and women can be employed. But even in this instance, women are not equally represented at the top levels of the party and men are not equally represented as daycare or other caring workers.

If we examine the second explanation, differences in human capital, we see that there are substantial human capital differences in every location as well, that only one government system has been able to partly overcome. The two major components of human capital, education and job experience are overwhelmingly preferential toward men in almost every locale; however the government may have less to do with this than a common Confucian and Legalist heritage does, since there are common policies that support education for all children in every society in the book. In every case except Singapore, men have more higher education than do women, mostly because families choose to educate sons rather than daughters, especially when there are not enough funds to do both. In Singapore, even though more women than men are obtaining educational forms of human capital, the government is actively encouraging educated women to bear more children, a strategy that may keep them from gaining as much job experience as men since the current government childcare policy does not provide adequate childcare for all of the current children, let alone the number of spaces that would be needed if more women bore children.

As an explanation of different employment patterns of men and women, a dual labor market does not seem to fit the Chinese experience as well as some of the other theories. The support for a dual labor market may be murky because of lack of clear data from some locations. In most of the locations in this volume it is clear that women do occupy different jobs from men, but it is not at all clear, with the exception of Taiwan, that they do so because they choose to enter those jobs because they expect to leave for childbearing. Most of these women do not expect to return to part-time jobs. Either they expect never to return to the labor market (Taiwan) or they expect to continue to work full time with little or no leave for childbearing (Hong Kong, Singapore, PRC).

In many cases it appears women have been pushed into separate jobs either for gender stereotypical reasons or because others expect they will have childcare responsibilities and do not want them to have opportunities to compete for better jobs. This last type of reason fits the discrimination explanation which is found in every setting regardless of government type and regardless of legal structure. In spite of the governments that have enacted legal and policy structures against gender discrimination, no system reported in this volume has enforced the laws on the books in ways that result in equal employment experiences for Chinese women. In several cases the lack of protectionist laws that are sometimes used as excuses not to hire women have actually resulted in better employment opportunities for women, when compared to locations where laws are present but not enforced. The Taoist images of women as dark, negative forces and Confucian images of women as secluded, inferior-status beings have not been overcome by any government legal or policy forces that create an environment in which women are able to create images of strength, competence and power in Chinese paid public spheres.

If we look at the Chinese traditions we see that there are few overt legacies of Taoist visions of women as foundations of being or forces of evil, but many remaining assumptions of looking at situations as containing both light and dark, good and evil, as well as ways of being in the world that seek to be at one with the natural forces of the universe. Chinese women today are still profoundly influenced by the Confucian traditions of inequality with their male counterparts, regardless of the government system in which they live. They have benefited from the Legalist tradition of education and competitive examination as access to the civil service, since if they do well in school, opportunities for careers and occupations and jobs can open to them that otherwise might be unavailable. The Buddhist tradition of tolerance and suffering rather than protest makes it difficult to speak out against inequality, but there are a few bright examples that point to hope for the future.

In examining the governmental and policy alternatives, PRC, Hong Kong and most recently Taiwan have legal and/or constitutional bases of equal opportunity for women, and Singapore, even without such laws, seems to be passing individual policies that support women's rights in certain areas. Access to education and health and safety, especially for preg-nant or nursing mothers, are the legal protections most commonly offered to women, but these protections are a double-edged sword when they are used by managers and business owners as an excuse not to hire female employees or not to enforce these policies because of the expense.

The recommendations for the future differ for each nation state. Some of the recommendations are specific to the location, but in many cases rec-ommendations might be useful in other locations as well. In Chapter 4, T.K. Peng and Tsai-Wei Wang state that the Taiwanese government must further encourage equal opportunity in training and development, ensure a harassment-free work environment and encourage better daycare services for minors and the elderly. Work in these policy areas will assist women's employment opportunities in ways that will encourage occupational segre-gation to decline and women's employment qualifications to improve. They believe that members of society will need to continue placing pressure on the government to take a more active role in taking care of women's well-being in order to accomplish this goal.

The author of Chapter 5, Irene Hau-Siu Chow, reminds us that the gov-ernment often lacks women's perspective in designing and implementing its social policies, and thus it is not aware of the problems facing women. In Hong Kong, a Women's Commission advises government policy makers on women's issues to try to combat this deficit, but this has not been sufficient to eliminate sex discrimination and promote equal opportunities even with an Equal Opportunities Commission and a Bill of Rights Ordinance pro-hibiting explicitly discriminatory practices.

Dr Chow recommends a critical analysis of the political, social and insti-tutional framework of Hong Kong, called 'gender mainstreaming' an approach to advancing gender equality that involves addressing gender inequality in all aspects of development, across all sectors and programs: 'It calls for setting up an integrated network of structure, mechanism and processes designed to arouse more gender-awareness, increase the number of women in decision-making roles, facilitate the formulation of gender-sensitive policies, plans and programs, and promote the advancement of gender equality and equity.'

In addition to gender mainstreaming, Dr Chow suggests using two new indices, the Gender-related Development Index and the Gender Empowerment Measure, to measure gender inequalities in key areas of political and economic decision-making structures to provide more detailed statistics and information for policy decisions.

The next set of recommendations for Hong Kong is useful to reorient the institutional process for the planning, implementation and monitoring of government policies to accommodate women's concerns. Dr Chow suggests that long-term strategies should be developed to promote women's integration and equality in the workplace and to develop women through individual personal growth. Gender issues need to be integrated into the development of all government work plans and budget allocations. Follow-up on the implementation of the engendered work plans and reviewing key indicators on the status of women are necessary to reinforce the mission. Dr Chow also recommends the Hong Kong government provide tax incentives for companies that set up family-friendly programs for employees.

The lack of appropriate statistics was also a problem in Chapter 6 for Irene K.H. Chew and Naresh Khatri as they reported on Singapore, and their task of policy recommendation might be aided by regular collection and publication of appropriate data on the status of women. They believe that some legislation needs to be updated, but that the government can only work to create an environment and infrastructure to make it conducive for women to develop their careers. Policies implemented will have to take the form of incentives rather than punitive measures for the Singapore government to achieve its objectives effectively. For example implementation of more family-friendly policies for women re-entering the workforce should be encouraged with incentives and consultation services to the private sector.

The Singapore government also must realize the contradictory effects of a policy that encourages increased childbearing yet fails to provide childcare for every child on the island. There are several ways that the government could address this issue. First, the government could work on training a group of childcare professionals and improve the image of this profession. In addition, the government's three-tier generation flat-selection scheme should be supported. Grandparents could then help to take care of household responsibilities, thus allowing their adult children to devote more time to their careers.

Another group of recommendations for Singapore concern training. First incentives or subsidies could be given to companies who are sending a large percentage of their female employees for training or retraining. Second, training in how to overcome dual-role conflict and balance work – family demands could be supported for both men and women in couples where both are employed.

Dr Irene K.H. Chew and Dr Naresh Khatri acknowledge that the Singapore government already has many incentives in place to help women cope with work and family demands and hence career development. However they believe that the government also needs to increase women's awareness of such incentives as well as educate them on how they can take advantage of such incentives.

Recommendations about women and government policy in the People's Republic of China were very general at the national level in Chapter 3 by Yong-Qing Fang, Cherlyn Skromme Granrose and Rita V. Kong (Mei-Hui Jiang). These authors stated that 'Women in the rural segments of the country need more help from the government, but problems of urban women clearly indicate that all programs should not be targeted solely toward rural areas. Instead, a more holistic approach should be adopted to counter gender differences in employment in the PRC.'

The more detailed recommendations followed in an analysis of the implementation of national policies as provincial policies of PRC in Chapter 7, as stated by Yong-Qing Fang. While it is always dangerous to apply generalizations from one area of PRC to another, since Hebei contains both rural and urban areas, some of these recommendations are likely to apply to other areas of PRC as well as to other locations.

Their first and most serious recommendation applied to the large number (up to 48 percent in 1999) of women who no longer had full employment in a work unit: 'To solve this problem, every labor unit will have to take a serious and systematic approach toward the re-employment of *xiagang* workers . . . if women are not to suffer disproportionately from these efforts, there needs to be continued promotion of labor law and women's labor protection and regulations.'

The second set of recommendations addresses equal access to education: 'There is a need to adjust the curriculum so that school knowledge is relevant to the local conditions. There is also is a need to improve awareness of the law requiring compulsory education of girls through grade nine. If all of these efforts do not encourage girls to catch up and participate in the educational system, the province needs to offer remedial education to teenagers below 17 years of age who have not completed secondary education.'

The most positive evidence of their analysis of this province is that 'the evidence from 1978 to the present shows the positive effect on women's development and gender equality of governmental intervention, including implementation and execution of law and policies. This evidence shows that even under market conditions, governmental intervention has a positive effect on women's development.' Perhaps the most optimistic hints lie in the exemplary local programs that inform women of their rights, provide them with legal recourse and educate employers. The greatest caution lies in the need for more worker health and safety.

In summary, these recommendations provide suggestions for policies that might assist governments to serve women better. They include ideas for special women's commissions with real power, plans that embed gender into government budgets, statistical methods to measure progress, and legislation that would enable, not just protect women, as well as ideas for local implementation and rural market legal aid centers that provide legal education and women's help on the spot. What needs to be done next is unique to each location and defies summary here, but certainly one can borrow ideas from each of these chapter authors.

The government employment policies for women are slow to be enacted, and no system of government has implemented employment policies that include Western provisions for equal gender opportunity for selection, promotion and compensation. A Western perspective would say that until laws that protect women's rights to equal access to all aspects of employment are available to Chinese women, and until these are accompanied by policies that provide affordable childcare to all families without automatically assuming that women will be the primary childcare provider, Chinese women will not be able to hold up their half of the sky with their full energy and spirit. A Chinese perspective might say that a new way will have to be found that is more patient, more indirect, less dependent upon laws and government and more dependent upon multi-generational family structure, networks between educated women, and power not readily measured by the numbers that appear in tables and books but power reflected in the culture of art and emotion such as stories, poems and paintings, and harmony with nature.

REFERENCES

Bosanquet, N. and P.B. Doeringer (1973), 'Is there a dual labor market in Great Britain?' *Economic Journal*, **83** (330), 11–35.

Eagly, A.H. (1987), *Sex Differences in Social Behavior: A Social-role Interpretation*, Hillsdale, NJ: Lawrence Erlbaum Associates.

Geib, A.E. and L.B. Leuptow (1996), 'Sex, gender stereotypes, and work', in P.J. Dubeck and K. Borman (eds), *Women and Work: A Handbook*, New Brunswick, NJ: Rutgers University Press, pp. 243–6.

Mincer, Jacob (1962), 'Labor force participation of married women', in H.G. Lewis (ed.), *Aspects of Labor Economics*, Princeton, NJ: Princeton University Press, pp. 63–97.

Moen, P. (1992), *Women's Two Roles: A Contemporary Dilemma*, London: Auburn House.

O'Leary, V.E. (1977), *Towards Understanding Women*, Monterey, CA: Brooks-Cole.

Pleck, J.H. (1985), *Working Wives/Working Husbands*, London: Sage Publications.

Sullerot, E. (1971), *Women, Society and Change*, London: Weidenfeld & Nicolson.

Index